Journalism
IN A FREE SOCIETY

Journalism

IN A FREE SOCIETY

Verne E. Edwards, Jr.

Ohio Wesleyan University

WM. C. BROWN COMPANY PUBLISHERS

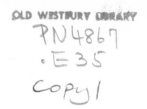
JOURNALISM SERIES

Consulting Editor
  Curtis D. MacDougall
  Northwestern University

Copyright © 1970 by
Wm. C. Brown Company Publishers

ISBN 0–697–04300–2

Library of Congress Catalog Card Number: 75-97604

Third Printing, 1972

Printed in the United States of America

To Dolores, Debby, and Nancy

Forewords

(A Broadcasting Executive's View)

The history of a free press in our country goes back some 200 years. Broadcast or electronic journalism, by comparison, is a newcomer of less than 40 years.

While hundreds of books have been written on both print media and broadcasting, the author of this book, a long-time educator in the field of journalism, has departed from the standard routine of treating the printed and spoken word as separate facets of communication. Instead, he combines the two and focuses broadly on the practice and problems of news coverage in general—whether print or electronic journalism. This is a highly comprehensive, thoughtful, balanced, and readable study of "journalism in a free society," and will interest not only students of journalism, but any person in public or private life who wants a better understanding of journalism, its importance and impact on our democratic form of government, and its vital role as an instrument of the public's right to know.

In his book, the author documents the constant and compelling threat to press and broadcast freedoms. Case histories range from the early days of both the print and broadcast media, and furnish a fascinating and informative picture of journalism's never-ending fight against the infringement of our First Amendment guarantees. One of the great dangers, as the author shows, is how easily these freedoms can be forfeited by public inaction or indifference. He goes on to underscore the need for Americans to recognize this threat and to avoid the common tendency to equate the trend toward greater government control of business with a parallel, far more dangerous trend toward government efforts to control the news media.

Only by recognizing this threat for what it is and preserving these freedoms, he writes, can newspapers and broadcasters carry on their watchdog role and protect against that greatest and most insidious enemy of democracy—government by secrecy. In particular, the author documents the need for greater access to government records and proceedings, and just as vividly shows how government officials try to seal off this access. He gives proper credit to the press and broadcast media for their long, so far successful record in overcoming such officials and other proponents of "hidden government."

This book constitutes, on the one hand, an important historical record of journalistic enterprise and result; it is also a veritable and valuable handbook on citizenship which shows how both the democratic rights of the public and of a free press are not only intertwined—they are all but indistinguishable from each other.

Frank Stanton
New York

(A FORMER PUBLISHER'S VIEW)

Verne Edwards's declared goals of inspiring respect for "press freedom's real meaning, more intelligent evaluation of press performance and belief in journalism's standing among civilized mankind's highest callings" make this a book worth studying. Indeed, it should be most useful to journalism students, to teachers and to those editors and publishers who are looking for a clear exposition of the press's function and its place in our democracy. It contains the most lucid and balanced statement of the community of interest and differences in status of all the major media of communications that I have seen.

In doing so, it supports the fundamental freedom guaranteed the press through the First Amendment, but with candid admissions of the frequent press failures to utilize that freedom responsibly. It draws the teeth of people in that rising chorus of criticism of press and electronic media and counters the demand that restraints be put upon them by legislators, administrators, judges or any others outside the media. That demand is not new: in 1938, when I served as president of the National Association of Broadcasters, I testified against the proposal by an FCC commissioner to impose cultural standards on radio stations. Culture has no common denominator; the devotees of Bach would hardly call Glenn Campbell, for instance—and he is one of the best in his field—an exponent of their type of culture. The proposal was defeated in 1938, but it keeps coming back in one form or another. More than three decades later, I was glad to see Frank Stanton and CBS refuse to yield to the prior restraint which Rhode Island's Senator John O. Pastore in effect proposed when he asked that NAB's Code Authority be allowed to censor network programs. Legislators, bureaucrats and even judges are more chary of tangling with the special status of the press, but the press, in turn, owes it to other media to support the principle of the First Amendment for them.

Print and electronic journalism are interwoven throughout these twelve chapters, instead of being treated separately as though the public and practitioners could ignore one medium or another in today's complex, fast-moving world. Naturally, I am glad that newspapers are recognized as the main medium.

The book dwells on journalism's opportunities to serve a free society rather than on boring listings of "vocational" statistics. Probably no two educators or practitioners could agree on exactly how much technique should go into this kind of book. Three chapters provide some things essential to understanding those mechanics which affect significantly the flow of news and opinion in a democratic society.

The treatment of advertising and public relations in terms of their effects on the flow of news and opinion seems especially appropriate in a book designed to introduce readers to the basics of mass communications.

The author appears to be saying that press independence is essential in a democratic society and that necessary improvements in press performance must come from men and women inside the press, spurred by intelligent laymen's demands. I like that.

Mark F. Ethridge
Moncure, North Carolina

Preface

If one word could describe this book's main purpose, it would be "inspiration." The book is aimed at inspiring belief in press freedom's real meaning, as opposed to ignorant payment of lip service or dangerous distortion of the principle into something befitting "guided democracy." It is aimed at inspiring more intelligent evaluation of press performance by both laymen and journalists. It is aimed at inspiring belief in journalism's standing among civilized mankind's highest callings.

I believe that a first, broad look at journalism's Fourth Estate role should be the same for all citizens—whether prospective journalists or not.

This book differs from most earlier "introductory journalism" textbooks by placing less emphasis on technical aspects. Whether the media deliver their offerings by using hand-set type and a flatbed press or by bouncing messages off satellites, the problems of collecting, writing, and editing those offerings remain paramount. The mechanics of Linotype machines and the marvels of video tape have been bypassed partly because those are boring in the abstract and partly because rapidly improving devices threaten to make such discussion quickly obsolete.

Another departure is the interrelating of broadcast and print journalism throughout, instead of treating each medium separately. The newspaper is emphasized because it is the oldest and because it remains the primary mass purveyor of information and opinion. America's ablest broadcast newsmen share this view.

Objectivity has been sought in treating such controversial matters as the roles of advertising and public relations, arguments about the "free press-fair trial" issue, and trends toward press consolidation. However, a fundamentalist view of press freedom is presented without apology. Those who believe Americans must surrender their most important freedom should find opportunities for stimulating rebuttal in these pages.

Risky oversimplifications are herewith confessed. For example, Chapter 10's sortie into civil libel was undertaken with strong misgivings. I decided that a little more knowledge would be safer than the assumptions otherwise evolved by many laymen and even by some practitioners. Those assumptions tend to range from "It must be true because he didn't sue" to "That wasn't true because he did sue." Including a smattering of knowledge about qualified privilege seemed better than leaving its interpretation entirely to the barbershop pundits. I apologize for skipping so lightly through the decades of American journalism (Chapter 3), but some perspective seemed essential to understanding the First Amendment.

Logic dictated the order of chapters. However, some readers might benefit from starting with Chapters 4, 5, and 6 before considering background material in Part I. Insofar as possible, chapters are designed to stand alone so that readers can skip about.

Flexibility was a primary goal. Each chapter is designed as an introduction to a phase of mass communications, rather than as an exhaustive study, of course. The "For Further Study" suggestions are intended to point toward more exploration, as desired by any reader or instructor. Choices in the "Suggested Readings" were made with a view to differences in library resources; those with limited sources should be able to find some of these, and those with access to good mass communications holdings should find better materials. [Volumes available in paperback are noted in brackets.]

Acknowledgments

Like most writers, I shy from acknowledgments. I have no adequate notes or tape recordings from which I can construct a complete list of those who have contributed, let alone evaluate a proper order of those who helped most. The project's beginnings can be traced to an older brother (John Arthur Edwards, later killed in World War II), who first interested me in journalism. Miss Dorothy Crane, my high school journalism teacher, helped solidify my interest in news work. Many men on the five dailies which used my "home-made news bureau" work belong on a proper list; so do many with whom I later served on the *Milwaukee Journal, Buffalo Evening News, Rochester Times-Union, Toledo Blade, Columbus Dispatch, Columbus Citizen, Detroit Free Press,* and other newspapers, and those with whom I served very briefly on two radio station news staffs.

Closer to the actual writing, I must mention Professors Neale Copple, University of Nebraska, and W. E. Garets, Texas Technological College, who read the entire manuscript and made valuable suggestions. I am grateful to Professor Curtis MacDougall, Northwestern University, who first encouraged this specific project and read part of the manuscript. As must any author, I rejected some of their suggestions and I may have mangled others; hence none of these should be blamed for shortcomings in this volume.

I am indebted to Ohio Wesleyan University's Committee on Faculty Personnel for recommending, and to its Board of Trustees for granting, a term's leave to work on this project. Thanks are also due Academic Vice-President Robert P. Lisensky for his encouragement and the Shell Faculty Assistance Fund for help with typing costs. Among those on campus who were most helpful, I must mention Marion E. Burton, lecturer in journalism (and vice-president of Howard Swink Advertising,

Inc., Marion, Ohio); Dennis E. Gaukel, director of broadcasting; Donald L. Noll, former manager of the O.W.U. Bookstore; and Mrs. Wilma Holland, secretary, and Mrs. Roberta Canegali, former secretary, of the Department of Journalism. Miss Mary Kathleen Jackson, who did most of the final typing, provided crucial help in meeting deadlines.

Gratefully acknowledged are various permissions and special aids provided by John K. Jessup of *Life*; Rufus Crater of *Broadcasting*; Robert U. Brown of *Editor & Publisher*; Richard H. Leonard of the *Milwaukee Journal*; Theodore M. Bernstein and Irvin S. Taubkin of the *New York Times*; Miss Catharine Heinz of the Television Information Office; James Boylan of *Columbia Journalism Review;* Richard W. Darrow of Hill and Knowlton, Inc.; George G. Huntington of the Television Bureau of Advertising; Buel F. Weare of *Congressional Quarterly*; Barton A. Cummings of Compton Advertising, Inc.; Robert Gunning of Robert Gunning Associates; Howard Mandel and Harold Niven of the National Association of Broadcasters; Roger Tatarian of United Press International; Rob Downey of the Radio Television News Directors Association; Edward M. Glick of the American Institute for Political Communication; Alexander Korn of the Federal Communications Commission; Robert E. Kenyon, Jr., of the Magazine Publishers Association and Miss Katheryn Powers of MPA's Magazine Advertising Bureau; Norman E. Isaacs and John C. Long of the *Louisville Courier-Journal;* James A. Fellows of the National Association of Educational Broadcasters; J. J. Graham and Miss Jeanne Brady of *Advertising Age*; Ted Boyle and Al Dopking of the Associated Press; Dennis Brown of the University of Missouri's Freedom of Information Center; Edward J. Reap of the *Los Angeles Times*; William J. Isam of the *St. Louis Post-Dispatch*; Mrs. Toni Dewey of North Advertising, Inc.; Frederick H. Teahan of the Public Relations Society of America; William E. Day and others of the *Toledo Blade*; Ted Smiley of the *Honolulu Advertiser*; J. R. Wiggins (then) of the *Washington Post*; Harold C. Reed of the *Delaware Gazette*; John L. Miller of WNBC-TV, New York City; Robert D. Thomas, Gus Bailey, Jim Flynn, and Ed Eakins of WBNS-TV, Columbus, Ohio; Herbert L. Block and Mrs. Jean Bonieski of Herblock Cartoons; Richard R. Clark, Russell B. Barber, and others of WCBS-TV, New York City; Gerald W. Johnson; the late Carl Lindstrom, long-time editor of the *Hartford Times*.

Let this last paragraph stand as an acknowledgment to the Forgotten Contributors—dozens of students, former students, colleagues, former colleagues, and others whose contributions have been blended into the whirl of words and ideas from which this book was fashioned.

Verne E. Edwards, Jr.

Contents

Part II. How Journalism Functions

Appendixes

Illustrations

Tables

Part One

Journalism's Magnitude
and Significance

Part One

Journalism's Magnitude and Significance

CHAPTER I

Profile of the Press

The press ranks near, if not at, the top of most lists of America's controversial institutions. In fact, the press and its adjuncts are often blamed for the faults of other institutions—government, schools, politics, industry.

Our uses of the terms "journalism," "press," and "medium" depend upon the broad definitions offered in *Webster's Third International Dictionary*—"the collection and editing of material of current interest for presentation through . . . publication or broadcast."

We will concentrate on the major mass media—newspapers, television, radio, and general magazines—which function within rigid time patterns. This is not intended to dismiss the importance of specialized magazines like those of the business press. Nor do we mean to dismiss books, motion pictures, pamphlets, and the like. Indeed, imaginative use of such "nonscheduled" media offers superb checks against dangers in modern trends toward press monopoly.

THE PRESS AS FREE ENTERPRISE

Freedom of the press may be the most abused phrase in the language. Laymen pledge their allegiance to the generalization and then renege when specific situations make it painfully meaningful. Journalists too frequently fail to defend it for fellow practitioners with whom they disagree. Press managers sometimes stretch its fabric dangerously to cover subsidiary business aspects of questionable pertinence. Government officials, sworn to uphold it, flout the principle and even attack it on grounds that real or alleged irresponsibility has somehow canceled the First Amendment.

A good starting point for understanding American freedom of the press is to compare government controls on printing and broadcasting

3

with government controls on the supplying of other goods and services. Table 1, an incomplete and oversimplified listing, should provide some guidance.

TABLE 1

RELATIVE FREEDOM FROM GOVERNMENT CONTROLS

I. Primarily Private
(For Private Profit)

a. *Publishers of books, newspapers, magazines*

b. Retailers (clothiers, grocers)

c. Restaurateurs, Tavern Keepers

d. Large Manufacturers (steel, automobiles)

e. Lawyers, Doctors

II. Franchised by Government
(For Private Profit)

a. *Broadcasters (FM, AM radio and UHF, VHF television stations)*

b. Public Utilities (railroads, airlines, electric companies)

III. Government Owned and Operated
(Nonprofit)

a. Public Universities

b. Public Schools

c. U. S. Post Office

d. U. S. Armed Forces

Since freedom of enterprise is not a factor within Classification III's nonprofit operations, we can point only to subtle, debatable refinements in the complete government control over each listing. For example, postal employees enjoy freedom to organize in unions and to quit their jobs at any time, options not open to military servicemen. Direct supervision and surveillance of public school administrators and teachers by government (i. e., the Board of Education and state education departments) are usually less comprehensive than are federal directions of post office operations. Still looser—in a majority of cases—is government supervision of public-university functions; important in our arbitrary rating scale, for example, is the fact that college teachers are not licensed by the state, whereas public school teachers are.

Some metropolitan school systems may function with less control than some state colleges. Other challenges to this list could be made. The important factor in Classification III is that potential government control is technically complete at all levels.

Classification II involves profit-making enterprises granted some degree of monopoly by the government, which in turn regulates their operations. Public utilities (II-b) must obtain government permission to raise or lower their rates, or to extend or curtail their services. The government allows no one to compete with the local electric company in supplying electric current and, in turn, holds the power to deny that company a rate increase which it believes would yield "excessive" profits. It can deny a rate decrease if it feels such a decrease threatens the welfare of the local gas company through "unfair competition." A railroad must have permission from the Interstate Commerce Commission to abandon a passenger stop; a public hearing might indicate that the community in question needs the service more than the railroad needs to cut that particular expense. A suburban bus company may be denied permission to pick up fares at certain points because the regulatory agency decides that such service would unfairly curtail business for another essential public carrier.

Classification II-a is especially set off from II-b in Table 1 because American commitment to the First Amendment has inspired for broadcasters important freedoms not allowed in parallel situations for public utilities. For example, the telephone company must service any legal enterprise in its domain; a radio station may refuse to service an advertiser so long as that station observes the equal-time rules. (The Democratic and Republican candidates for sheriff may both be denied time, but federal law does require that if one is granted time his opponent must have equivalent time if he wants it.) Nor are a broadcaster's advertising rates subject to direct government approval, as are the public utilities' profit-producing charges.

Nevertheless, the licensing requirement does drop broadcasting below the level of publishing in terms of freedom from government controls. The Federal Communications Commission determines who shall broadcast on what wavelength with what power and at what times. License-renewal proceedings enable the FCC to influence station policies, ranging from advertising techniques to the volume of "public service" programming. The FCC's restraint in exercising its powers and the Federal Communications Act's clear statement against censorship have maintained the main substance of press freedom on the air thus far. No one quarrels with the need to license broadcasters because broadcast bands are limited, but experts do disagree on how far the FCC should go in forcing those licensees to "serve the public interest." (The mere defining of "public interest" leads to savage debate.) Choosing among applicants for a valuable new license raises the power-tends-to-corrupt specter for the seven-member FCC. Decisions on such policy matters as whether publishers should also own television and radio out-lets can have a profound effect on America's total journalistic well-being. (In 1968 publishers owned 22 per cent of America's television stations.)

For example, should a city's single AM radio outlet be granted to the local newspaper publisher or to an outside broadcasting "chain"? This involves policy questions, complicated by the specific situation— the value of competing local editorial voices versus the disadvantages of absentee ownership; an established broadcasting enterprise's proven know-how versus the publisher's ability to build onto his basic news operation; a chance for competitive advertising rates versus a threat to the newspaper which might need total community advertising support. If the chain applicant wins, the community might be subjected to in-appropriate packaged programming and unfair advertising competition (underwritten by other chain units) that would wreck its local news-paper. If the publisher wins, the community might be denied business-stimulating competition in advertising rates, a wholesomely different approach to the news, and an inspiring clash of local editorial opinions.

Classification I (the "primarily private" sector) offers more room for argument about our arbitrary gradations. Understanding, if not set-tling, those arguments is essential to grasping the significance of journal-istic freedom in a democratic society. Americans have accepted strict government supervision of medical practitioners as necessary to protect the public from charlatans and incompetents. Both licensing by the state and quasi-governmental controls by medical societies are generally welcomed by the public. In cases where organized medicine's discipline of a physician is opened to public scrutiny, public opinion tends to sanction the discipline or, at the very least, to regard control over indi-vidual practitioners as a necessary evil. Neither lawyers nor medical doctors advertise (beyond placing discreet cards) not because every single practitioner opposes that means of seeking clients and patients, but because his organized peers consider advertising "unprofessional" and effectively forbid it. We placed "large manufacturers" (I-d) below the retailers of I-b and I-c because their enterprises bring them more often into confrontation with government. Interstate involvements make them subject to more state laws and place them under more federal surveillances. Restaurateurs were ranked below other retailers because government controls to protect patrons from such dangers as contami-nated food are considered necessary. (The restaurant owner who serves alcoholic beverages is still more closely supervised—e. g., in the ages of patrons, hours of operation, and sometimes even the design of his front window.)

The primary justification for placing publishers atop this list stems from the First Amendment to the U. S. Constitution, which also accounts for the special, though lesser, placement of broadcasters. Like the other freedoms covered there, that of the press belongs to the people, but inevitably the businessman-publisher benefits. As the first-line bene-factor, he has a moral (but only a moral) obligation to use that privilege for informing the public fully—sometimes incurring the wrath of friends and foes with disturbing news, sometimes sacrificing extra profits to get the main job done. Extended to all fifty states through the Fourteenth Amendment and "seconded" by similar provisions in state constitutions, the press's freedom is unsurpassed by any other in American society. Naïve people overinterpret what it means, and cynics scoff at it as mean-ingless, but in terms of barring prior restraint, it is strong indeed. Gov-ernment prosecutions for abusing that freedom (criminal libel, obscenity charges, contempt of court) are significantly infrequent. Nor can any reasonable man charge that threats of such penalties seriously deter American publishers in this last third of the twentieth century.

In refereeing clashes between the rights of publishers to print and those of private citizens to be let alone or to be protected from false and otherwise unfair damage to their reputations, the judicial branch of government has been consistently solicitous of press freedom. Civil libel is an abridgement of press freedom (as at least one U. S. Supreme Court justice has argued), and so are such threats of penalty after the fact as prosecutions for sedition, obscenity, and blasphemy. In an age of few absolutes, one could say that the fortress of American press free-dom contains a few soft spots and that it has been outflanked on occa-sion, but it remains the strongest bulwark against government control yet standing in the private sector.

Publishers, as businessmen, are "interfered with" by government, of course. They are subject to most of the same zoning ordinances, mini-mum-wage laws, tax obligations, and growing business controls faced by other profit-seekers.

The significant difference between publishers and other entrepre-neurs or professional practitioners exists in the government's basic hands-off policy toward the quality and scope of what is produced for sale. A restaurant can be closed down because the City Board of Health considers that restaurant's fare dangerous to public health, but govern-ment efforts to keep a publisher from "poisoning the public's mind" have been rare and even more rarely successful. A famous illustration of American posture with regard to freedom in printing is the case of *Near vs. State of Minnesota*: A District Court had adjudged the *Saturday Press*, a purveyor of anti-Semitism and intemperate attacks on govern-ment officials, as a "public nuisance" and ordered it closed down; the U. S. Supreme Court in 1931 reversed the lower court, declaring Minne-sota's press-restricting law unconstitutional. A butcher may be fined for selling beef bootlegged past government meat inspectors, but American information inspectors have been largely confined to the front lines in wartime. (Even there they have faded in the two great conflicts—Korea and Vietnam—since World War II.)

Noting exceptions to "the basic hands-off policy" is important as a guard against idealistic naïveté about American press freedom. Like most exceptions to a general rule, they help illustrate that rule by their contrast. And they should remind observers of the constant threats to press freedom. The U. S. Post Office has occasionally exercised partial censorship by blocking distribution of publications allegedly promoting lotteries or containing obscenity. The Post Office kept abolitionist materials from circulating in the South prior to the Civil War. During World War I it employed the dubious practice of banning a given issue of a publication from the mails and then barring that publication permanently on grounds it had failed to maintain its second-class mailing schedule. In *Schenck vs. United States* (1919), the U. S. Supreme Court articulated the "clear and present danger" doctrine, in effect justifying temporary suspension of the First Amendment. The highest court's surprising affirmation of Ralph Ginzburg's 1967 conviction for sending obscene material through the mails was an exception to developing court liberality in that difficult area of press freedom. (Significantly, the publisher of *Eros* lost his appeal on grounds of demonstrated intent rather than on judicial evaluation of the magazine's content.)

On balance, however, publishing's freedom from government control surpasses that of other enterprises in terms of what it can offer the public. Government requires safety features on automobiles, but specifies no protection against "scare headlines." A careless surgeon can be sidelined by the State Medical Board, but a sloppy publisher is accountable only to private citizens. Government regulates the components of Grade A milk, structural steel, and "100% wool," but allows publishers to mix world and local news or devote their columns to pap, as they choose. The government permits a man to practice law only if he has passed the state bar examination and maintains his license; no test or licensing law stops any citizen from publishing. Two good and related reasons justify this special privilege:

1. Measuring truth and significance in man's communications is not possible, as it may be in determining public school teachers' qualifications or sanitation standards for food distributors.
2. Our democratic tradition holds that government control of the press would destroy the press's main purpose: to check on government and report back to the people.

Examples of why publishing operates within this special sanctuary belong to Chapter 2, but one modern illustration is useful here. Since broadcasting now rivals printing as a major channel of information and influence, broadcasting's necessary control by the FCC must be watched and reported on by an agency free from government interference. Newspapers and magazines are in a safe position to criticize FCC policies and actions, whereas radio and TV stations are potentially subject to penalty by the FCC. However unlikely the political majority of commissioners might be to favor license-applicants of their political persuasion, they are more unlikely to do so at the risk of press exposure. However unlikely they might be to refuse license renewals for stations that embarrassed the FCC, they are ultimately less likely to do so with a free press looking on. Those who argue that America should have "an FCC" for publishing since the FCC has not harmed broadcasting's freedom overlook the deterrent power of the unlicensed Fourth Estate.

An example of the press's watchdog role over the FCC occurred in 1958. The House Subcommittee on Legislative Oversight's chief counsel was dismissed after publicly charging the subcommittee with trying to whitewash his findings of questionable behavior by FCC members. Press disclosure—including the text of the counsel's charges in the *New York Times*—spread the issue before the citizens. Eight weeks later one commissioner, accused of accepting gifts and loans from the attorney for a Miami television station applicant and then casting the deciding vote for that applicant, resigned. The ex-commissioner and the attorney were subsequently indicted, and the conduct code of the seven commissioners underwent wholesome review. The attorney was finally acquitted, and charges against the former commissioner were dropped. Because the free press was able to watch on behalf of free citizens, the corrupting potential of power was observed, and a reasonable confidence in government integrity was maintained—as neither could have been in a closed society where the press is beholden to government.

So long as Americans intend to rule themselves, rather than trust some authoritarian government, unfettered press surveillance will remain crucial. The right to vote and to petition for redress of grievances means little to citizens without unrestricted information on government policies and practices.

FUNCTIONS OF THE PRESS

America's first newspapers and magazines concentrated on information and influence, but today's journalistic mass media perform four major functions. Over the years entertainment and paid advertising have become rivals of the first two functions. Let us set down some arbitrary definitions of the four functions. The designations are determined on the basis of "declared" primary intent, although any function's final effects can overlap the effects of others:

Information includes all reports of real-life occurrences, except those involved in the pursuit of leisure. It covers all news of government and politics, foreign affairs, weather, accidents, war, business, labor, education. It covers most of what is offered in news broadcasts and news columns of newspapers and magazines. It excludes sports, hobby columns, theater reviews. It includes network broadcasts like "Issues and Answers" and local forum ("roundtable of the air") shows, and parts of variety-discussion programs like "Tonight" and "Girl Talk."

Influence here means presentation of opinion as such—either editorials representing the views of the newspaper, station, or magazine, or some clearly identified individual journalist's views or a layman's views as in a letter-to-the-editor. It includes editorial cartoons and broadcast commentaries designated as such. It excludes "slanted" news or any other form of indirect influence—accidental or otherwise. Here we are speaking only of "labeled" attempts at directly influencing readers and listeners within the space and time not sold to advertisers.

Entertainment includes all fiction (comic strips, dramatic shows) and that factual material (sports, theater reviews, hobbies) dealing primarily with leisure. (A suit to stop transfer of a professional football franchise, however, would fall into our information category.) Entertainment in the journalistic media is important both because it competes for space and time with other functions and because its content can exert indirect influence and impart information incidentally.

Advertising is most easily identified. Usually, it is commercially oriented ("Buy Acme Toothpaste" or "Stay tuned to this station"). Occasionally, it is a public-service message ("Drive safely") or a piece of advocacy ("Why this strike is unreasonable"). But always, under this definition, it is set off by distinguishable sight and/or sound patterns on the air or by different typography in print.

With these loose definitions loosely applied, Table 2 was designed to indicate something about the proportions that the major media devote to the four functions.

TABLE 2

Estimated Allotments to the Four Functions

	Newspapers	Magazines	Radio	Television
Information	20%	°	16%	11%
Influence	4%	°	2%	1%
Entertainment	16%	°	57%	66%
Advertising	60%	52%	25%	22%

°NOTE: Major magazines vary so widely in their content patterns that "averages" for the first three categories would be totally meaningless.

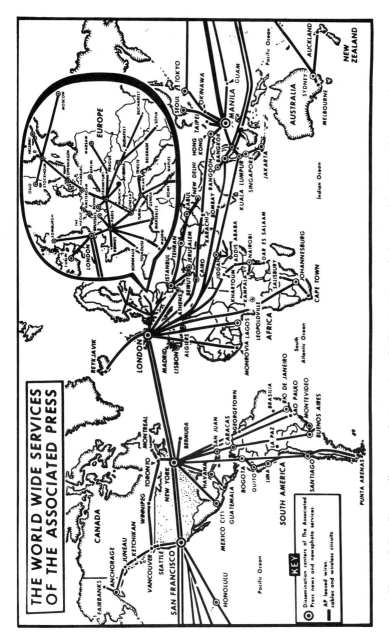

Figure 1.1. Five million words (counting duplications) are fed over this AP world network every day. They are collected and processed by 3,500 full-time employees, aided by thousands of part-time reporters and photographers, and include material collected by member newspapers and broadcasting units.

11

Caution should outweigh comparison in use of Table 2 figures. To begin with, the estimates are based on inadequate samplings. (Publisher and broadcaster organizations are hesitant to provide basic figures because of quarrels over definition and fears of unwarranted conclusions.)

Even a casual observer should recognize that broadcasting's greater concentration on entertainment is as understandable as publishing's bigger percentage of paid advertising because readers can choose from newspapers and magazines, whereas audiences cannot monitor broadcasts in anything like the same fashion. (Classified advertising in a newspaper, for example, can have no reasonable counterpart on the air.)

Misleading comparisons between media—and between outlets within one medium—can be avoided only by careful attention to differences both apparent and otherwise. A 30-second newsfilm of a Vietnam battle may deliver war information more effectively than half a column of type, partly because of its moving-picture impact and partly because the audience is "forced" to watch the film, whereas readers can skip the printed version. Or the edited film can distort the total story more grossly because printed words are subject to greater reader evaluation. Radio's daily percentage devoted to information is exaggerated in Table 2 because hourly newscasts—as any cross-country motorist with a car radio knows—contain a heavy percentage of repetition.

In the face of certain argument, let us rank the four media in carrying out the four functions of the press (Table 3). Rankings are based on a blend of each medium's relative effort, estimated use by the public, and the total reach of each medium. Among arbitrary considerations applied are estimates of such unmeasurable factors as what kind of people get most of their news from any medium.

TABLE 3

MEDIA RANKINGS BY FUNCTION

INFORMATION	INFLUENCE	ENTERTAINMENT	ADVERTISING*
Newspapers	Newspapers	Television	Newspapers ($5.2 billion)
Television	Magazines	Radio	Television ($3.1 billion)
Radio	Television	Magazines	Magazines ($1.3 billion)
Magazines	Radio	Newspapers	Radio ($1.1 billion)

*NOTE: Advertising totals for 1968.

One documented quarrel with Table 3's first column comes from Roper Research Associates, which reports that since 1963 a majority of Americans say they get most of their "news about what's going on in the world today" from television. A Television Information Office release of Roper's 1967 findings indicated that 64 per cent listed television against 55 per cent for newspapers. (Footnotes explained that "multiple answers accepted" accounted for totals greater than 100 per cent and further reported that "college educated and upper income groups" followed the same patterns.) Several psychological factors could mislead respondents. The phrase "in the world" might cause them to overlook local police and school news. The impact of "moving-picture headlines," especially when seen before the more detailed versions are read, could cause reader-viewers to confuse "most" with "startling" and "first." It is even possible that some respondents consider knowledge of major TV entertainment shows—which dominate so much conversation—part of "news about what is going on."

In any case, common sense dictates that informed citizens have to depend upon print for the major share of their total news information because television newscasts simply cannot carry that much bulk, nor could viewers assimilate it if they did. After weeding out news-illiterates from the Roper totals, a searcher for the truth would want to analyze those "multiple-answer" statistics and recast the basic question.

Any discussion of the four functions comes back inevitably to the overlap factor. Information can be written and edited in such slanted fashion that it exerts more influence than printed editorials or broadcast commentaries. (Under our definition, *Time* magazine would score 0 in the Influence row of Table 2, yet *Time's* editors admit—in fact, proclaim —that they present information in opinionated form.)

One television official, challenging the author's definitions, asked: "If you live in a big city, how much of 'Bonanza' is pure entertainment?" That adult western's information is of a more historical than journalistic nature, but many of its episodes do focus "the moral of the story" on respect for the law and property rights or against vigilante justice, thus exerting an influence. Some entertainment features in all media deliver information on the side. The comic strip "Buz Sawyer" has made startling revelations about naval weaponry on occasion. Millions have learned rudiments of courtroom procedure from "Perry Mason" (though lawyers often object to inferences laymen draw from the hero's fictional achievements). Entertainment, in an incidental fashion, has taught many people a little about geography and something about subjects ranging from aquatic safety to zoological trends. And almost all entertainment influences audiences. The late Harold Gray's "Little Orphan Annie" preached conservative political economics during four decades of dodging the Communist enemies of her billionaire foster father. Walt Kelly has supplied "Pogo" with swamp-animal acquaintances that were extremely non-flattering representations of the late U. S. Senator Joseph McCarthy in the early 1950s and President Lyndon B. Johnson in the 1960s. Demonstrating college students were brutally caricatured in Al Capp's "L'il Abner" as "SWINE" ("Students Wildly Indignant about Nearly Everything").

Serious sociological study has been devoted to entertainment's role in shaping American opinions and prejudices. Mass-communications scholars have cited numerous themes in movies, comic strips, slick-magazine fiction, and radio and television shows as having much to do with what Walter Lippmann calls "the pictures in our heads." The theory suggests that fictionalized versions of muddleheaded teachers, "Amos 'n' Andy" Negroes, and pompous Englishmen help create monumental opinion blocks against editorials and factual reports that might encourage better public-school teachers' pay, improved civil rights, and strengthened Anglo-American relations.

Recent entertainment-formula changes may loosen some of the stereotypes, if the theory is correct and if the changes are sustained. At one time, Negroes were reportedly brushed out of movie street scenes where they accidentally appeared (the "Invisible Man" treatment) and were portrayed mostly in "Stepin Fetchit" roles. By contrast, two 1968 Academy Award films, "Guess Who's Coming to Dinner" and "In the Heat of the Night," starred Sidney Poitier in hero roles. The integration of prime-time television adventure shows may have started changing the attitudinal backgrounds against which journalists must report the news and construct their opinion pieces.

Entertainment is perhaps most important to journalism as the magnet which attracts and holds large mass audiences. Its domination of commercial broadcasting is overwhelmingly apparent. Its vital role in selling newspapers and magazines by the millions is only slightly less apparent. Sports pages, comic strips, astrology columns, advice to the lovelorn, and crossword puzzles are essential to the average newspaper's survival as a mass medium. Only the *Wall Street Journal* among the circulation giants gives negligible space to entertainment, and it is a highly specialized daily. It has been estimated that the *New York Times* could increase its Sunday circulation a quarter of a million by adding a colored-comics section; certainly its sports and theater sections contribute to its circulation standing among the top 10. And it seems safe to assume that the tabloid *Daily News,* New York City's only other morning daily, has held a better than two-to-one lead over America's most highly rated newspaper at least partly because the *Daily News* offers a wider assortment of entertainment features. The importance of entertainment to magazine circulation can be inferred from the correlation between circulation size and entertainment content of the top 100 (see Appendix A). The few which offer little entertainment as such are subscription-with-membership types or special-interest journals like *Business Week* (not intended for diversified masses). A larger number, like *True Story,* *Sports Illustrated,* and *Photoplay,* are devoted almost exclusively to entertainment.

Entertainment is often valuable in its own right, of course. Certainly, serious theater and criticism of it are more valuable to society than trivial information (e. g., divorce-case hijinks among the jet set). And lesser offerings provide necessary escape from life's real problems. Its power to deliver sugar-coated pills of information and influence to lazy citizens is tremendous. Entertainment-oriented conversation shows on radio and television air—sometimes accidentally, sometimes with malice afore-thought—pungently expressed opinions on issues in which large numbers of mesmerized regular fans would otherwise remain abysmally uninterested. Dr. George W. Crane's popular-psychology column regularly strays from advice on how to pick a mate to perils of the welfare state.

The entertainment function's greatest threat to good journalism is its competition against information and influence for media space and time and consumer attention. An extra page of comic strips may add circulation and accompanying advertising revenue, thus enabling the newspaper to add editorial material—or, it may simply crowd out eight columns of news and commentary. A second lovelorn column not only steals space from significant offerings but also tempts more readers away from the remaining substance.

The entertainment-versus-information problem is more pronounced with broadcasting. America's broadcasters, unlike Britain's, have basically allowed advertisers to shape programming. This has tended to push much important journalism into the "ghetto hours" and concentrate situation comedies and variety shows in prime time. Momentous events get newspaper coverage more readily because publishers can add pages and juggle makeup in their format, but live broadcast coverage and unscheduled specials usually cost broadcasters heavy losses of advertising revenue for shows knocked off the air. Proposed all-day coverage of Pope Paul VI's visit to America in 1965 would have cost $1 million in sacrificed advertising revenues plus $300,000 in production costs, it was estimated for one television network. The three-day coverage of the aftermath of President John F. Kennedy's assassination in 1963 cost the three television networks an estimated $9.5 million in loss of advertising revenue alone. In addition, a conscientious broadcaster imperils his ratings since viewers, angered by cancellation of favorite soap operas and game shows, might switch channels. And stockholders resent both the immediate profit loss and the threat of bigger losses if ratings are damaged.

Pitted against such commercial-entertainment arguments is the duty of serving a democratic society responsibly—in return for permission to use the airwaves and the special privileges of the First Amendment.

Happily, there is some evidence that hard news pays off commercially for media in the long run. Between 1949 and 1955, when television's full impact as a competing medium hit newspapers hardest, newspapers with the highest concentration of news and commentary suffered least. For example, the tabloid *New York Daily News* dropped 234,000 (a 10 per cent loss) while the *New York Times* ended the six-year siege with 17,000 more subscribers (a 3 per cent gain). The *Times* continued to gain in nearly every one of the next 12 years, too, adding 309,000 more for a phenomenal 60 per cent growth to 870,000, while the *Daily News* lost another 21,000 to wind up the 18-year span with a net loss of 11 per cent at 2,074,000.

Examination of the 100 biggest-circulation magazines in Appendix A also reveals that information and argumentation on significant, timely issues rival entertainment in attracting mass circulation. Among highly specialized types, the news weeklies top others by wide margins (see Table 4).

TABLE 4

Magazine Specialty Rankings
(Top 100 circulators only)*

7,921,181—*Time, Newsweek, U. S. News & World Report, National Observer**

5,453,347—*Popular Mechanics, Popular Science, Mechanix Illustrated, Family Handyman, Popular Electronics*

3,569,966—*True Story, Modern Romances, True Confessions*

3,227,868—*Photoplay, TV-Radio Mirror, Modern Screen, Motion Picture*

---

*NOTE: Circulations for first half of 1967.
**NOTE: Three school-circulated news magazines—*Senior Scholastic, Junior Scholastic, NewsTime*—totaling another 4,950,648 are omitted as "forced" circulation.

Information and influence play big parts in the success formulas of the largest general interest magazines. A good half of *Reader's Digest's* editorial space is devoted to articles and opinion pieces about government, foreign affairs, current morality issues, and education. Nearly a fourth of the nonadvertising space in *McCall's* is focused on information and influence.

Important indicators also point to the salability of journalistic substance on the air. Successful operators of small-town radio stations find
that comprehensive local news coverage is the single best device for
luring local listeners from the programming of nearby metropolitan
stations. An estimated 50 million Americans regularly watched the early-
evening network television newscasts in 1968. Audience totals reached
record levels for their time with live coverage of the Kefauver Senate
Crime Committee hearings in 1951, the Army-McCarthy hearings in
1954, and the Kennedy-Nixon presidential-campaign debates of 1960.
The International Radio and Television Society, whose 1,300 executives
"encompass the business and decision-making areas of the industry,"
awarded five of its first eleven Gold Medals to news-related individuals.
In presenting the 1968 awards to the three network news chiefs, IRTS
President Edward P. Shurick declared that "the news and information
capacity of the medium . . . is fast challenging, perhaps surpassing,
entertainment as the cornerstone of television in America today."

Advertising's role as a crucial function of America's basic mass media
is both pleasantly and painfully obvious. It provides the largest part of
the revenue to finance the world's most elaborate and technically sophisticated press system. Advertising pays for all broadcasting by 82 per
cent of the television stations and all broadcasting by more than four-
fifths of the AM and FM radio stations. (The broadcasting percentages
financed by advertising are even larger in terms of total broadcasting
hours and total audience.) Advertising produces more than two-thirds
of the revenue to operate America's daily newspapers and more than
half of the two billions required annually to publish and circulate the
major "general and farm" magazines. In addition, business magazines,
nondaily newspapers, many school publications, and even some school-
operated radio stations depend partly on advertising revenue.

Advertising supplies essential marketing information to the public
and helps inform businessmen of changes within their fields.

Although laymen complain about advertising "static" on the air and
its clutter in newspaper and magazine pages, they have learned to depend upon it for guidance in their material way of life. Servicemen over-
seas during World War II objected to the absence of advertising from
their special editions of favorite magazines. A relatively new service, in
terms of volume and subject-matter breadth, is the "ad-itorial"—which
enables laymen to present controversial views beyond the typographical
limitations of the letters column. Once confined largely to political campaigns and occasional use during labor-management disputes, it has
spread to citizen concerns over civil rights and U. S. foreign policy. The
1964 U. S. Supreme Court decision in the *New York Times-Sullivan* case
(which involved an "ad-itorial" on civil rights in Montgomery, Alabama)
has encouraged this form of public debate in the mass media.

Allegations against advertising as a basic press function range from fears of advertisers' controlling the media to contentions that advertisements directly mislead a gullible public. These matters are discussed in Chapter 8, but for now we might weigh alternatives. Subsidization by political parties, like that of the late eighteenth and early nineteenth centuries, appears both impractical and undesirable. A religiously pluralistic society militates against real mass circulation of a denominational effort. Except for the *Christian Science Monitor*, religious bodies have chosen to concentrate largely on magazines aimed at their memberships. Nor have foundations come forward, as urged by the late press critic, A. J. Liebling. Sporadic efforts to publish without paid advertising have demonstrated convincingly that omnibus newspapers and multifaceted magazines with any chance for saturation circulation are too expensive to produce without advertising revenue. The most dramatic twentieth-century attempts were New York's *PM*, an experimental tabloid financed by the late Marshall Field, and *Reader's Digest*, the pioneering pocket-sized reprint magazine. *PM* operated without advertising from 1940-1946 but added the fourth function two years before it died. *Reader's Digest* avoided much of the typical magazine's production expense and reaped a good profit by selling millions of copies at a relatively high price for most of its first thirty-three years. However, a poll of *Digest* subscribers brought a four-to-one vote for adding advertising over increasing the price, and the *Digest* has been a leading advertising medium ever since. The 1955 conversion of America's most widely circulated periodical scores more heavily on the side of advertising as an essential function than its ad-less third of a century scores on the other side.

THE REACH OF THE MASS MEDIA

America's millions acquire their information and are jogged toward their opinions by an amazing variety of communicators—from neighbors across the back fence and taxicab drivers, from small-town weeklies and metropolitan dailies, from Kiwanis Club programs and speakers on the lecture circuits, from college FM radio stations and 50,000-watt clear channel AM radio stations, from Public Broadcast Laboratory offerings on UHF television and the Huntley-Brinkley VHF television network newscasts, from soap-box orators and door-to-door campaigners, from news magazines, from chamber of commerce bulletins, from trade union papers, and from nonfiction books.

The major mass disseminators are listed in Table 5.

Despite some nonsensical declarations by proponents of both sides, no citizen can be well informed today without relying on both print and electronic media. A few who think they get all they need from newscasts are in fact partially rescued from news ignorance by neighbors and

TABLE 5

Major Mass Media
(1967-1969)

Newspaper	Number	Circulation
A.M. Newspapers	328	25,838,270
P.M. Newspapers	1,443	36,697,124
Total Daily Newspapers	1,752[a]	62,535,394
Sunday Newspapers	578	49,692,602

(Above figures from *1969 Editor & Publisher Year Book*)

Weekly Newspapers	9,705[b]	27,000,000 (est.)

(Number of weekly newspapers only from *1968 N. W. Ayer & Son's Directory of Newspapers and Periodicals*)

[a]19 all-day newspapers counted only once.
[b]The Ayer Directory listed another 672 "newspapers" published from three times a week to every other month.

Magazine	Number	Circulation
General, Farm Magazines	276[c]	225,661,797

(Figures supplied by Magazine Publishers Association, compiled from Audit Bureau of Circulation listings)

[c]Number represents single titles and groups of titles. Does not include comics or magazines with non-audited circulations. Ayer listed 10,204 "periodicals" for 1967.

Radio	Stations	Receivers
AM Broadcasting	4,235[d]	58,500,000
FM Broadcasting	2,276[d]	36,250,000 (est.)
Total Radio Units	6,511[d]	58,500,000

[d]Includes 359 noncommercial FM stations and about three dozen non-commercial AM stations.

Television	Stations	Receivers
VHF Broadcasting	581[e]	57,522,300
UHF Broadcasting	259[e]	37,500,000 (est.)
Total TV Units	840[e]	57,522,300

(Radio, television figures from *1969 Broadcasting Yearbook;* FM and UHF receiver estimates by *Broadcasting's* editorial director)

[e]Includes 75 VHF and 94 UHF noncommercial stations.

friends who relay what they have read in newspapers and magazines. Those who eschew broadcast journalism sometimes escape debilitating lags in information the same way.

Many Sunday morning newspapers on March 30, 1952, ignored President Harry Truman's announcement that he would not seek a second full term, in favor of less newsworthy material in his Jefferson-Jackson Day dinner speech the night before in Washington. They were early editions based on advance copies of his prepared address, which did not contain that news bombshell. At least one Sunday newspaper went so far as to headline its coverage to the effect that Truman had remained "mum" on his presidential campaign plans! It is hard to imagine how Americans could have waited for newspapers to report the Sunday afternoon (Central and Eastern time zones) attack on Pearl Harbor December 7, 1941. Having to wait a few hours for printing and delivery of major news breaks in this nuclear age is unthinkable. Responsible relaying of news within minutes, or even seconds, is essential both to inform our complex society of important developments in time and to protect it against dangerous rumors that could create crippling panics and seriously damage public confidence in government within hours. The dimensions of sight and sound add enormously to the total truth which good journalism constantly seeks.

On the other hand, intelligent citizens cannot function effectively in a democratic society with the necessarily abbreviated information that radio and television can deliver or the limited details those citizens can assimilate from evanescent newscasts. A 30-minute television newscast delivers less information than half a newspaper's front page. It is impractical for broadcasters to carry more than a small fraction of the stories newspapers offer, and normal citizens would find it impossible to listen to all those stories at the time of broadcast, let alone grasp such details as precinct voting results and vital statistics about news principals.

And because daily, or hourly, packaging of the news twists developments out of focus, thoughtful citizens need the slower-paced writing and editing of magazines. News-of-the-week-in-review sections of Sunday newspapers and the weekly news magazines give millions better perspectives on news events and their interrelationship. Because newspapers rarely devote 80 column inches to a single story, the 4,000-word treatments of a *Harper's* provide an important source, especially for the most influential elements in a democratic society. Sometimes full-length books —such as Ralph Nader's *Unsafe at Any Speed,* dealing with automobile safety, and James Boyd's *Above the Law,* reviewing the censure of U. S. Senator Thomas J. Dodd—produce major thrusts in the journalistic surveillance of society.

Recognizing the advantages and special limitations of various media is as important to laymen depending upon them as it is to journalists operating them. Yet many newspaper readers are unaware of time differentials between morning and afternoon newspapers. Some TV newscast fans assume that a given station's local newscast covers the same material as the network newscast at a different hour. Readers denounce "*The Herald*" for failing to cover a subject given top play in "*The Chronicle*"—not realizing that the morning "*Herald*" went to press before the story broke on "*Chronicle*" time. Dependent upon a newspaper's judgment of what is important, readers should understand that some evening newspapers move a top story down or inside simply because morning newspapers got the break on it. When North Korea seized the U. S. S. Pueblo in early 1968, listeners to radio stations with one press service immediately heard bulletin treatment while those listening to other stations with only the competing service missed the story's gravity for hours.

Those who confine their journalistic sources too narrowly fail to reap the full benefits of our marvelously complex mass communications system. That system has developed its own checks and balances, born of competition between press associations, among the major media, and between units within each medium. Its total multimillion-dollar efforts tend to level the mountains of exaggeration and fill the valleys of neglect within the patterns of major news. Dedicated journalists (i. e., the non-venal, noncynical variety) and intelligent lay citizens not only must strive against those mountains and valleys in the established news patterns but also must seek to chart truths in areas of human affairs where news patterns remain undeveloped. Among modern journalism's most encouraging trends has been development of probing, in-depth treatment of problem areas (like the poverty of migrant workers) before those problems explode into news of violence, and explorations of human achievement (like the sacrificial services of a dedicated country doctor) when no "news hook" suggests such coverage.

Declining competition among newspapers has been a major journalistic concern of the twentieth century, but other factors have somewhat counterbalanced this regrettable trend. The growth of radio and television and the expanded reach of modern newspapers and magazines have established an adjusted system of checks and balances. The adjusted system leaves something to be desired at the community level, but offers new strengths at broader levels. Even at the community level, one researcher found greater total media competition in the 1960s than existed at the high-water mark of newspapers in 1910. Professor Guido Stempel, III found local ownership competition—between media or between units within a medium—in 48 per cent of the 2,947 American communities served by any local medium—"about twice the number" of 1910. (His report in the *Columbia Journalism Review* is listed under Suggested Reading at the end of this chapter.)

In any event, examples of existing competition's effectiveness are legion. A small-town Wisconsin weekly suppressed information about the city clerk's embezzlement, but a nearby metropolitan daily delivered the story to its hundreds of subscribers there. Dailies and local stations in a major eastern city overlooked (intentionally or otherwise) illegal gambling, so widespread it even involved uniformed policemen—until a network television special shocked that city and the nation with a filmed exposé. Both dailies in a large southwestern city looked the other way when a country club canceled its annual invitational tennis tournament rather than invite a top-ranked Negro star, but *Sports Illustrated* told the story to a million subscribers, including several thousand in the metropolitan area where the story had been suppressed. When television network news executives resigned to protest cutbacks in news coverage, the public—whose informational welfare was at stake—learned the details from newspapers and magazines.

ORGANIZATIONAL STRUCTURE OF THE PRESS

Corporate and organizational structure of media is important in terms of commitment to public service. If the newspaper's owner wants to inform his readers, as does John S. Knight, the republic can be well served. If the owner is a Frank A. Munsey, ruthlessly practicing his amateur economic theories on newspapers, readers will have less choice in journalism. If he is a William Randolph Hearst, seeking political power, they will be better entertained than informed. If the small-town radio station owner decides to have a disc jockey "rip and read" five-minute press-association reports on the side, he may turn an easy profit while his listeners' citizenship atrophies. If a television station owner wants to cater only to the laziest masses, he can replace "Meet the Press" with re-runs of some should-be-forgotten Western series like "Judge Roy Bean."

It is not simply a matter of profits versus public service. Under our press system, the journalistic enterprise must turn a profit to operate as an effective mass communicator. And, among the outstanding financial successes in American newspapering, especially in the twentieth century, public service looms larger as a major feature than it does on newspapers of lesser economic accomplishment. The history of broadcasting has been too short to render any similar judgment, but the early television dominance of the Columbia Broadcasting System—with its pioneering emphasis on significant news—may point in the same direction.

Rather, the question may be one of short-sightedness in seeking quick, easy profits. Unfortunately, newspaper monopolies enable venal owners to indulge in greedy irresponsibility with little apparent risk to their long-range economic security. One of American journalism's relatively unsung marvels is the number of monopoly publishers who do spend "more than they have to" on news and editorial comment. *The American Newspaper Markets* annual reports show significant correlation between percentage of households buying monopoly newspapers and the journalistic quality of those newspapers. However, 55 per cent coverage can turn a tidy profit with little strain, whereas responsible news-gathering effort to reach 75 or 80 per cent involves initial budgetary risks and sometimes disturbs the publisher's relations with the local power structure. (Where the geography of neighboring competition is right, the uncommitted publisher can have it both ways—minimum editorial effort and heavy circulation.) The threat of a new competing daily is virtually removed because of prohibitive initial costs and often because the prospective competitor cannot obtain enough popular syndicated features to meet the demands of today's mass subscribers.

One clue to a newspaper's posture with respect to profits and its special responsibilities may be found in the relationship of chief news executives to other administrators. Perhaps the most comprehensive study of newspaper organization ever made was that by Professors Donald J. Hornberger and Douglass W. Miller of Ohio Wesleyan University in the 1930s. Their findings "that there is no standard or uniform way of organizing a newspaper property" and that "far more distinction between corporate officials and major operating executives exists in the newspaper field than in the usual industrial" hold to this day. Reflecting the most important difference between journalistic enterprise for profit and other corporate enterprise for profit was this conclusion:

> The [newspaper] organization set-up is usually warped to reflect the type of control being exercised, that is, whether the paper is controlled from the viewpoint of news and editorial policies, or from a financial angle.

Overseeing corporate officials—the president, vice-presidents, secretary, and treasurer—may function in ways ranging from proper support to crippling interference. The Hornberger-Miller study found more than a third of the newspaper corporations had inactive presidents, reflecting an unusual hands-off tendency. (An example of the other extreme led a few years ago to an "efficiency study" of a metropolitan daily's newsroom. Recommendations for reducing that 200,000-daily's news staff demonstrated a complete misunderstanding of how reporters must function to carry out the newspaper's primary purpose. Such "business" attitudes toward newspapering recall William Allen White's famous 1925 comment on the passing of Frank A. Munsey, who, with "the talent of a meatpacker" and "the morals of a money-changer," had tried to change "a once-noble profession into an eight per cent security.")

The accompanying "Skeleton Operating Organization Chart of a Metropolitan Daily" (Fig. 1.2) represents no single newspaper. It is designed as a hybrid of fact and fancy, merely to illustrate some internal relationships.

The Owner may be a corporation or one man, and in the latter case he may be his own Publisher and Editor. The Editor frequently guides both news and editorial-page policy. He may run the editorial page or leave that to an Editorial Page Editor (or Editorial Director or Chief Editorial Writer). The Managing Editor normally runs the news side, supervising the News Editor, City Editor, and all other news-department chiefs. (On some papers the News Editor ranks just below the Managing Editor; on others he is only a Copy Desk Chief with little policy power, outranked by the City Editor and sometimes others.) The City Editor—now sometimes Metropolitan Editor—is generally the most important of the lower-echelon news executives. Some major dailies divide the Wire Editor's job into National ("Telegraph") and Foreign ("Cable") designations. Growing challenges by the suburban press have inspired some metropolitan papers to create an important Suburban Editor's post. Depending upon the daily's circulation pattern and news attitudes, the State Editor's importance ranges from major to little more than that of an Assistant City Editor.

A crucial determinant of any newspaper's worthiness involves relationships between the business and editorial departments. If the chain of command makes news executives subservient to whims of the advertising department, the newspaper's integrity is destructively compromised. If the Promotion Director is regularly allowed to commandeer prime news space for "Cappy Dick Contest" or Reader's Insurance propaganda, the editors' ability to win reader confidence is deservedly depressed. A Circulation Director, intent on a special drive, may suppress important stories or significant editorials where "business orientation" is dangerously short-sighted. Even a Personnel Director, insistent on employing only "The Organization Man," can dilute the newspaper's total editorial potential. The author knows one small daily where the Mechanical Superintendent, intent on early press runs, sometimes overrules the Managing Editor on story placement and page corrections—a condition traceable to the Owner's profit-only interest in the newspaper.

Whereas little moral objection can be raised against the shoe retailer who drops his only quality line in favor of another cheap money-maker, strong moral protest should be hurled at the publisher who features publicity releases and cheesecake pictures instead of expensive-to-produce news. Other shoe retailers in the area can supply the quality brand of shoes, but no competing newspaper exists down the street in 95 per cent of the cases to cover the City Council and the School Board

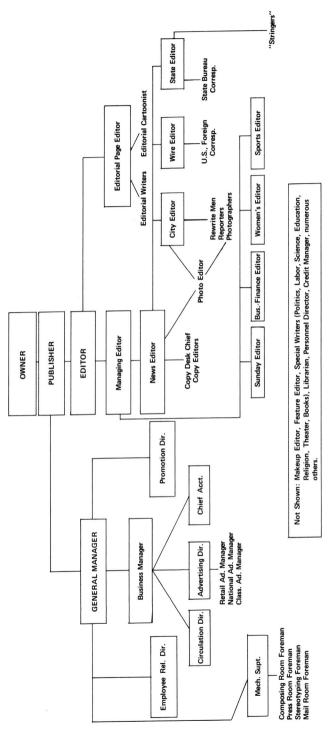

Figure 1.2. Skeleton operating organization chart of a metropolitan daily. The chain of command down the middle and to the right is of greatest concern, whatever the titles. The owner's dedication to public service, whether on the scene or through delegation, determines the level of performance.

OWNER

PUBLISHER

EDITOR

GENERAL MANAGER

Managing Editor

Promotion Dir.

Business Manager

News Editor

Editorial Page Editor

Editorial Writers

Editorial Cartoonist

City Editor

Wire Editor

State Editor

Copy Desk Chief
Copy Editors

Photo Editor

Rewrite Men
Reporters
Photographers

U.S., Foreign
Corresp.

State Bureau
Corresp.

"Stringers"

Sunday Editor

Bus.-Finance Editor

Women's Editor

Sports Editor

Employee Rel. Dir.

Circulation Dir.

Advertising Dir.

Chief Acct.

Retail Ad. Manager
National Ad. Manager
Class. Ad. Manager

Mech. Supt.

Composing Room Foreman
Press Room Foreman
Stereotyping Foreman
Mail Room Foreman

Not Shown: Makeup Editor, Feature Editor, Special Writers (Politics, Labor, Science, Education, Religion, Theater, Books), Librarian, Personnel Director, Credit Manager, numerous others.

25

the way responsible citizens need to have them covered. The broadcaster who blacks out a significant network news special to run "Ma and Pa Kettle at the Fair" deserves more denunciation than he gets.

Both the broadcaster and the publisher enjoy a degree of monopoly —one granted by the people through the FCC, and the other granted by the people's economic vote of confidence. Such franchises, delivered with the First Amendment's special privileges, add up to a public trust calling for corporate commitment to something more than just the stockholders' profits. Using the Hornberger-Miller report's terms, newspapers should be "controlled from the viewpoint of news and editorial policies," and not "from a financial angle."

Analysis of broadcasting and magazine organizations is less meaningful since news and editorials play smaller roles in their total pictures. Still, the relative position of a station's news director (Does it even have one?) and the place of a network's chief news officer provide some clues to the legitimacy of broadcasters' claims on the First Amendment and their monopoly of our limited channels.

The *1967 Annual Report to the Shareholders of Columbia Broadcasting System, Inc.*, placed the CBS News Division on a third-echelon par with the New York Yankees among its eighteen diversified corporate entities. The CBS News president was not among the parent corporation's fourteen vice-presidents, but he did sit on the Board of Directors, whereas the administrators of the Yankees and Creative Playthings did not. The news chief's place on the board and the demonstrated news commitment of CBS Board Chairman William S. Paley and CBS President Frank Stanton made things look promising for network news. However, Fred W. Friendly, who had quit as CBS news chief the year before, sounded warnings in his *Due to Circumstances Beyond Our Control* . . . Friendly reported that Paley and Stanton had turned important news-policy decisions over to Friendly's immediate superior, an executive steeped in sales rather than news. Such a move could hardly fail to give income-per-share considerations an added advantage over hang-the-expense approaches to imaginative, expensive news coverage. And the news chief was missing from the CBS Board of Directors in the 1968 annual report.

As corporate mergers grow more complex, journalism's main functions face growing threats of getting lost in the organizational charts.

FOR FURTHER STUDY

1. Add to Table 1 a Primarily Private (Nonprofit) classification. Where would clergymen and rabbis rank in freedom from government controls? Private schools and colleges? Charitable and research foundations?

2. In 1962, the late Rachel Carson's book *Silent Spring* triggered a national debate on the dangers of pesticides. Ralph Nader's *Unsafe at Any Speed* did the same thing on automobile engineering a few years later. Check the current best-seller list for nonfiction titles of similar journalistic topics and note coverage or lack of it in the four major mass media.

3. Measure allotments to the four functions (as in Table 2) for your favorite newspaper, magazine, or broadcasting outlet—or one which disappoints you. Count column inches for newspapers or pages and fractions for magazines, rounding off liberally to save time. Or count the minutes and fractions recorded for advertising messages in a station's log (open to public inspection) or use a stopwatch; subtract ad totals from the three kinds of programs and then compute all four percentages for the broadcast day. (Conversational programs such as "Tonight" should be measured internally for information and entertainment.) In comparing your findings with Table 2, remember that allotments vary seasonally for all media and by the day of the week for newspapers and broadcasting stations.

4. Compare broadcasting's information delivery with that of newspapers by jotting down a list of stories presented in one 30-minute newscast. Compare the total count with the number offered in your daily newspaper. Are any of the nonbroadcast newspaper's stories important to a good citizen? How many of the broadcast stories were insignificant?

5. Check the statistics in Tables 4 and 5 against more recent figures. (*The World Almanac* lists print media under "Circulation"; broadcasting figures usually require a bit of searching under both "Radio" and "Television." *Editor & Publisher Year Book* and *Broadcasting Yearbook* carry pertinent newspaper and radio-TV figures, respectively, in the front parts of their annual editions.) Check Appendix A also, noting changes in circulation totals and rankings. For example, Curtis Publishing Company killed its high-ranking *Saturday Evening Post* in 1969.

SUGGESTED READING

COLLE, ROYAL D., "Negro Image in the Mass Media: A Case Study in Social Change," *Journalism Quarterly*, Spring, 1968 (Vol. 45, No. 1), pp. 55-60.

COPPLE, NEALE, *Depth Reporting*, Englewood Cliffs, N. J.: Prentice-Hall, Inc., 1964, Chapter 22. Appropriately titled "Nightmare of the Newsroom," the chapter analyzes what has happened to the typical daily's news hole since 1900.

FRIENDLY, FRED W., *Due to Circumstances Beyond Our Control . . .* , New York: Random House, 1967. [Available in Vintage paperback.] Friendly's two-part adaptation from his book in *Life*, March 17 and 24, 1967 (Vol. 62) offers an interesting evaluation of entertainment-advertising dominance over information in television.

MERLIS, GEORGE, "An Afternoon Paper New York Didn't Get," *Columbia Journalism Review*, Spring, 1968 (Vol. 7, No. 1), pp. 30-33. This illustrates the clash of corporate thinking with the needs of journalism.

O'HARA, ROBERT C., *Media for the Millions*, New York: Random House, 1961. Chapter 16 offers good treatment of entertainment's role in influencing the masses.

PETERSON, THEODORE, *Magazines in the Twentieth Century*, Urbana: University of Illinois, 1964. (A capsule version of magazine-industry peculiarities is cited in the following entry.)

PETERSON, THEODORE; JENSEN, JAY W.; and RIVERS, WILLIAM L., *The Mass Media and Modern Society*, New York: Holt, Rinehart & Winston, Inc., 1966. Chapter 5 deals with structure of the communications industries; the segment on magazines, pp. 68-71, is particularly valuable.

STEMPEL, GUIDO, III, "A New Analysis of Monopoly and Competition," *Columbia Journalism Review*, Spring, 1967 (Vol. 6, No. 1), pp. 11-12. This suggests that electronic journalism's growth has resulted in more competition at the local level than existed early in the century.

REFERENCE ANNUALS

American Newspaper Markets' Circulation (Box 182, Northfield, Ill. 60093) annually gives newspaper circulations, including percentage of households covered, for every county in U. S. Includes major magazine circulations for metropolitan areas, too.

Broadcasting Yearbook (1735 DeSales St., N. W., Washington, D. C. 20036) annually reports most comprehensive information on all radio and television stations, related information.

Editor & Publisher Year Book (850 Third Ave., New York, N. Y. 10022) annually provides the most comprehensive information on daily newspapers, related information.

N. W. Ayer & Son's Directory: Newspapers and Periodicals annually lists almost every periodical, from alumni magazines to zoological journals, with officers, circulations, page size, etc.

Television Factbook (2025 Eye St., N. W., Washington, D. C. 20006) attempts to do for television coverage what American Newspaper Markets' annual does for newspaper circulation county by county.

[For additional readings, see PRICE, WARREN C., *The Literature of Journalism*, Minneapolis: University of Minnesota, 1960 (2nd Printing). Chapter IX, pp. 354-366, lists books on newspaper and magazine management; Chapter XI, pp. 387-393, lists some on radio and television.]

CHAPTER 2

The People's Need
to Know

. . . were it left to me to decide whether we should have a government without newspapers or newspapers without a government, I should not hesitate to prefer the latter.

—*Thomas Jefferson, 1787*

The only security of all is in a free press.

—*Thomas Jefferson, 1823*

The greatest danger to American press freedom stems from good citizens' ignorance of their need to know. Their tendency to equate needs for government controls on business in general with suggestions for government controls on the press misses the whole point of the press's purpose in a democratic society. The press serves as the people's watchdog of government. That watchdog function is destroyed when the government is permitted to leash or muzzle the press. Nor can that watchdog serve the citizens if government is allowed to fence itself off from the press, operating with secret meetings, secret orders, and secret trials.

Take the hypothetical case of a blue law through all three branches. The citizens need to know when such a bill is in the works so that those who feel strongly can rally for or against it. The people need to know whether it is being pushed by religious groups to force observance of their particular Sabbath or by downtown retailers trying to block some suburban competitors' seventh-day advantage. They need to know how their elected representatives voted on the bill and why, so they can reward or punish those representatives at the polls next time. The press can report these details and provide forums for debate—if it has access to proceedings and freedom to function.

After the bill becomes law, citizens need to know how it is being enforced. Those who were uninterested in the bill may become excited by what the law produces. Is it being enforced in one jurisdiction and not in another? Are some violators arrested and others merely warned? Does the pharmaceutical exemption give one druggist wide latitude beyond prescription-filling and another none? An alert free press provides the best check for all the people on whether laws are being administered fairly.

When blue-law cases reach the courts, what penalties are meted out? The press can tell the people, who must then decide whether judges are assessing only token fines (which fail to discourage breaking the law) or whether judges are handing down maximum penalties (too severe for technical violations of a hypocritical law).

At the law-enforcement and law-interpretation stages, thoughtful citizens thus get second and third chances to evaluate the merits of the law—and to call for amendments to strengthen it or to call for its repeal. Their evaluation may be based on selfish interest in shopping convenience or on religious prejudice, but it is certain to be better when fully informed than when poorly informed.

In this nineteenth decade of our republic, American press freedom from government control remains strong. The necessary evil of licensing broadcast media has not been seriously abused—largely, it could be argued, because unlicensed printing stands guard. Censorship of broadcasts is expressly forbidden in the federal Communications Act of 1934 (although its Section 315 "equal time" provision could be considered a kind of reverse censorship). Prior restraints on printed journalism have been negligible—no licensing, limited wartime censoring of front-lines dispatches (but not of periodicals as such), and only occasional interference in the form of stretching second-class mailing regulations to cripple circulation of "offending" journals. (Attempts at censoring publications for alleged obscenity at the local level have been numerous, but appellate-court rulings have discouraged these of late. Required filing of foreign-language periodicals' translations during World War I was designed to restrain opposition in the press. Censorship of publications from outside the United States is another matter.)

The government's power to punish the press after it reports and comments—and thereby to discourage press freedom—has also been held in abeyance. Prosecutions for criminal libel have been significantly rare. Even in civil-libel actions, the odds are stacked against government officials who sue the press. Contempt-of-court citations against journalists are infrequent. Statutes on obscenity are not stretched to harass journalists concentrating on general news and opinion; in fact, the judicial branch has vigorously curbed that deviation from the First Amendment for primarily literary material in recent years. (Associate Justice Hugo Black's insistence that the First Amendment's "no law abridging freedom of the press" means no law has not carried the day, but the U. S.

Supreme Court's liberalized approach has edged in that direction.) The only major government attempt to punish opposing newspapers by excessive taxation—a 1934 Louisiana statute—was forcefully struck down by the highest court.

Less reassuring is the status of press access to government activities and records—so that full reporting and informed commentary can be made. Too much government business, particularly at the local levels, is conducted in secret. Citizens sometimes are not even told of government decisions. Or they learn of those decisions when it is too late to exercise democratic influence. Voters often cannot find out which representatives supported and which opposed a particular action, let alone their elected servants' reasons for support or opposition. City Council members have been known to meet privately, thrash out a proposal on which they are split 4-3, then march into the public meeting and vote 7-0 as if the other side had never existed. This not only directly mocks democracy but also damages the Council members' image in terms of deliberative capability and responsibility. School boards have bowed in the direction of open-meeting laws by announcing when they will meet but not where. Although better press vigilance has broken many federal moves toward secrecy, enough have succeeded since World War II to make the problem at that level a far greater threat. Something like 40 per cent of congressional committee sessions (where the action is) are closed to the press—and therefore to the public. As the executive branch has grown in relative power, its tendencies toward secrecy have also grown, compounding threats to truly democratic government. Clark Mollenhoff, Washington correspondent for the Cowles publications, has written two books, detailing how Congress has been denied critical information about the executive branch. In fact, he reports, secrecy has so pervaded some powerful executive-branch agencies that the President, himself, could not find out what was going on. (See "Suggested Reading.")

NEED-TO-KNOW EXAMPLES

Government officials can be expected to follow their natural tendencies toward secrecy. Thus, if newsmen do their duty to democracy, the survival of government by the people—which rests on a free press—will depend upon those people. More accurately, the minority of conscientious and informed citizens (called "local influentials" and "cosmopolitan influentials" by some social scientists) will decide whether George Orwell's novel *Nineteen Eighty-Four* was a warning or a prediction.

Let us examine two similar instances of government secrecy. In the first, the press did its duty. The case was reported in a 1955 pamphlet

The People's Right to Know by Allen Raymond, issued by the American
Civil Liberties Union:

> In 1951, reporters for the *Albany Knickerbocker News* [then a mem-
> ber of the Gannett Newspapers group] discovered that investigators for
> the Bureau of Internal Revenue had found liquor being adulterated in
> 368 saloons within the capital area, and had levied fines totaling
> $37,465.33 upon the offending saloon keepers, without bringing them
> into court, by a process known as "confidential compromise."
>
> The city editor, Charles L. Mooney, was then startled to learn that
> although a large proportion of the saloon keepers in Albany were cheating
> their customers, and were being tried and fined for this knavery by a
> Federal agency, neither the press nor the public in Albany was entitled
> to learn from the Federal government which saloon keepers were guilty,
> or the amount of any fine. The amount of the fines, of course, averaged
> slightly more than $100 per offender, a sum that could hardly have been
> a deterrent against the saloon keepers' continuing to bilk their customers.
>
> An editorial by the *Knickerbocker News* commented: "For a Federal
> Bureau to deny information to the public on saloons it has found water-
> ing liquor and substituting cheap brands for expensive ones puts it in the
> position of aiding and abetting the guilty by concealing their wrong-
> doings. . . . The people go into public places to spend their money.
> . . . They have a right to know whether the proprietors of these places
> are conducting their business legitimately."
>
> The editor of the *Knickerbocker News* then sent this information
> to James S. Pope, Executive Editor of the *Louisville Courier-Journal,* then
> chairman of the Freedom of Information Committee of the American
> Society of Newspaper Editors. Mr. Pope exchanged correspondence—
> which was fruitless—with Charles Oliphant, chief counsel to the Treasury
> Bureau. Mr. Pope asked Mr. Oliphant on what grounds the Bureau kept
> secret the identity of guilty saloon keepers.
>
> Mr. Oliphant replied that compromises of charges against tavern
> keepers accused of adulterating their product were not matters of public
> record under the provisions of the Administrative Procedures Act. "In
> general," he said, "compromises are in the interests of the individual con-
> cerned and of the Bureau. The compromises are offered (by the tavern
> keepers) and accepted by the government in cases where liability to tax
> is doubtful. The authority to compromise thereby enables the Bureau to
> reach, by negotiations, a type of case which otherwise might escape cor-
> rective action."

Raymond raised several questions:

> In such an atmosphere of secrecy do all the so-called settlements
> find their way into the U. S. Treasury? Or are agents of the Alcohol Tax
> Unit of the Internal Revenue Bureau periodically shaking down saloon
> keepers all over the United States—as they did in Albany—and permitting
> these tavern keepers to go on robbing the public as long as they settle
> for a few dollars occasionally after some star chamber trial from which
> the public is barred? . . . is there any guarantee that revenue agent and
> saloon keeper are not whacking up the small sum of shakedowns, as petty

graft to protect illicit enterprise? Does not this government practice bring the whole Alcohol Tax Unit of the Bureau of Internal Revenue under justifiable suspicion? Does it weaken or strengthen the people's faith in their government?

Other questions could be raised, but let us use another case to get at those. This one has few specific details since it was not exposed by the press. A state law specified butterfat levels for cheese. One manufacturer (and probably others) found it less expensive to pay occasional unpublicized fines than to meet the law's requirements. He actually budgeted an amount for those fines. Possible results include:

1. If the butterfat requirement was proper, consumers were cheated out of what they paid for. That state government's executive branch was failing in its sworn duty to enforce the law. Dairy farmers were cheated out of proper earnings by illegal depression of the proper market.
2. If the butterfat requirement was bad, open opposition by cheese manufacturers might have forced a change, in the best democratic traditions. But, by making it easier for manufacturers to "bribe" their way around it, the bad law was allowed to stand.
3. If the law was bad, the secret fines increased the manufacturers' costs and therefore the retail price. The process also wasted tax money, financing fake enforcement of a worse-than-unnecessary law.
4. As in the watered-liquor case, agents collecting unreported fines could be tempted to pocket $50 and turn in $50. The payer of the fine and the agent's superior had no reliable checkpoint. Nor did the payer of the $100 fine know whether his competitor got off with $50.
5. Whether the law was good or bad, naïve (i. e., honest) manufacturers faced unfair competition, having to cut their profit margins or charge a higher price to cover higher costs. (If the law was good, his cheese may have sold better; if the law was bad, he may have suffered on both counts.)
6. Because publicity is often worse than the legal penalties in such cases, unscrupulous agents could in effect demand "protection money" from honest manufacturers. The honest manufacturer who refused to pay the blackmail might be in the ironical position of being "exposed" as an accused cheater while his dishonest competitors remained protected from exposure through "confidential compromise."
7. Poorly enforced laws, especially bad ones, breed disrespect for other laws. ("If the state doesn't mean it with the butterfat law, maybe it doesn't mean it with the income tax. If Ed can shortchange on the butterfat in his cheese, I ought to be able to shortcut on sanitation in my restaurant.") The Eighteenth "Prohibition" Amendment and the accompanying Volstead Act demonstrated that tendency nation-

wide from 1920-1933. Without effective enforcement and full exposure, rumor replaces fact and cynicism replaces respect in public
discussion and attitudes concerning the law.

The only effective protection against such dangers is to make government accountable to the people. And the best device yet found for
that is an independent press system, reporting fully on all three branches.
The press is an imperfect instrument, of course, since it is subject to the
same human frailties which beset men in government, from City Hall to
Capitol Hill. The checks and balances among the legislative, executive,
and judicial branches militate against corrupting power within any one
branch. The "fourth branch," operating outside the government, can help
the citizens referee those checks and balances—first, by reporting the
actions and discussions which busy citizens cannot watch for themselves
and, second, by providing a wide range of commentary on government
affairs.

POLITICAL REASONING

In late 1962, then Premier Nikita Khrushchev of Russia delivered
an impressive diatribe against corruption in his country. In eighty-seven
single-spaced pages, he charged party racketeers with selling diplomas,
putting in the fix for pensions, peddling apartment permits for bribes,

Figure 2.1. A South Vietnamese military policeman bars Associated
Press photographer Eddie Adams from entering Danang's soccer
stadium where three suspected Viet Cong sympathizers were about
to be executed. (Associated Press photograph)

and assigning plots of land out of order. He blamed the tyrant, Joseph Stalin (safely dead for nine years), and explained: "The wonderful system of control which had grown up during the first five years of Soviet rule was replaced by a bureaucratic control apparatus divorced from the masses." The Russian press, operated by the party in power, could not have reported to those masses anything about destroying the earlier "wonderful system" since it had been an integral part of the later "bureaucratic control apparatus." When Khrushchev was deposed in October, 1964, such key editorial figures as his son-in-law Aleksei Ad-zhubei, editor of *Izvestia*, lost their jobs. Suddenly, the Russians were told of Khrushchev's "hare-brained scheming, bragging, and phrase-mongering." The Russian press had said nothing like that during Khrushchev's decade at the top, anymore than it had reported anything unfavorable about Stalin's rule in the preceding decades.

Only a stumbling step removed from the Communists' at-the-source control is the old-fashioned authoritarian press system. That system prevailed pretty much worldwide from the invention of printing in the fifteenth century through most of the eighteenth century. Great Britain and her offspring, the United States, established free-press systems only two centuries ago. Utilized in the Western World, the concept is far from safely entrenched there. In much of the world, rigid controls on the press still prevail. (Freedom-of-the-press ratings throughout the world are discussed in Chapter 12.)

Meanwhile, attacks on liberty of the press continue apace at the fountainheads. They range from government-news blackouts to serious suggestions for press-restriction laws. A senior member of Congress in 1968 recommended "suspending" the First Amendment. Professor Curtis D. MacDougall presents an alarming list of proposed laws in his *The Press and Its Problems* (see "Suggested Reading"). These included bills in state legislatures to subject newspapers to regulation as public utilities, to license newsmen, to force the printing of government replies to criticisms, and to punish minor officials who talked to newsmen. A bill before Congress in the 1930s would have banned from the mails newspapers carrying unsigned editorials. Another would have made "deliberate falsification" a criminal offense.

Whether press freedom will be yielded, as we said earlier, depends upon the electorate's attitude. When the United States faced its first "cold war" during the John Adams Administration, public opinion rejected that Administration's blatant attack on press freedom. The people saw quickly that the Alien and Sedition Acts of 1798 were designed to silence the opposition. The "dangerous" aliens to be deported were those opposed to the party in power, particularly unfriendly editors. The "false" utterances and printings forbidden by the Sedition Act turned out to be unprovable opinions against the Administration. Public reaction against that departure from the First Amendment is credited with helping Thomas Jefferson to defeat Adams in the election of 1800. Dissenting patriots who had been victimized by that disgraceful law were pardoned and had their fines repaid with interest after the measure had expired.

Whether modern public opinion could be rallied against similar law-making "efforts to protect the United States from the dangers of a free press" is open to question. Such blatant attempts as those in the Alien and Sedition Acts probably would bring a public outcry. (Historians Charles A. and Mary R. Beard considered the 1918 Sedition Act worse than the 1798 version, but our entry into World War I did differ from the "cold war" test 120 years earlier.) A modern Congress and Administration would be unlikely to move that far without a declared war. But step-by-step approaches to press control are another matter. Advocates of "some" control point to the fact that today's press is not as open to would-be editors as was that of the late eighteenth and early nineteenth centuries. They also argue that jet air travel, nuclear weapons, and intercontinental missiles make today's cold-war dangers vastly more threatening than those during the time of John Adams. Mushrooming domestic problems—from civil-rights strife to air pollution—make undirected mass communication a luxury we can no longer afford, according to those arguments.

American majorities invariably declare their dedication to press freedom, but evidence often indicates that this dedication is more to a mystique, than to the hard realities. Among the most comprehensive surveys in this field was one made by Charles E. Swanson of the University of Minnesota in 1949. Swanson found that more than 90 per cent of a Midwestern city sampling favored allowing their daily to present "all" ideas. That reassuring result faded with a check of specifics. Not a single specific, ranging from such innocent practices as book criticism to such delicate matters as criticizing a religion, was considered allowable by all of those who favored freedom in the abstract. Less than 80 per cent would have allowed the newspaper to attack the mayor and less than two-thirds would have allowed it to attack the President. One-third would have forbidden criticizing an employer's labor policy, and barely half would have permitted criticizing a gasoline's quality.

College students tend to score even worse in realistic commitment to press freedom. The tendency is partly explained by their relatively recent (and often only partial) emergence from authoritarian domination by parents and school officials. They pay relatively less attention to news and editorials since their campus-life concerns fall outside the substance of those. (Among five age groupings, from 15-20 to 55-and-over, the 15-20 group scores lowest in average newspaper readership, according to studies made for the American Newspaper Publishers Association.) Compounding this danger to free-press commitment among tomorrow's opinion leaders, this author believes, is the widespread practice of mangling the principle's meaning on most college campuses.

Whether either public or private colleges can afford to grant editorial freedom to college-newspaper editors is a subject too involved for full discussion here. Idealists argue that even when the newspaper is published by the college, students should be totally free in their editorial control. The more traditional view was succinctly expressed by the head of a large Midwestern school of journalism: "The man who pays the bills must take responsibility for what is printed and therefore must have control over what is to be published." A number of colleges in effect evade the issue by allowing an off-campus "dummy corporation" to publish the newspaper and control editorial policy. Even there, some conservatives argue, use of the college's name vests some owner control with the college.

The larger problem, in this author's view, is one of nomenclature. Proclaiming that the student newspaper is "free" or "independent" and then censoring it in the name of "responsibility" is the evil. In fact, the possible inference that a controlled student newspaper has real press freedom is dangerous. The college which controls its student newspaper should take steps to prevent such an erroneous assumption. An adviser who has censoring power should perhaps be identified as the publisher —indicating that he controls the student editor just as the publisher outranks the editor on a commercial staff. If limited areas of freedom do exist (e. g., coverage of student government), those could be spelled out. Some college papers might be labeled "Laboratory Newspaper" in their mastheads or flags when they are in fact controlled by a journalism department.

The danger lies in teaching future citizen-leaders that "press freedom" really means something different from what the First Amendment intended. One political science professor at a Western university seriously argued that the student newspaper should not have reported the Student Council's 5-4 division over raising the activities fee. He insisted that the newspaper's job was to sell the majority decision and that it was failing its mission by even reporting arguments against that decision. The author once heard a city manager denounce the local daily with just such an argument. He related how his university's student government had functioned so much more smoothly than the city's because the student editor, who was "both free *and responsible*," had refrained from reporting minority views on issues "too complicated" for those outside the government. The professor and the city manager argued that once the electorate's representatives had made a majority decision democracy had been satisfied, and the community press's job was to help government in both its news and editorial columns. This parallels frighteningly the "Soviet Communist" system as outlined in *Four Theories of the Press* (see "Suggested Reading").

In a coast-to-coast survey of college-press policies a few years ago, the author found overwhelming evidence of specious freedom claims. The questionnaire carefully indicated that it was not another sheep-and-goats check on "campus press freedom." Policy-identification choices included a respectable "laboratory" designation and one other favorably phrased option. Yet only 30 per cent chose a category other than "real freedom of the press." Another 29 per cent split the truth by marking "real freedom" and a contradictory choice as the distinguishing characteristic. Total replies of the remaining 41 per cent, who claimed "real freedom" alone, revealed outrageous discrepancies. One claimant, for example, indicated that "all copy must be shown to a faculty adviser" and page proofs as well. In response to the question "Are editors pushed toward making their own, even risky, decisions?" he took the trouble to type in "Never." Only a fourth of the claimants indicated in their total answers that they meant it. A follow-up check on that 10 per cent would have reduced the actual total, of course. Results of that survey thus indicated that the American meaning of press freedom was being grossly mistaught on at least 60 per cent of those campuses. And chances are, some of the 30 per cent who did not claim "real freedom" in that professional, no-names survey did falsely claim it on their own campuses. This dangerous burlesque of an important democratic device is approached only by the operation of some student governments, whose supposed control of certain student affairs is actually an exercise in what dictators call "guided democracy."

The issue of press freedom is rarely raised with regard to college broadcasting stations. The fact that programming is primarily beamed to off-campus audiences, rather than to the college community, is probably the primary reason. Full-time nonstudent professionals usually play direct roles different from that of a newspaper adviser. The administration's holding of the broadcasting license more clearly identifies it as the responsible owner than is the case with student newspapers. (The *Columbia Missourian*, where University of Missouri journalism students work under faculty professionals on a competitive commercial-style newspaper, is like most college broadcasting operations in this respect.)

CONFUSIONS OVER FREEDOM

Contributing to reservations about general press freedom are several areas where the Fourth Estate functions weakly or not at all. Certain government operations have been traditionally exempted from full press surveillance. Diplomatic negotiators have been expected to operate secretly. Press disclosures of police strategy which might help fugitives from justice are not knowingly made by responsible journalists. Military facts that could help the enemy plan strategy are voluntarily embargoed by the press itself. Therefore, officials suggest and laymen often wonder, why not "lay off" other sensitive matters?

Adding to this factor are isolated instances of voluntary news black-outs in specific situations, which seem to suggest that still more might be helpful. Chicago broadcasters subscribed to a code on riot coverage to keep some of the lunatic fringe from flocking to disturbance sites. Washington newspapers for a time ignored American Nazi Party disturbances on Capitol Hill to avoid inspiring the storm troopers with publicity "rewards."

The answer to why-not-more views of the foregoing lies partly in the dangers of those very suppressions themselves. Those dangers should give free-society devotees pause in blindly calling for more blackouts, and they should warn against letting government (rather than the press itself) control the blackouts. Two United States senators almost succeeded in blocking American military commitment during early NATO treaty discussions, but alert reporting exposed their position in time to allow for public debate. That public debate surprised the senators in revealing that Americans, fresh out of World War II, wanted a meaningful NATO alliance to protect Western Europe from Russian threats. If no reports are made on police efforts to apprehend criminals, public confidence in police protection may be dangerously depressed. (During the sixty-five days between Martin Luther King's assassination, April 4, 1968, and the capture of the prime suspect, news coverage of the search served two purposes—to combat charges that the FBI was not trying to catch the man and to enlist the public's help in finding him.) Detailing exact troop movements near battle positions could help enemy intelligence, but withholding the number of United States troops in South Vietnam or West Germany would only deny to American citizens what foreign military commanders already know. Does "protecting" the people from shocking pictures of dead American soldiers, as in World War I and much of World War II, inspire the most useful citizens' attitude toward the total war effort? Do law-abiding citizens have a right to be warned about riot areas that might rival the value of keeping such information from thugs? Should the American Nazis be denied their publicity "rewards" at the expense of failing to alert other Americans to their threat? (Might the promptly reported facts about Nazi shenanigans be less frightening than unchecked rumors, which could inflate the Nazis' importance?)

Secret juvenile-court proceedings shield youthful defendants from the scars of bad publicity, but present other dangers. One California teen-ager (from the wrong side of the tracks) was serving time in reform school when a reporter accidentally unearthed evidence that freed the boy. Had the original trial been public, that evidence—that the little girl whose testimony convicted the boy was a pathological liar—might have spared the teen-ager from something worse than embarrassment. A South Dakota case offered a reverse situation. An enterprising reporter exposed the authorities' failure to punish several young men (from the right side of the tracks) who had brutally raped and beaten a girl with lesser social connections. Gossip exaggerating the facts of cases involving young offenders, or assigning guilt to the wrong parties, is a seldom-recognized by-product of such secrecy. If the sociological benefits of the practice outweigh its evils, those evils should at least give pause to those who would extend such secrecy to other government affairs.

To be an effective democratic instrument, the press must be trusted by the people. Conspiracies of silence, no matter how well intentioned, imperil the press's important ability to allay unwarranted public fears and suspicions. People tend to be panicked by wild rumors in inverse proportion to the completeness of press coverage. Wartime army camps, where secrecy dominates, are breeding grounds for wildest rumor. Where citizens believe the local press is hushing up news unfavorable to The Establishment they develop a debilitating distrust which seriously handicaps efforts toward community progress. Even a mild quarantine on unfavorable angles in coverage of a local issue may boomerang against a worthwhile project. One aftermath study of two recent attempts to establish metro government suggested this. The press in both areas had supported the plan with editorials. Voters approved the plan in the area where antimetro forces had received full news coverage. Voters in the other area, "protected from divisive appeals," turned it down. The study indicated mass feelings of vague mistrust, a fear that "they were trying to put something over on us" in the latter case. Inoculations of "bad" news into the body politic's information stream build important protections against the dangers of infection by rumors and doubt.

Full coverage tends to protect press freedom itself. Studies by Swanson and others have indicated that citizens support coverage and comment somewhat in proportion to their exposure. Swanson found only 12.6 per cent would forbid criticism of books and movies (which they had seen in their daily), whereas 40.5 per cent would forbid criticism of gasoline quality (which they had not seen). A majority of both students and faculty at one college of 2,000 enrollment opposed campus-newspaper coverage of faculty meetings before it was instituted. After three years of such coverage, the balance had shifted to majority support in both groups.

DEFENSE BY THE PRESS

Canon II of the American Society of Newspaper Editors code of ethics declares: "Freedom of the press is to be guarded as a vital right of mankind." (The Radio Television News Directors Association's Code of Broadcast News Ethics points in the same direction in Article Six [See Appendix B].) This canon seems less subject to varying interpretations than do the other six. One might argue about fine points of access, like cameras in the courtroom, but it does seem to require opposing prior restraints on the press.

Yet the 1925 Minnesota "gag law"—allowing bans on "nuisance" journals—stood unattacked by that state's press until after the U. S. Supreme Court struck down the statute in 1931 (*Near vs. State of Minnesota*). A federal law requiring registration of all printing equipment (including mimeograph machines) by groups on the attorney general's list of subversive organizations was challenged only by the *St. Louis Post-Dispatch* at the time it was rushed through Congress during the "Red scare" following World War II. The real test of commitment to this, or any other, freedom lies in one's support of the principle for those with whom he disagrees.

On the other side, strong newspaper support helped broadcast journalism remove the equal-time straitjacket on newscast coverage of political figures in 1959. The FCC had ruled, 4-3, that a Chicago station had to give Lar "America First" Daly twenty-two seconds on a news show to balance filmed coverage of Mayor Richard Daley's greeting a foreign dignitary. The decision was based on the fact that both were candidates in Chicago's mayoralty contest. Frank Stanton, president of CBS, led a well-covered fight against the decision. He was supported by at least ninety-eight newspaper editorials, numerous columns, and editorial cartoons from coast to coast. Under heavy pressure, Congress changed the rule, exempting noncampaign news coverage of an incumbent candidate. The next year, Congress temporarily suspended part of the remaining equal-time restrictions to allow televised debates between the two primary presidential candidates, John F. Kennedy and Richard M. Nixon. In civil-libel cases involving potentially important precedents, news media do tend to close ranks for freedom of the press. The 1964 landmark success of the *New York Times* in its U. S. Supreme Court appeal of the Sullivan case, for example, was supported by the *Chicago Tribune*, despite sharp differences in editorial opinions. The Inter-

American Press Association maintains an impressive vigilance in behalf of press freedom throughout the Western Hemisphere, defending oppressed journalists and attacking authoritarian efforts like a 1968 bill to require registration of newspapers and magazines in the Virgin Islands.

Greater vigilance and more submergence of political prejudice and competitive selfishness are needed to advance and protect liberty of the American press. A state-capital daily of Republican persuasion violated at least the spirit of Canon II when it ridiculed a Democratic governor for opening his cabinet meetings to press coverage in 1959. Equally blinded by political prejudice was a Midwest morning daily when it attacked the "editorial faux pas" of a nearby college newspaper. The editorial had "invited" President Harry Truman to join that college's history faculty when he finished his term, and this had reportedly incensed Old Guard alumni, still smarting from Truman's 1948 upset victory over Thomas E. Dewey. Noting that the college's alumni fund had "suffered" (actually it was 25 per cent ahead of the preceding year's), the metropolitan daily suggested that student editorials "be more carefully screened in the future . . . one boner like that is enough for one lifetime." Even foes of editorial freedom for student editors could hardly consider the editorial an example of irresponsibility calling for censorship. It remained for the college's publicity director (a Republican nonadmirer of Truman) to lecture the professional editor on the rudiments of free speech and the extra perils of attacking it with hearsay evidence.

When the commercial press challenges student journalists' claims to press freedom—as it may properly do—it should consider the whole situation, lest it appear to oppose the principle by which it supposedly lives. If the editorial writer likens the college administration and trustees to his own publisher and owner in rebutting students' freedom claims, he should consider chastising that administration for falsely advertising, or implying, that its student newspaper is free. His concern should be with protecting the real meaning of press freedom, not with "putting down some college kids" as is so often the case.

Nor should the obvious connection between freedom of the press and freedom of speech so frequently elude professional editorialists. Neither freedom can exist without the other. Yet the records of both print and electronic journalism are filled with yawning silences in the face of state-college speaker bans and municipal maneuvers against renting halls to minority advocates. Shamefully, one can find outright journalistic support for violating the First Amendment.

Among the infrequent editorials supporting free speech are too many with a halting, almost apologetic, tone. One such, offered by a chain of more than a dozen newspapers, noted the U. S. Supreme Court's 1968 ruling that an Illinois high school teacher had been unjustly fired for writing a letter to his newspaper. After seven paragraphs of reviewing the case and unenthusiastically accepting the opinion, the editorial concluded: "Moreover, [the plaintiff's] comments were constructive, according to his viewpoint, which is more than can be said about the statements and actions of some college professors who helped incite recent student riots—and got away with it." The editorial thus appeared more concerned with who "got away with" free speech than it was pleased by that victory for free speech.

The press could well emulate—as indeed some elements have—the American Civil Liberties Union's posture on the First Amendment. The ACLU has been called "ultra-liberal" and "left-leaning," but the truth is that it has defended basic freedoms from attacks on both flanks. The late Senator Joseph R. McCarthy once badgered a witness with the false allegation that the attorney general's list of subversive organizations included the ACLU. The senator's mistake grew out of the fact that right-wing assaults gave the ACLU most of its business during those years right after World War II. However, even then, the ACLU's efforts included a formal protest against a Seattle radio station's refusal to sell time to McCarthy.

In the 1960s, the ACLU was very busy defending the rights of extreme conservatives against the assaults of panicked liberals and others. Against an all-star lineup of forty politically liberal groups (including the NAACP and the state AFL-CIO and Council of Churches), the ACLU's Pennsylvania affiliate supported the right of the Rev. Carl McIntire's fundamentalist Faith Theological Seminary to acquire a radio station license in Media, Pennsylvania. Records show that the ACLU supported segregationist Mississippi Governor Ross Barnett's demand for a jury trial on contempt-of-court charges and challenged the U. S. Justice Department's treatment of ultraconservative Major General Edwin A. Walker following the University of Mississippi desegregation riots in 1962. It has backed the rights of the John Birch Society, the American Nazi Party, British fascist Oswald Mosley, and others to speak and to be accorded due process of the law.

A 1963 struggle over a Playboy Club application for a New York City cabaret permit offers an appropriate sample of ACLU work. The ACLU's side lost in the New York Supreme Court's Appellate Division, but along the way the ACLU showed dedication to freedom for all. After New York's license commissioner denied the application, the Playboy Club took its case to court. The New York Civil Liberties Union filed an *amicus curiae* (friend-of-the-court) brief supporting the club's petition for a writ of mandamus to reverse the commissioner. The brief contended that the denial had involved prior restraint and violated due process because the applicant had satisfied the three conditions specified by law for such a permit. It contended that refusal had been based on prejudiced assumption that the club would violate other laws later. The *Brooklyn Daily*, which opposed licensing the club, editorially denounced the NYCLU for intruding in the case. However, Kings County Supreme Court Justice Arthur G. Klein praised the brief in his decision ordering that the permit be granted. Thereupon, the *Brooklyn Daily* lambasted Klein, hinting at questionable motives on his part. Klein referred the editorial to the Brooklyn Grand Jury, which returned a criminal-libel indictment against the newspaper. Immediately, the NYCLU leaped to defend the newspaper. Before Justice Klein dropped his charges, Counsel Emanuel Redfield prepared another *amicus curiae* brief. In it, he declared: "Ironically, the Union is now defending its critic against the complaint of its admirer. This seeming inconsistency is readily explained in that the Union adheres to principle objectively, free from emotional appeals and personalities, and has done so repeatedly throughout its history."

WHAT THE PUBLIC WANTS

Since American press freedom rests ultimately on public opinion, a review of pressures on that opinion may help indicate whether that freedom can survive this century. In several crisis periods, significant masses—if not majorities—of American people themselves moved to curb freedom of speech and the press. Their mood endorsed, and sometimes led, governmental antifreedom moves. Prior to the Revolutionary War, several Tory newspaper editors were driven from business. Even Patriot and neutral editors who dared to print stories or letters favorable to the other side were subjected to mob attacks. From the 1830s to the Civil War, Abolitionists fought countless costly battles with Northern citizens who feared that antislavery journalism would foment war. Various "citizen committees" and just plain mobs wrecked printing offices and assaulted editors. The Rev. Elijah P. Lovejoy kept his *Observer* going after mobs destroyed his presses three times, but he was killed in a fourth attack at Alton, Illinois, in 1837. (Government suppression of Abolitionists in the South precluded much chance for popular censorship there.)

Mob actions against newspapers carrying unpopular views continued during the Civil War, but overt violence by private citizens largely de-escalated to individual incidents from the last third of the nineteenth century onward. Mobs lynched a German Socialist in Illinois and a union official in Montana during World War I, but propaganda-incited citizens resorted mostly to burning editors in effigy by that time. Private mass attacks on press freedom now occur in more civilized forms. Economic boycott, like that which ruined P. D. East's antisegregationist *Petal Paper* in Hattiesburg, Mississippi, is the modern vigilante device for silencing dissent in the press. Some reactionaries developed a new wrinkle on this in California during the 1960s. Working in relays, they harassed smaller dailies by tying up telephone lines to hamper ad sales and news-gathering and by choking office functions with deluges of useless mail.

On the whole, public opinion has shown a better tolerance toward press freedom during the past four decades, in terms of private behavior toward journalistic dissent in times of crisis. The Great Depression of the 1930s brought no serious threats from either the people or their government. The *Chicago Tribune* prospered in a highly competitive market despite sometimes inflammatory attacks on an exceptionally popular President, Franklin D. Roosevelt. During World War II, neither the people nor their government moved against coverage of, or possible dissent from, American involvement on the scale they had under the much smaller provocation of World War I. In both the Korean War of the 1950s and escalated involvement in Vietnam during the 1960s, acri-monious dissent was well tolerated. (Private attitudes and public be-havior during the Red scare of the 1950s might win no First Amendment prizes, but performance on both fronts was significantly superior to those during the similar panic of the 1920s.)

Still, just as observers may question whether today's vastly im-proved press is good enough to cover today's vaster problems, one may ask whether the American public's improved tendency not to lynch dis-senting editors is good enough to protect press freedom from subtler and more complex pressures for government controls. These pressures might be grouped under three general headings.

1. IMPATIENCE WITH IMPERFECTIONS

No reasonable observer of American journalistic history can doubt that today's press is infinitely better than the one which the Founding Fathers blessed with unique protection from government interference. But to arguments about whether it is "better enough" for an infinitely different age has been added the "rising expectations" factor. Just as improving the lot of oppressed peoples tends to make them more, rather than less, demanding, so do press improvements tend to call for more. The abandonment of purely partisan news columns has led to involved concerns about "slanting" the news. The demise of truly sensational journalism like that of the 1890s and 1920s has led to a looser use of the "sensationalism" charge. Good televised documentaries have helped inspire the "vast wasteland" attack on the balance of television's 126-hour-a-week offerings. Increasing demands, of course, are necessary to continuing improvement, but ever present is the danger of impatience outrunning reasonable improvement. The danger is that citizens may employ the quick cure of government control, to which press freedom is fatally allergic.

The "fair trial versus free press" controversy affords an example. Pretrial coverage has improved sharply from the sensational offerings of the 1920s and 1930s, but lapses like that in the 1954 case of Dr. Samuel H. Sheppard have produced cries for press restrictions. Sheppard served ten years for the bludgeon slaying of his wife Marilyn in suburban Cleveland before being acquitted in a second trial in 1966. The U.S. Supreme Court's order for the second trial cited "prejudicial publicity" as having blocked a fair·trial the first time. Among page-1 shockers had been such *Cleveland Press* headlines as "Quit Stalling and Bring Him In" (prior to Sheppard's arrest) and "Who Speaks for Marilyn?" (above coverage of defense testimony during the trial proper). Fears that innocent defendants may be convicted by prejudiced juries and that guilty men may escape conviction through press-caused mistrials have inspired pressures against press surveillance of law-enforcement and judicial proceedings. Many civil libertarians favor parts of the American Bar Association's Reardon Report as necessary to uphold the Sixth Amendment's guarantee of a "trial by an impartial jury" but oppose other parts as violating that amendment's provision for a "public" trial as well as the First Amendment. They favor court moves to curb prejudicial pretrial statements by lawyers and police officers. But they look with suspicion on enlarged contempt-of-court threats against the press and increased secrecy in court proceedings. This issue, further discussed in Chapter 10, represents a major test of America's commitment to press freedom.

Critics have leveled the "one-party press" charge throughout much of the twentieth century. The ("Hutchins") Commission on Freedom of the Press synthesized important aspects of this in its 1947 report, *A Free and Responsible Press*. The basic complaint is that mass communications is big business and tends, therefore, to side with big business's views to the exclusion, or unfair subordination, of other views. The American Newspaper Publishers Association's formal condemnation of the proposed Child Labor Amendment in 1935 is a frequently cited example of newspaper-owners' propensity toward the status quo. The overwhelming editorial-page support for Republican candidates since 1920 is charged to business control of the press. In nine of the ten past presidential campaigns, a majority of newspapers have endorsed the Republican candidate (1964 was the exception) by percentages ranging from 55 to 67 per cent, according to *Editor & Publisher*. In terms of circulation, the Republican-favoring percentages ran even higher—probably well over 80 per cent in several instances. Meanwhile, however, news-column coverage of candidates and issues has been found basically well balanced. In his study of thirty-five dailies' coverage of the 1952 campaign, Professor Nathan B. Blumberg found only six clearly guilty of news-column partiality (see *One-Party Press?* in "Suggested Reading"). Radio and television coverage, among other factors, has discouraged blatant favoritism. Many party-lining editorial pages offer syndicated columns and letters-to-the-editor which favor the other side.

From the Hutchins Commission to the late A. J. Liebling, critics generally ruled out government controls as a cure for political imbalance. However, some newer critics have been looking toward legal force like that of the federal Communications Act's equal-time rule. Professor Jerome A. Barron of George Washington University's Law School proposed in the June, 1967, *Harvard Law Review* that government should guarantee right of access to the press for individuals and groups. Although more opinions get wider circulation now than during any previous period in history, critics argue that it is not enough. In fact, some say, America has suffered too much already from suppression of news and views by the press-owners. Further risks, they say, are too dangerous in these more perilous times. Press-freedom proponents argue that government power to control news space would threaten the Fourth Estate's watchdog function directly and indirectly. Even well-intentioned officials could cripple newspapers and magazines by ordering enough "press access" material to choke the news hole. Radio and television faced that kind of threat in the 1959 Chicago mayoralty affair, they contend, and its correction might not have been made without help from the unlicensed print media. They point to the feebleness of broadcast editorializing as an example of what government-enforced "fairness" might do to newspaper and magazine editorializing. The indirect threat feared is that a kind of Law of Increasing Government Power would operate: "If you can force something 'good,' why not stop something 'bad'?" With no segment of the press safe from potential bureaucratic revenge, the FCC and its print counterpart might try to "correct" more than mere political imbalance.

2. OPPOSITION BY FALSE ANALOGY

Some laymen's reservations about full exercise of press freedom rest on false analogies and confusion about journalistic operations. Newscasters who also deliver commercials tend to blur the lines between objective news coverage and outright advocacy for listeners. Newspapers which identify a syndicated columnist as a "*Gazette* columnist" confuse readers over who's doing what in their paper. Ignorance of libel-law rudiments causes readers and listeners to judge some journalism unfairly;

of legal privilege, they regard coverage of wild accu-
he Senate floor and reluctance to cover wild accusa-
here as mere lack of fair play. (The libel defense of
ıssed in Chapter 10.)
e most dangerous lay attitude stems from the tendency
ate matters with public affairs. The private citizen who
ghbors to think he earns more (and his creditors to think
he earns) than he actually does sympathizes with the city manager
who objects to having his exact salary revealed to the public. Businessmen who appreciate the advantages of private dealing side with public
servants who prefer to deliberate and decide behind closed doors. Ob-
serving the golden rule, good citizens sometimes oppose police-court
listings, lest it happen someday to them. Privately employed experts
appreciate government-employed experts' objections to the perils of
being misinterpreted by outsiders. The ultimate in all this is the "We
elected them to govern; now let them govern" attitude.

Then there is the lowest-common-denominator doubt about press
freedom. One serious error among thousands of accurate reports is cited
by some as a compelling argument against allowing unrestricted news
coverage and comment. For example, a major network newscast's report
that Negro James Meredith had been killed on a "freedom walk" in the
South, when he had been only wounded, could have sparked major race
riots, extreme censorship proponents argue. More widespread is the
tendency to lump all press performance with that of the worst. Use of
a double standard in covering bad news by some editors hurts public
confidence in the entire press's avowed watchdog role. A prominent
Southwestern editor openly declared that he kept names of the "best"
citizens out of his police-court reports because their good reputations
were too valuable to besmirch. (How he determined the cutoff on his
protected list was not explained.)

Because mass media seek full coverage partly to obtain salable
goods, laymen sometimes dismiss free-press pleas as mere profit-seeking,
rather than defenses of the democratic process. The fact that two goals
—one "selfish" and one noble—can overlap escapes some press critics.
The 1953 vice trial of Minot F. Jelke illustrated that overlap when the
New York Times joined with its tabloid morning rival, the *Daily News*,
to protest the judge's having barred the public and press from the courtroom. More important than news-media access to scandalous testimony
about call girls was the defendant's right to a public trial. American
tradition holds that testimony which can deprive a man of his liberty
must stand the test of full public scrutiny, lest dishonest or incompetent
witnesses be used to "railroad" defendants. (The New York State Court

of Appeals reversed Jelke's conviction twenty-two months later. He was convicted in a new, public trial three months after that.)

Fortunately, millions of American citizens do distinguish between private and public business and between good and bad journalism. Most public officials, albeit grudgingly, recognize the people's need to know government business, from the City Hall custodian's pay to policy disagreements between the Pentagon and the State Department. Major dangers lie in temptations to force "bad" journalists to conform to "good" journalists' standards and differences over just how much detail of governmental affairs the people need to know. Do the people need to know that a visiting traffic expert will be paid $200 a day? Do they need to know that City Council members debated the costs versus the needs for his services? A democratic purist would say yes to both so that citizens can govern themselves properly. If the facts are not reported, rumors may distort the picture, or citizens may ignorantly oppose proper tax support for managing their community. They need to know what their public-school employees are paid to determine whether they are competing for the best or what's left. Accurate, uncensored reports of who was penalized how much for what offense can help assure citizens of even-handed justice, good police performance, and some degree of traffic safety. Unexpert though they may be, citizens in a democratic society must choose between the recommendations of opposing experts in matters ranging from sidewalk-placement to nuclear-testing policies. The system, inefficient and perilous as it seems, has worked better than its opposites in Hitler's short-lived Third Reich, Stalin's tyranny-controlled Russia, and Franco's economically depressed Spain.

The press, as a profit-making enterprise, is assailed by critics who fail to distinguish between its business mechanics and its First Amendment-protected product. Since government regulates both the butcher shop and the purity of the meat it sells, they reason, it should do the same with the press and the quality of its product. The press has contributed to this concept, both understandably and foolishly. Labor-relations laws applied to the press do have a third dimension beyond their nominal reduction of freedom for the employer and the employee. For example, the First Amendment is knicked if a fundamentalist is barred from news work because his religion forbids union membership, and the government in effect has forced the employer to operate a union shop. (Technically, the private owner who bars union-favoring employees is not violating the First Amendment since he is not the government. Ethical responsibility is another matter.) Antimonopoly regulation which prevents press owners from broadening their economic base could conceivably be used as a club against a strong free press. In a marginal market, for example, government insistence on separate broadcasting and newspaper ownerships might weaken both by dividing limited advertising revenues and denying combined-operation efficiencies.

Left to their own devices, publishers often have demonstrated ruthless opposition to local competition. Some have refused to carry advertising of merchants who patronized competitors. Others have forced advertisers to buy their morning and evening combinations or go without, thus discouraging business for struggling newcomers. Established operations have offered deficit-producing subscriptions and ad rates in order to bankrupt junior competitors so that they can reap larger profits over the longer, noncompetitive run. Such behavior has brought government interference on the business side to protect editorial freedom from private economic conspiracies. Thus, a question of which is the lesser evil has evolved.

Whatever the merits of business-side protection, the free-press banner has been dangerously tattered by being so wildly waved against child-labor laws, the Wagner Labor Relations Act, efforts to curb questionable advertising, and antimonopoly enforcement. What looks like—and often is—outright economic greed has been confused with legitimate concerns about freedom to gather and report the news and to comment upon it fearlessly. Some proponents of change now insist that increasing government regulation in other sectors justifies the same for press performance as well as business operations.

Actually, with government operating so many more controls over citizen life, the need for surveillance by an agency independent of that government has grown.

Within the press itself, the twentieth-century rise of electronic journalism—subject, as it must be, to licensing—has increased the need for print-media freedom from government control. Already it has taken an act of Congress to make possible broadcast debates between the major presidential candidates—presentations that were economically risky under regular FCC rules. (Suspension of the equal-time rule still bothers some who are concerned about fair treatment of minority parties.) If Roper polling results are anywhere near correct in their finding that a majority of citizens depend mostly on televised news, the dangers of government control have grown year by year. Newspapers and magazines must remain absolutely free of any possible government penalty for reporting and criticizing that government's broadcast-licensing procedures.

With local governments more closely limiting use of private property through zoning laws, the need for free-flowing information and unrestricted debate is greater than it was in the less crowded days of the Frontier, to which the disenchanted citizen could escape.

With state governments setting ever-tighter standards for local schools, the Fourth Estate has larger obligations to provide information and viewpoints—free of censorship—to the citizens who must evaluate those standards and their enforcement.

With the federal government empowered—as it was not during its first one and one-half centuries—to overrule an employer's right to fire an employee, unfettered press surveillance on behalf of the concerned public is more, rather than less, necessary. Federal income taxes, authorized by constitutional amendment only since 1913, present for Fourth Estate reporting and debate a vast field which did not even exist when the Founding Fathers recognized the need for a free-press check on government.

Growing citizen dependence on public utilities, vastly more complicated and dangerous than those of the past, has increased the free press's surveillance duties. If an incompetent public utilities commission permits the gas company to operate without good safety standards, alert news work can provide the best hope for exposure and correction. Newsmen with access to records and freedom from government control offer important protection against crooked commissioners' selling franchises for their benefit instead of the people's.

Protections within the government's own checks-and-balances system are limited by political loyalties and other conflicts of interest. Where political loyalty is not in the way, suspicions of political rivalry becloud an official's warnings. The press is often the safest instrument a civil servant can use to expose chicanery by his colleagues or superiors.

3. "RESPONSIBILITY VERSUS FREEDOM"

A favorite thesis of those who believe America has outgrown press freedom is that irresponsible press performance has destroyed the grounds for freedom. The almost humorous horror of this tack lies in the contradictory views of what is "responsible." When news of a homosexual scandal struck President Lyndon Johnson's Administration on the eve of the 1964 election, the media were denounced on one side for "irresponsibly" reporting such a thing at all and on another side for "irresponsibly" withholding and then underplaying the story. When a similar scandal touched California Governor Ronald Reagan's staff three years later, the same patterns emerged. During the Red-scare era of Wisconsin Senator Joseph R. McCarthy, foes of McCarthy held the "irresponsible" press guilty of having created the senator's power, and followers of McCarthy held the same "irresponsible" press guilty of having hampered the senator. Much of this obviously springs from the critics' blind partisanship.

Former *Washington Post* Editor James Russell Wiggins identified many pleas for a "responsible" press as in fact pleas for a press "responsive to the power of government, the power of the establishment, the power of the profession." A truly free press is as certain to err—sometimes irresponsibly—as is any human institution. It will err against custom as well as government. In approving of America's press system in 1834, Alexis de Tocqueville wrote: "In order to enjoy the inestimable benefits that the liberty of the press ensures, it is necessary to submit to the inevitable evils that it creates." He warned: "There is no medium between servitude and license." More than one and a third centuries later, Wiggins issued a parallel warning. Declaring "I am not indifferent to the problems," he said he believed that power to curb them "once organized in any governmental or nongovernmental agency will be used to compel the conformity and coerce the compliance of precisely those newspapers which struggle to maintain in our society an element of dissent."

A special aspect of the responsibility-first, freedom-later view of press performance relates to the "bad news/bad press" syndrome. Many are afflicted with a vague idea that if the press would stop reporting so much bad news—or at least stop "playing it up"—life would be better. President Lyndon Johnson once cited a specific example during widespread dissension over his Vietnam-war policies. He pointed out that "10,000 American boys" had volunteered for military duty during the same week that a mere handful had staged an antiwar protest at the Pentagon; yet news broadcasts and front pages had featured the latter and ignored the former. CBS Commentator Eric Sevareid, among others, replied by explaining the nature of news, suggesting that it would be a sad day when protests became so commonplace that they would no longer be newsworthy. The Russian people, who are spared news of dissension and even news of disasters, lack both the discontent and the political vigor of their American counterparts. Eternal vigilance is the price of liberty, and the price has never been a comfortable one.

A natural human tendency to link bad news with the messenger who delivers it has always imperiled freedom of the press. In times of increased stress, like this era's racial revolution, public tolerance of press freedom is especially strained. Citing the "sheer volume of bad news," a 1968 report by an American Society of Newspaper Editors committee warned: "As the press is continually blamed, the danger is that more and more people will begin to feel that what they want is less freedom of information." Some critics blamed the press for a wave of prison riots in the 1950s, contending that news coverage inspired others to follow preceding examples. The factor overlooked in such cases is that of rumor, a far more dangerous source of bad inspiration. Detroit's record-breaking race riots of 1967 were blamed on news reports of rioting in Newark ten days earlier. Roger Tatarian, vice-president and editor of United Press

International, replied to the charge in the *U.P.I. Reporter* November 30, 1967. If "the real story of Newark" (26 dead, 1,500 injured, and 1,000 arrested) had been kept from the press, he asked: "Does any reasonable person think that Detroit would therefore not have heard about it? On the contrary, it would have heard about it by the grapevine. And by the time it reached Detroit it would have become far worse than it really was because rumor is always worse than the fact."

Distressed citizens often can find no handier whipping boy than the newscast or newspaper which first apprised them of a misfortune. Or they associate previous coverage with a tragic ending, as did the woman who telephoned *Akron Beacon Journal* Editor John S. Knight at 4 A.M. after the 1968 assassination death of Senator Robert F. Kennedy in California, screaming, "I hate you! I hate you! I hate you!" When America's long-heralded first space shot fizzled, leaving Russia with her embarrassing space lead, the press was denounced for having built the Free World's hopes too high. (When America began catching up in the propaganda phase of the race, partly through the impressive technique of calling her shots in advance, the press did not share in the congratulations.) When a government leader issues a shocking or frightening statement, the press which delivers it is first in line to catch the backlash. Politicians often float trial balloons to test public reactions. If public reaction is bad they retreat behind "clarifications" or quoted-out-of-context smoke screens, leaving only the press associated with the unpopular proposal and "dishonestly" at that. In the darkest hours of the Korean War, President Harry Truman answered a reporter's question by saying the United States had been considering use of the atomic bomb. Emergency sessions of parliaments from London to New Delhi were among the shock waves that brought clarifying explanations from Washington—and denunciation upon the press.

The whole problem was illustrated in an exchange between Milwaukee Mayor Henry W. Maier and *Milwaukee Journal* Editor Richard H. Leonard. Mayor Maier challenged press coverage of Milwaukee's racial strife in a speech before the 1967 United Press International Editors Conference. His remarks, reported in the September 23, 1967, *Editor & Publisher*, brought a letter of reply from Leonard.

Maier charged that "we are being stage-managed out of city government" by press emphasis on "dramatic" demonstrations. Milwaukee had suffered retail-business and other losses under the pressure of protracted "open housing" marches and attendant clashes between civil rightists and their foes. "The non-spontaneous event is staged to look spontaneous," he contended. "This has certainly been true in Milwaukee. After the riot, we were proceeding on a 39-point Little Marshall Plan, but suddenly we found ourselves in the position of an Austrian carpenter trying to

build a platform in the middle of a revival meeting. And the more flam-
boyant and extreme a statement made by anyone who calls himself a
'leader,' the stronger the charge, the louder the voice—the more likely
it is to take over the front page or the lead spot on a television show.
The public official who is concerned about civil peace and order along
with justice finds it difficult to restore any sense of proportion and balance. We may be seeing in some of our cities the portents of a new, and
perhaps different, kind of civil war. In a time like this, it is dangerous,
in the name of usual news procedure, to over-dramatize events which
contribute to the hardening of prejudice or play on violent emotions; to
echo every extreme statement whether false or true; to play down positive efforts which are being made to help solve our deepening racial,
economic, and social problems. Or to indulge in loose reporting."

He praised an editorial which had decried the "tiresome" tactics
of some demonstrators and then observed: "But guess what dominated
the front page of that same paper? A picture of teen-age protestors taking
to the streets. . . ." His main point was:

> This is no time for business as usual, nor is it a time for news as
> usual.

Leonard's letter, in the October 14, 1967, *Editor & Publisher,* gives
the other side:

> Milwaukee's Mayor Henry Maier, in his speech at the UPI Confer-
> ence, called on editors and publishers to show more concern for saving
> their central cities. He also declares that a period of civil rights strife
> is not a time for "news as usual." He further implies that the news judg-
> ment of elected officials is superior to that of the nation's editors.
>
> I disagree.
>
> All the editors and publishers I know couldn't be more concerned
> about the future of their central cities for a very good reason—they know
> that they will prosper if their city prospers, and decline if it fails.
>
> Elected officials may come and go, but a newspaper is firmly rooted
> to its city. It is anchored there for better or worse and has an intense,
> permanent interest in the welfare of this home base, which is the source
> of most of its revenue and the home of most of its readers.
>
> A politician can move on to a variety of jobs. A newspaper's very
> survival is dependent upon the strength of its city.
>
> Printing "news as usual" means to me that a newspaper is carrying
> out its time-honored mission of keeping the public advised as to what
> is happening. When is there a greater need for full and honest informa-
> tion than in a period of social conflict? Such a time of crisis is no time
> to open up a credibility gap.
>
> It is understandable that the mayor is disturbed by demonstrations
> in support of open housing in Milwaukee. The city's reputation and its
> economy are being harmed. Furthermore, the mayor and the aldermen

believe that most voters are opposed to open housing—and the mayor and the aldermen are aware that elections will be held in the spring.

Now, who is in the better position to judge news of Milwaukee's civil disturbances more objectively, public officials who face re-election or editors concerned solely with the over-all welfare of the community? I think the answer is obvious.

FOR FURTHER STUDY

1. Should campus courts be open to campus citizens? To the student press? How do campus-court procedures differ from those of regular courts?

2. Conduct some small polls on press freedom. Begin with a question about the principle and then ask about recent controversial stories or editorials. (Be sure to distinguish between whether the press "should" and "should be allowed to" for a fair test of the respondents' attitudes.) How do respondents compare as between age groups, men and women, intelligence levels?

3. Interview an editor or broadcast-news director about public pressures either to suppress or force coverage of events.

4. Check the files of a newspaper or news magazine for fairness in covering a campaign or issue. How much balance do you find among news stories, editorials, columns, letters-to-the-editor?

5. Study the coverage of a criminal case for pretrial reports that might prejudice prospective jurors—confessions by the defendant, police statements about his guilt, and charges by his lawyer.

6. Should a student newspaper be a part of student government?

SUGGESTED READING

BLUMBERG, NATHAN B., *One-Party Press?*, Lincoln: University of Nebraska Press, 1954.

Commission on Freedom of the Press, *A Free and Responsible Press*, Chicago: University of Chicago Press, 1947. Pages 6-11 offer an excellent philosophical look at press freedom and problems.

ESTRIN, HERMAN A., and SANDERSON, ARTHUR M., *Freedom and Censorship of the College Press*, Dubuque: Wm. C. Brown Company Publishers, 1966. [Paperback.] A comprehensive offering of views on this controversy.

MACDOUGALL, CURTIS D., *The Press and Its Problems*, Dubuque: Wm. C. Brown Company Publishers, 1964. Pages 68-71 list recent proposals for government controls on the press.

MOLLENHOFF, CLARK R., *Despoilers of Democracy*, Garden City: Doubleday & Company, Inc., 1965. Gives detailed case studies of news suppression by federal officials.

———, *Washington Cover-Up*, Garden City: Doubleday & Company, Inc., 1962.
  [Available in Popular Library paperback.] Earlier material on federal
  secrecy.
ORWELL, GEORGE, *Nineteen Eighty-Four*, New York: Harcourt, Brace & World,
  Inc., 1949. [Available in Signet paperback.] The first five chapters of
  this dystopian novel are especially appropriate reading for one interested
  in freedom of speech and the press.
SIEBERT, FRED S.; PETERSON, THEODORE; and SCHRAMM, WILBUR, *Four
  Theories of the Press*, Urbana: University of Illinois Press, 1956. [Avail-
  able in Illini paperback.] Chapter 3 on the "Social Responsibility Theory"
  challenges the practicality of "libertarian" press freedom.
SWANSON, CHARLES E., "Midcity Daily: What the People Think a Newspaper
  Should Be," *Journalism Quarterly*, June 1949 (Vol. 46, No. 2), pp. 173-
  176.

[For additional readings, see: PRICE, WARREN C., *The Literature of
Journalism, Minneapolis: University of Minnesota Press, 1960 (2nd Printing),
pp. 295-311 and xi-xiv.]

CHAPTER 3

A Brief History
of American Journalism

Omission rivals oversimplification in this brief sketch of American journalistic history. It has been arbitrarily divided into four periods to emphasize major thrusts during more than two centuries. Other divisions could have been made—for example, at the beginnings of the radio and television eras. More detailed coverage could have been assigned developments other than the rise of the penny press and the yellow press. Nor should one assume that the periods designated actually either ended or began with the dates assigned to them. The "Seekers of Freedom" go back at least to the inspirations for John Milton's *Areopagitica* of 1644, and modern "Seekers" may face stiffer challenges, relatively, today than they did during the John Adams Administration. Certainly "Political Organs" were important before and after the 1800-1835 period assigned here. Political ambitions accompanied the editorial fervors of great editors from Horace Greeley to William Randolph Hearst. A number of current press owners exhibit editorial dedication matching, if not exceeding, their prowess as entrepreneurs.

This treatment seeks to highlight evolutionary processes. Thus, basic freedom was in a sense won with popular defeat of the Alien and Sedition Acts in 1800. By 1835, mass circulation was providing newspapers with independent support, displacing political-party patronage. By 1900, in the wake of the Pulitzer-Hearst circulation war, fat omnibus newspapers—produced in expensively equipped plants with huge payrolls and other enormous business problems—had precluded the success of any more Benjamin Days, Greeleys, or James Gordon Bennetts who could start with a few hundred dollars and depend upon ideas to establish newspapers.

SEEKERS OF FREEDOM: 1690-1800

Colonial rulers' attitudes toward informing the masses were typified by Virginia's governor in 1671: "I thank God we have no free schools nor printing, and I hope we shall not have these hundred years. For learning has brought disobedience and heresy and sects into the world, and printing has divulged them and libels against the government. God keep us from both."

The colonists themselves were busy with elementary survival problems throughout the seventeenth century. Mother England's first real newspaper, the semiweekly *Oxford Gazette* (later the *London Gazette*), was not established until 1665—almost 200 years after William Caxton had imported a printing press from the continent. In the latter part of the seventeenth century, British newspapers and American reprints of them were occasionally circulated in the colonies. News of outstanding events was disseminated by ballads, and pamphlets were sporadically issued. At least one newspaper-like effort by colonial authorities was an undated one-page "Present State of New-English Affairs"—issued to combat rumors.

Generally recognized as America's first newspaper is Benjamin Harrison's *Publick Occurrences Both Forreign and Domestick*, printed in Boston September 25, 1690. Only three of its four pages (little larger than those in this book) carried printing. Horrified colonial authorities stopped this abortive monthly after its first issue on grounds that Harrison lacked a license. Historical evidence suggests that two stories particularly bothered authorities. One deplored cruel treatment of French prisoners by Indians who were allied with the British. The other concerned a scandal about the king of France.

Fourteen years elapsed before another newspaper was attempted, this time successfully. John Campbell, postmaster, obtained government permission to issue the *Boston News-Letter* in 1704. Fifteen years later, William Brooker obtained permission to print the *Boston Gazette,* which became America's second successful newspaper.

The first newspaper outside Boston appeared that same year, 1719, when Andrew Bradford began Philadelphia's *American Weekly Mercury.* James Franklin started something important when he created Boston's third newspaper, the *New England Courant,* in 1721. He began the audacious practice of criticizing constituted authority. Franklin served a jail term in 1722 for questioning government efficiency in curbing pirates. Six months later he insulted "His Majesty's Government," and a warrant for his arrest was ordered. Direct censorship by the province's secretary was ordered as a guard against further insults by the publisher, but he turned the paper over to his seventeen-year-old brother, Benjamin. (Benjamin eventually went on to greater journalistic fame in Philadelphia, and James later moved to Newport and started another colony's first newspaper, the *Rhode-Island Gazette,* in 1732.) Significant in this first sustained press-government clash was Andrew Bradford's editorial support of Franklin in his *American Weekly Mercury,* perhaps the first example of American press cooperation in seeking freedom from government censorship.

New York City got its first newspaper in 1725, when Andrew Bradford's father, William, began publishing the *New York Gazette.* Eight years later, leaders of a colonial party opposed to New York Governor Cosby, prevailed upon John Peter Zenger to start his *New York Weekly Journal.* The ensuing battle between Bradford's pro-Cosby *Gazette* and Zenger's anti-Cosby *Journal* led to a milestone in the fight for press freedom.

Zenger was arrested in November, 1734, on a charge of printing a seditious libel. Andrew Hamilton, a Philadelphia lawyer brought in to defend Zenger, delivered one of the all-time great courtroom arguments during the trial eight months later. He convinced the jury—and eventually political philosophers on both sides of the Atlantic—that two assumed legal principles commonly used in seditious libel proceedings were wrong. Whereas English law held "the greater the truth, the greater the libel," Hamilton insisted: "Truth ought to govern the whole affair of libels." Criticism, he argued, was "a right which all free men claim"; therefore, only *false charges* could be restrained by the law. Equally important to Zenger's defense was Hamilton's contention that the jury should decide not just the fact of Zenger's publication but also the law —that is, whether the published material was seditious libel. The chief justice ruled against Hamilton on both points, but Hamilton's argument and citations of precedents carried the day. Among his telling points was his contention that if a jury could decide whether a defendant's having killed another man (fact) was murder or manslaughter (law), surely the jury should decide whether a man's action in publishing something constituted libel or justifiable criticism. Hamilton's arguments and Zenger's acquittal were widely hailed both in England and the colonies, but the two important principles—basic to press freedom—were not formalized for many decades. The jury's right to decide the law was established in England by the Fox Libel Act of 1792, and Lord Campbell's Act of 1843 recognized the admissibility of truth as a defense. America's own infamous Sedition Act of 1798—at the insistence of Alexander Hamilton (not to be confused with Andrew)—did recognize both principles in its otherwise anti-free-press clauses.

By the middle of the century, modest weekly newspapers were operating in seven colonies, from Massachusetts to Virginia. Their influence was greater than either their size or numbers might suggest. When

Benjamin Franklin produced his famous cartoon, "Join or Die," in his *Pennsylvania Gazette* in 1754, it was immediately copied in four other newspapers. The drawing of a snake, divided into eight parts, was an appeal for unified colonial defense in the impending French and Indian War. Franklin presented a plan for union of the colonies at a congress in Albany that year. Although it was rejected by both the colonial assemblies and British government, it contributed to the concept of unity which newspapers had fostered as they were circulated from colony to colony. The war itself, from 1754-1760, taught Americans how to cooperate in a common cause.

In 1755, Connecticut became the eighth colony to have a newspaper with the founding of the *New Haven Gazette*. By 1758, the colonial post office found it necessary to start charging for transporting newspapers, which had been carried as a courtesy. By 1775, eleven of the thirteen colonies had newspapers—and Delaware and New Jersey were well served by those nearby. Approximately three dozen newspapers, mostly weeklies, were serving the two million or so colonists by 1775.

Charles A. and Mary R. Beard declare in *The Rise of American Civilization*: "The political and cultural significance of this early American journalism, crude as it appears to the sophisticated of modern times, can hardly be overestimated. If narrow in its range, it was wider and freer than the pulpit and the classroom. . . ."

Meanwhile, the accession of George III in Great Britain in 1760 and British efforts to tighten the empire from 1763 on sparked discontent in the American colonies. Freed of the French threat after the Seven Years' War (and therefore less dependent upon British troops for protection), the colonists were in a better position to resent actively impositions from London. Thus, the Acts of Trade, curbing economic liberties of American merchants, and provisions for permanent British troop garrisons brought open opposition from many colonists. The successful newspaper fight against the 1765 Stamp Act was a key move on the path toward independence. The *Pennsylvania Journal and Weekly Advertiser* came out on October 31, 1765 (the day before the tax began) with its front page made up like a tombstone, bidding farewell to "liberty of the press." Refusing to pay the half-penny or penny base rate plus two shillings on each advertisement, most colonial newspapers fought the tax vigorously. Some suspended publication, and others were printed without their titles. A colonial congress in New York that fall formally protested taxation without representation and other matters to the British. Letters denouncing British colonial policy were printed in many papers and copied in still others; sometimes these were collected and issued again in pamphlet form. Protests were also carried forward exclusively in pamphlets—an important journalistic device of that era. Parliament repealed the Stamp

Act in 1766, but other taxation and control measures brought new protests, effectively articulated by pamphleteers and letters-to-the-editor authors. The Townshend Acts of 1767 particularly enraged the colonists. Parliament dropped all the duties except one on tea in 1770, but this stubborn maintenance of principle inspired an equally stubborn resistance by the colonists.

Leading the journalistic crusade was the *Boston Gazette*, published by Benjamin Edes and John Gill, and supplied with columns of protest by Samuel Adams and his followers. During this period, the *Gazette* reached a record circulation of 2,000, and its effectiveness drew fire from colonial officials and Loyalist sympathizers. The Massachusetts House of Representatives refused the governor's appeal to move against Edes and Gill, and his request for a libel indictment was rejected by a grand jury. By 1773, Sam Adams was emboldened to the point of calling for "an independent state—an American commonwealth."

Not all of the press or the colonists took the Patriot side during this critical period, of course. John Adams estimated that one-third of the principal men in the colonies opposed the revolution. About one-fifth of the newspapers supported the Tory cause, and another fifth remained essentially uncommitted. The *Boston News Letter*, a government organ from its beginnings, was the Tories' main spokesman. Several newspapers attempted to print both sides, but the deepening crisis found neither Patriots nor Tories willing to tolerate editorial neutrality. The *Boston Chronicle*, which became New England's first semiweekly in 1768, was driven to the Tory side by Patriot mobs. It had printed John Dickinson's famous "Letters from a Farmer in Pennsylvania" and other Patriot declarations, but Publisher John Mein's opposition to proposed boycott of English imports brought violent harassment from the Sons of Liberty. Mein was hanged in effigy, and he and his partner were attacked in the streets. Loss of readers forced the *Chronicle*'s discontinuance in 1770. A reverse situation drove Isaiah Thomas's *Massachusetts Spy* to the extreme Patriot side in the early 1770s. Thomas had printed letters from both sides, but when Tories learned that Thomas himself was a Patriot they withdrew support and attacked him. He began printing a version of Franklin's "Join or Die" snake confronting a British dragon across his front page in 1774 and made the *Spy* probably the Patriots' most rabid supporter. James Rivington's *New York Gazetteer* started in 1773 to print material from both sides, but in 1775 Patriots hanged him in effigy, and his pro-Tory sympathies (like Thomas's pro-Patriot sympathies) soon took over. With the war underway late that year, Rivington fled to England. He returned in 1777 to publish the *Royal Gazette*, which became infamous for printing such untruths as a report that George Washington had been captured and killed.

Against the background of violent crisis, especially from 1770 to the final break in 1775, mass intolerance of the other side or even neutrality is understandable. The Boston Massacre in March, 1770—both in its toll of five dead and behavior of the mob which provoked it—demonstrated the depth of feeling. The burning of a grounded British gunboat by Rhode Islanders in 1772 and the Boston Tea Party of late 1773 helped put the dispute beyond the discussion stage for both Tories and Patriots. By September, 1774, some Tories were so desperate that they circulated pamphlets among British troops urging them to kill Boston's "trumpeters of sedition" and "plunder their effects" to make them the "first victims of the mischiefs they have brought upon us." That same month, the first Continental Congress in Philadelphia (representing all colonies but Georgia) made the last peaceful, but firm, demand of the British. All but New York agreed to cut off British imports within three months and to end exports to Britain within a year.

Open conflict erupted in April, 1775, at Lexington and Concord. The Second Continental Congress met in May and appointed George Washington commander of the American Continental Army.

The war touched every colony between the battle of Bunker Hill (where 1,000 British and 440 American troops died) in June, 1775, and Cornwallis's surrender at Yorktown in October, 1781. The American victory is one of the marvels of military history, considering the British superiority in arms and the Americans' division and lack of discipline. It has been estimated that at least 25,000 American Loyalists fought for the British—a tenth of the largest total estimated under arms for the Patriots! Thousands of ill-equipped, poorly trained soldiers deserted Washington at critical points during the more than six years of conflict. Washington's eventual victory drew heavily on help from France, his logistical advantages, and bungling by British generals. But it could not have been won without what historians Allan Nevins and Henry Steele Commager called the "superb fighting spirit" of American troops at crucial junctures. Nor could the war against such great odds have been sustained without dedication to the cause by a majority of American civilians, suffering the physical and psychological privations of violent separation from their motherland.

Journalists played a major role in rallying both troops and the populace, as they had in the disputes which led to the war. Thomas Paine's pamphlet *Common Sense* in early 1776 called for independence in such compelling terms that it boosted wartime morale by proposing a new goal while the lesser goal still looked elusive. More than 100,000 copies were circulated within three months. Dr. Benjamin Rush said it had an "effect which has rarely been produced by types and paper in any age or country." Washington applauded its "sound doctrine and unanswerable reasons." A college president rebutted Paine's arguments against reconciliation and for independence with a series of letters in the *Pennsylvania Gazette* that spring. His letters, signed "Cato," were answered by Paine in a *Pennsylvania Packet* series over the pen name "Forester." The "Cato-Forester" letters were widely reprinted throughout the colonies, demonstrating a remarkable journalistic objectivity on an incendiary matter during wartime. Reconciliationists lost the ensuing argument as Virginia voted for independence that May and carried its proposal to the Continental Congress in June. The Declaration of Independence was adopted July 2 and proclaimed July 4.

Paine's first *Crisis* paper was printed in the *Pennsylvania Journal* December 19, 1776, in perhaps the darkest hours of the war. It was read to Washington's often beaten soldiers just before they attacked Trenton and routed 1,400 Hessian troops. Its lines remain stirring to this day:

> These are the times that try men's souls. The summer soldier and the sunshine patriot will, in this crisis, shrink from the service of their country; but he that stands it now deserves the love and thanks of man and woman. Tyranny, like hell, is not easily conquered; yet we have this consolation with us, that the harder the conflict the more glorious the triumph. . . . Heaven knows how to put a proper price upon its goods; and it would be strange indeed if so celestial an article as Freedom should not be highly rated. . . .

As the fortunes of war surged back and forth, so did those of the press. When the Americans occupied Boston after March, 1776, two Patriot papers returned and a third was started. When the British took New York City that fall, three Patriot editors moved their operations and a fourth closed down. One of the former, Hugh Gaine, returned in a few months to resume control of his *New York Gazette and Weekly Mercury*, converting it to a Loyalist sheet. The aforementioned James Rivington returned from England in 1777 to serve the British journalistically. Patriot hatred of Rivington was summed up by Philip Freneau (the Poet of the Revolution) when he labeled Rivington "the inventor as well as the printer of lies." Benjamin Towne of Philadelphia's *Pennsylvania Evening Post* built perhaps the most disgraceful newspaper record of the war. Fiercely Patriot from 1775 to 1777, his was the first newspaper to print the Declaration of Independence. When the British occupied Philadelphia in September, 1777, he stayed on by changing his politics while three other Patriot editors fled. When the Americans returned in June, 1778, he switched again while two Tory editors left. (Towne was indicted on treason charges after the peace of 1783.) Generally, along the eastern seaboard newspapers stuck with their commitments, fleeing from enemy occupations and returning when the enemy departed. The British started a number of newspapers during their various occupancies.

By the formal end of the war in 1783, approximately three dozen newspapers, mostly weeklies, were functioning. Many had perished since 1775, but enough war-born ventures had survived to match the prewar total. New York and Philadelphia had semiweeklies, and triweeklies had been attempted. Circulation claims during the preceding decade included 3,500 for Thomas's *Massachusetts Spy* and 3,600 for Rivington's *New York Gazetteer* before the war. Hartford's *Connecticut Courant* had claimed 8,000 in 1778. Most, however, had circulations in the hundreds. Frank Luther Mott estimated total prewar circulation at 40,000, though newspapers reached a far wider audience through coffeehouse reading and passing from one family to another. Their importance in the American way of life was established beyond argument.

Magazines were slower in developing. A half dozen monthlies, none lasting even two years, had been attempted by the war's end. In the journalistic boom that followed the war, Mott reports, about seventy-five new ones were started, of which four lasted for periods of six to eight years.

Newspapers enjoyed a great surge, however. Sixty new ones were started during the mid-1780s, according to Mott, and about 450 altogether between 1783 and 1800. By 1800, about 200 newspapers were operating.

Daily newspapering got a shaky start in America in May, 1783, when the famous turncoat editor Towne converted his semiweekly *Pennsylvania Evening Post* into a daily. Nearly seventeen months later, in September, 1784, John Dunlap and David C. Claypool changed their thriving triweekly into the *Pennsylvania Packet and Daily Advertiser,* and Towne's sputtering effort died a month later. New York's first daily was the *Morning Post,* converted in February, 1785, but the *New York Daily Advertiser,* started the next month, was more successful. By 1800, Philadelphia had six dailies, New York five, Baltimore three, and Charleston two. Two attempts in Boston failed. With a largest city of only 25,000, America was eight decades behind England in this phase of journalism.

Newspapers, at four to six cents a copy, were aimed at an elite mercantile class. Later, primarily political journals were priced more cheaply, but the offerings—whether commercial or political—and the prices were not geared to truly mass audiences. The press easily turned its capacities for disseminating political debate, developed by the long Tory-Patriot battles, to the problems of American independence.

The loose 1781 Articles of Confederation allowed a myriad of problems to develop among the thirteen sovereign states, ranging from needs for treaties with foreign powers to unreliable currencies. Quarrels erupted over state boundary lines, troubles with the Indians, and debtor-creditor settlements. A serious depression in 1785-86 deepened the new crisis. An abortive rebellion, led by Daniel Shays against the government arsenal at Springfield, Massachusetts, in 1786, provided a kind of climax to the growing concern over lack of a strong central government. Except for the farsighted Northwest Ordinance of 1787, the Confederation's Congress achieved little. A 1785 conference between Virginia and Maryland concerning navigation on the Potomac and Chesapeake Bay led to a broader interstate-commerce meeting in 1786. Alexander Hamilton, at the latter meeting, led a move to hold a full-scale constitutional convention, and it was scheduled for May, 1787.

With more newspapers and greater frequency of publication, the press was well equipped to carry the ensuing debates between the forerunners of the Federalists and Anti-Federalists to citizens throughout the thirteen states. Pamphlets played a lesser role in these national debates. After delegates approved the new constitution and the Continental Congress forwarded it to the states in September, 1787, debate filled the newspaper columns for months. Best known of the anonymous letter campaigns in this period was the series first published in the semiweekly *New York Independent Journal or General Advertiser*. Written by Alexander Hamilton, James Madison, and John Jay, the collected works are known as *The Federalist* papers. They were widely reprinted in other newspapers. The first series ran from October, 1787, to April, 1788, and another ran from June to August, 1788.

The fight was bitter. The presses of one New York newspaper, opposed to ratification, were wrecked. Several antiratification newspapers charged that Federalists had used their control of the post office to hamper circulation of opposing papers. It took thirty-two months to secure all thirteen ratifications. Delaware became the first state to ratify in December, 1787. Pennsylvania and New Jersey followed within the next two weeks. Georgia and Connecticut approved in January, 1788. Massachusetts marked the two-thirds point toward the goal of nine ratifications, but on a narrow 187-168 vote, in February. More than two months elapsed before Maryland ratified; South Carolina followed in May, and one month later—on a 57-46 vote—New Hampshire delivered the crucial ninth ratification. Rhode Island, which had boycotted the convention, finally ratified the Constitution May 29, 1790, on a 34-32 vote, after it had already been in force nearly fifteen months.

Following the bitter struggle over ratification, Madison moved to reassure constitutional doubters by proposing a series of twelve amendments in the House of Representatives. The first Congress quickly approved and forwarded them to the states. Ten amendments—the "Bill of Rights"—were ratified and put into effect within two years. Thus, by the end of 1791, freedom of the press—guaranteed in the First Amendment—was incorporated into the fundamental law of the land.

Emerging from the constitutional struggle were the beginnings of two political parties—the Federalists and the Anti-Federalists (later known as Republicans and finally as Democrats). Alexander Hamilton, spokesman for the Federalists, and Thomas Jefferson, spokesman for the opposition, both encouraged editors of their persuasions. John Fenno established the Federalist *Gazette of the United States* in New York in 1789 in time to cover Washington's inauguration. When the capital was moved to Philadelphia in 1790, Fenno moved his semiweekly *Gazette* there. James Madison prevailed upon Philip Freneau to establish the *National Gazette,* an opposing semiweekly, in Philadelphia the next year. Jefferson encouraged the project by giving Freneau a translator's job in the U. S. State Department, which he headed in Washington's Cabinet.

Thus, the stage was set for newspapers as political organs, our designation for the next period. Differences between Jefferson and Hamilton began etching political-party lines quickly. As Treasury secretary and Washington's closest adviser, Hamilton pushed through strong government measures, including an excise on distilled liquors. Jefferson, representing the Republican-oriented agrarian citizens, opposed such measures. Hamilton's dominance was demonstrated by the dispatching of 15,000 troops to smash western Pennsylvania's Whiskey Rebellion in 1794. (The excise was repealed during Jefferson's tenure as President.) War between France's revolutionary republic and Great Britain in 1793 divided the two parties further. Republicans sympathized with the French, who were feared by the Federalists. Washington declared America's neutrality, whereupon the French minister, Citizen Genêt, carried the French cause to the American people. Washington asked for his recall, and Genêt retired from diplomacy and remained in the United States. British seizure of American ships headed for the French West Indies brought calls for war. But Washington instead sent John Jay to London to negotiate. Jay brought back a treaty promising the British would consider damage claims for the ships and that they would abandon trading posts in the Northwest Territory, which they had held in violation of the 1783 Treaty. They also granted trading privileges in the British East Indies and West Indies. None of this satisfied the Republicans, and Jay was burned in effigy as opposition newspapers denounced the Washington Administration, and anti-British orators called for war.

During the John Adams Administration, the war danger reversed. Angered by Jay's treaty, France threatened Adams's minister with arrest, and Foreign Minister Talleyrand refused to deal with special commissioners sent by Adams. Publication of the "X-Y-Z" papers, charging a covert $250,000 blackmail offer by French agents, brought cries for war

—this time from the Federalists. A series of naval battles with the French took America to the brink of war. America's army and navy were both enlarged in preparation. In such an atmosphere, Republican sympathies with the French appeared dangerous to angry and frightened Federalists.

As a result, Congress passed the Alien and Sedition Acts in 1798. The new laws extended the residence requirement for naturalization from five to fourteen years and empowered the President to deport aliens he considered subversive. A majority of the 25,000 aliens happened to be pro-Republican, making that law's intent clear. Two shiploads were deported, and some active anti-Federalist aliens went underground. John Burk, publisher of the *New York Time Piece*, was among the latter.

The Sedition Act, a clear violation of the six-year-old First Amendment, provided: "That if any person shall write, print, utter, or publish . . . any false, scandalous, and malicious writing . . . against the government of the United States, or either house of the Congress . . . or the President . . . with intent to defame the said government . . . or to bring them . . . into contempt or disrepute . . . shall be punished by a fine not exceeding $2,000 and by imprisonment not exceeding two years." Section 3 did provide, reportedly at Hamilton's suggestion, that "the truth of the matter" could be introduced by the defense and that the jury "shall have a right to determine the law and the fact." But neither these bows toward the revered example of John Peter Zenger's 1735 acquittal nor the Act's designation of "false" writings protected reasonable journalistic dissent.

One man was fined $100 for saying he wished that wadding from a cannon salute to the President had struck the President's breeches. Another served eighteen months for posting signs protesting the Alien and Sedition Acts; he was kept in jail when he could not pay the accompanying $400 fine. Respecters of the written law might countenance the conviction of an editor for printing a rumor that Hamilton was trying to silence a Republican newspaper by buying it with British gold—an allegation "absolutely destitute of foundation," according to Hamilton. But jailing and fining a congressman for charging President Adams with "ridiculous pomp, foolish adulation, and selfish avarice" in a letter-to-the-editor hardly meets the "false" test. The Federalists, in strong control of all three branches, were demonstrating the inevitable tendency of power to corrupt. In all, two dozen persons were arrested, fifteen indicted, and ten or eleven tried. The ten convictions under the Sedition Act and four others under common law involved a majority of editors. Historians generally regard the thirty-two-month assault against the opposition press as a failure in that Republican editors kept up a strong attack. How much fear of the law may have discouraged a stronger attack cannot be assessed, of course.

In any case, the Alien and Sedition Acts provided a target for counterattack by Jefferson and his followers. In November and December of 1798, Jefferson teamed with Madison to secure resolutions in the Kentucky and Virginia legislatures, calling for state nullifications of the Acts. These resolutions were printed in newspapers throughout the land. Although a majority of the papers, being Federalist-oriented, attacked the resolutions, widespread printing of both views stimulated discussion among the previously ineffectual majority of citizens. The state legislatures from Maryland north rejected the resolutions' appeal, some citing the federal judiciary as the proper instrument for challenging a law's constitutionality. But the Federalists' excesses in prosecuting the law, combined with skillful propagandizing by the Republicans, sealed the Federalists' doom in the elections of 1800. Spring elections in New York signaled the end as voters filled both houses with Jefferson supporters, sure to choose electors for him that fall. A quirk in the electoral system left Jefferson tied with fellow Democrat Republican Aaron Burr at seventy-three electoral votes each, throwing the choice into the House of Representatives. Eight states backed Jefferson, six Federalist delegations chose Burr, and two remained split for thirty-five ballots. A Vermont Federalist abstained finally, and Vermont went to Jefferson. (The Twelfth Amendment, ratified during Jefferson's first term, removed further chance of vice-presidential candidates' tying with ticket-leaders for the presidency.)

Thus did the citizens of the United States pass their first test of commitment to press freedom. The Alien and Sedition Acts expired on schedule in March, 1801. President Jefferson pardoned all those convicted and sought to repay with interest fines levied under the law, thus symbolically eradicating this stain on the First Amendment.

POLITICAL ORGANS: 1800-1835

Evolution of the press in this period is summarized by the Beards' *The Rise of American Civilization*: "When . . . the alignment between the Federalists and the Republicans was clearly defined, every newspaper of importance became a party organ, exchanging advocacy for patronage and praise."

Political-party dominance of newspapers was underway before the elections of 1800 "settled" the issue of press freedom. By the time Jefferson's Administration took up residence in the new capital at Washington, two Federalist and two Republican newspapers were on the scene. The main Administration voice was that of Samuel Harrison Smith's triweekly *National Intelligencer*. (Smith's detailed coverage of House proceedings, beginning with the Seventh Congress's second session, provided a new journalistic service widely depended upon by other newspapers. His fight for permission to cover the House was an important contribution to freedom of information.)

Editors had begun replacing printers as newspaper-operators, although basic content followed the same patterns. Editorials began rivaling pen-name letters as major providers of influence. News, as it was to be developed in the next period, remained secondary. Advertising, growing in importance, was even blamed for a preponderance of Federalist newspapers at this period's beginning. However, the twelve-year reign of the Federalists (granting printing contracts) and natural sympathies of the mercantile-paper editors provide more logical reasons. Interestingly, one Federalist editor contended that Republican papers in New York carried more advertisements than their Federalist competitors. The rise of magazines tended to diminish newspaper attention to literary entertainment, leaving more room for concentration on political views. Frank Luther Mott's *American Journalism* states that several hundred magazines, ranging from weeklies to quarterlies, were published for varying terms during this period. Probably the most important journalistically was *Niles Weekly Register,* published in Baltimore by Hezekiah Niles from 1811-1849. Historians still lean on reprints of that ancestor of today's news magazine.

Vitriol and violence marked the extreme partisanship of this journalistic period. One historian has called the journals of this period "viewspapers." The legacy of the bitter Patriot-Tory struggles of 1765-1783 and the postwar political fighting was preserved and intensified in this period.

No important leader, from Washington on, escaped scurrilous attacks. Washington was accused of seeking to become "king" of the country; Jefferson was denounced as an atheist; Hamilton was charged with being in the pay of British agents. Typical of the calumny was that involved in the period's most famous criminal-libel case. Harry Croswell, editor of *The Wasp* at Hudson, New York, was indicted by New York in 1804 for having reprinted a charge that Jefferson had hired James Callender to smear Washington as a traitor, robber, and perjurer. Croswell appealed his conviction, and Hamilton stepped forward to defend him. Hamilton made an eloquent appeal on behalf of truth as a defense, but this principle remained unestablished even sixty-nine years after the Zenger trial. (Apparently, Hamilton believed Callender—a disenchanted Republican editor—could prove that Jefferson had paid for the attacks on Washington. Callender had denounced Jefferson after Jefferson refused to make him postmaster of Richmond.) Croswell lost his appeal, but the New York Legislature passed a law the next year establishing both truth as a defense and the jury's right to decide the law in criminal-libel cases.

A newspaper story led to the duel in which Aaron Burr killed Hamilton shortly after the Croswell case, in 1804.

The partisan press's viciousness was decried by most of America's early leaders at one time or another. Washington once wrote that a chief reason for his leaving public life was to escape unprincipled attacks in the newspapers. John Adams wrote bitterly of the "foreign liars" who had vilified him as President. Even Jefferson, the strongest advocate of press freedom, became discouraged with the outrageous lies promulgated against him. Earlier, Benjamin Franklin had written from France that he felt compelled to lay aside some American newspapers rather than let friends over there see how disgraceful they were.

When the long-threatened involvement in the French-English conflict became a reality with the War of 1812, journalists treated it like any other partisan dispute. Federalist papers, particularly in New England where pro-British sentiment prevailed, called it "Madison's War." Boston's *Columbian Centinel* repeatedly derided the "waste of blood and property" in a "useless and unnecessary war." The *Centinel's* editor even endorsed a movement for New England to secede from the Union. Madison's Administration tolerated the opposition, but private reaction was another matter. Mobs destroyed the building and press of Baltimore's antiwar *Federal Republican* and later attacked one editor's home. Two Revolutionary War generals, helping defend the home, were among the casualties. James Lingan was killed, and "Light Horse Harry" Lee was crippled for life.

By this time, Mott reports, there were 366 newspapers in the United States. Perhaps thirty dailies were scattered from New England to New Orleans. The Republican press had cut into the heavy lead that the Federalists had held through the Washington and Adams Administrations.

The James Monroe Administration, 1817-1825, was labeled "The Era of Good Feelings" by a Federalist editor, as his party faded from the political scene. But partisan controversy heated up newspaper columns toward the end of Monroe's second term. The jockeying for position in the campaign of 1824 led to attacks, inane and otherwise, on the principals. A Philadelphia newspaper, for example, charged John Quincy Adams with sloppy dress, alleging that he sometimes attended church barefoot. Partisan bitterness was encouraged by the awkward outcome of the 1824 election. Andrew Jackson led a four-man field with 156,000 popular votes and 99 electoral votes, but the lack of a majority threw the election into the House. Adams, who had run second with 105,000 popular votes and 84 electoral votes, was elected in a cloud of controversy. The campaign of 1828 and the approach to it plumbed old depths. The President's son, John, was assaulted by a newspaperman while on an official errand in the Capitol. His attacker had taken umbrage at a reported remark by young Adams about press treatment of his father. Stories that Jackson's mother had been a mulatto and that Adams's wife was an English subject, only pretending American citizenship, typified the low level of partisan journalism.

After Jackson took office in 1829, the *United States Telegraph* (which Adams called "scurrilous and abusive") became the Administration's paper and its publisher Duff Green was printer for both houses of Congress. Suspected of favoring John C. Calhoun, Green fell from favor, and the semiweekly *Globe* was set up under Francis P. Blair to serve the Administration. Blair, Business Manager John C. Rives, and another *Globe* man, Amos Kendall, formed Jackson's famous "Kitchen Cabinet" during Jackson's second term. Blair and Rives also got the government printing contracts, and the *Globe* held its favored position through Martin Van Buren's Administration, 1837-1841.

The earlier press's baptism of fire in revolutionary times may be blamed for some of the press's political extremism. Another important factor was many editors' dependence on party success for their economic welfare. If the newspaper's side won, the editor shared in the spoils; if it lost, the editor faced something worse than editorial disappointment. Mercantile papers naturally tended to tune their political coverage to that of the party organs. In addition, Federalist and Republican differences appeared larger than most major-party divisions of later decades. One side viewed the choice as lying between civilized government and rabble-rousers' anarchy; the other saw it as a choice between grinding oppression by propertied aristocrats and government for the people. Moreover, the Old World—to which Americans still felt ties— offered few examples of political moderation, what with the bloody overthrow of Louis XVI and war between France and England.

Overall, press performance was disgraceful by present-day standards. Yet that performance served to prove Jefferson's theory: that democratic government could prosper under the severest assaults by an unbridled press. No new government in the past three centuries has developed more effectively and swiftly than did that of the United States.

Near the end of this period, 1,200 newspapers were serving a population of about 13,500,000. Perhaps 70 or 80 were dailies. Most were four-pagers printing six or seven columns per page, with advertising dominating pages 1 and 4. Circulations averaged around 1,000. Among established newspapers the *New York Courier and Enquirer* led with 4,500. Most dailies charged subscribers $10 a year, beyond the reach of laborers making $8 or $10 a week. Single-copy sales at six cents were not encouraged. (In the last two years of this period two upstart papers began revolutionizing this, but they belong to the next period.) The fastest press in New York could produce only 2,000 papers per hour, though work was advancing on one with double that capacity. Two important Abolitionist organs—Benjamin Lundy's *Genius of Universal Emancipation* and William Lloyd Garrison's *Liberator*—were functioning. Beginnings of a labor press were noted, and 100 church papers were circulating.

EDITORS' PRESS: 1835-1900

On September 3, 1833, Benjamin H. Day brought out the first number of his *New York Sun*, America's first totally successful mass-circulation newspaper. Its four pages (at 7 1/2 by 10 inches, slightly smaller than a sheet of typing paper) were divided into three columns each. It sold for one penny and offered a radically different news diet, emphasizing local and human-interest stories. Page 1 of the first issue carried this:

> *A Whistler.*—A boy in Vermont, accustomed to working alone, was so prone to whistling, that, as soon as he was by himself, he unconsciously commenced. When asleep, the muscles of his mouth, chest, and lungs were so completely concatenated in the association, he whistled with astonishing shrillness. A pale countenance, loss of appetite, and almost total prostration of strength, convinced his mother it would end in death, if not speedily overcome, which was accomplished by placing him in the society of another boy, who had orders to give him a blow as soon as he began to whistle.

Attempts at cheap, mass-circulation papers had been made for several years. Boston had three successful $4 dailies by 1831, but they did not aim quite as directly at the mass audience, either in circulation technique or in basic content. Horace Greeley, later to become the most famous of the early editor giants, had been associated with an abortive penny-paper effort in New York nine months before the *Sun* appeared.

Day improved on all the foregoing efforts and had the good fortune to be approached by George W. Wisner, who asked to cover police reports and double as a printer for $4 a week. Day also had the foresight to reward Wisner's Herculean efforts with reserved shares in the *Sun* if it proved successful. By the following spring, enough profits had accrued under Day's unusual arrangement to give Wisner half interest in the *Sun*. (Later, Day said, they quarreled over Wisner's insistence on inserting Abolitionist articles, and Day bought out Wisner for $5,000.) A sample of the *Sun's* quaint police-court coverage may reflect its appeal, in competition with the business and political news which dominated other newspapers:

> *Giving a Divorce.*—Yesterday morning, a little curly-pated fellow, by the name of John Lawler, was called up on a charge of kicking over the mead stand of Mary Lawler, alias Miss Donohue, alias Mrs. Donohue.

Magistrate, [to the complainant.] Mrs. Donohue, what were the circumstances of this affair?

Complainant. You will be so good sir, if you please, as to call me Miss Donohue. It is my maiden name, and I wish no other.

Mag. Very good, MISS Donohue, how came he to kick over your stand, and break your bottles and glasses?

Comp. Aye yes, now, I like that better. Every virtuous woman should be called by her own right and proper name.

Mag. Well, let's hear your story. Do you know the boy?

Comp. The boy did you say. Indade, sire, devil a bit o' boy is there about the baste, nor man neither, barring he drinks brandy like a fish. [loud laughter.]

Mag. Did you ever see him before?

Comp. Indade I guess I did. Many years ago he was my husband; but your honor sees, I gave him a divorce. That is, ye see, I gave him a a bit of paper, stating that I would'nt live with him no longer. [laughter.]

Pris. Its no sich thing, your honor. She used to go off with other men, and so I sold her for a gill of rum.

Comp. [shaking her fist at the prisoner.] A *gill* was it, you baste? I'll take my bible oath that it was a whole blessed pint. [laughter.]

Mag. Well, well, it matters not whether it was a gill or a pint.

Comp. Indade it matters a good deal—to say that a good vartuous woman like me isn't worth no more nor a gill of rum. [turning to the prisoner.] You baste of the earth. I'll bung out your 'tother peeper. [The prisoner had but one eye.]

Mag. [getting out of patience.] Madam, if you want this man punished you must tell me what he has been doing.

Comp. Indade then, I'll tell you what he has been doing. You see, I was down to the market, selling some mead and spruce beer, to get a little money to support my children with. Last night the brute came down where I was, and, says he, Mary, says he, will you go and live with me again. And says I, go along you divil, for you know I gave you a divorce. And then says he, if you don't go and live with me, I'll break every damned bottle of made that you've got. Then says I, John Lawler, if you touch my made I'll break your head. And then your honor, he up with his foot—O, my poor children—he up with his foot, and he kicked the bottles, and the glasses, and the pen-nuts—all into the dirt!

The prisoner was committed.

New York's mercantile papers had carried limited police-court reports, but reaction from their clientele had discouraged the practice. However, the *Sun's* new newspaper customers obviously liked it. By January, 1834, the *Sun* led in American circulation with 5,000. It doubled that before year's end, building a circulation lead it was to hold for a quarter century. An early imitator, the *New York Transcript*, reached 9,000 by 1835.

As novel as the content, size, and price was Day's business policy. Newsboys hawked the *Sun*, paying seventy-five cents per hundred on credit or sixty-seven cents per hundred cash in advance. Thousands of low-wage earners were thus encouraged to buy copies at one cent or subscribe for six cents a week, whereas other dailies had long only grudgingly sold copies at six cents apiece and concentrated on selling annual subscriptions at $8 or $10. Day also insisted on cash in advance for his $3 annual subscriptions and for advertising other than on yearly contracts, thus avoiding ruinous losses from defaulters, long a burden to publishers. The *Sun's* circulation climbed to 30,000 as he doubled the page size by 1836, and Day was clearing $20,000 to $25,000 a year.

Imitators, in addition to the *Transcript,* swarmed onto the scene. Mott estimated that a dozen of the thirty-four dailies started in New York City in the four years between the *Sun's* birth and the financial panic of 1837 were penny dailies. Penny papers blossomed in other cities. The *Boston Daily Times* quickly reached 12,000 in 1836 and was absorbed twenty-one years later by another, the *Boston Herald,* which became a top circulator in Civil War times. The *Philadelphia Public Ledger,* also founded in 1836, reached 20,000 circulation in its first two years. The *Baltimore Sun,* despite the financial panic clouding its birth year, 1837, reached 12,000 circulation quickly and continued on to greater success.

Thus, within half a decade, newspapers were spread to the masses. Prior to the penny press, Horace Greeley had estimated that "less than one-third of the adults" in New York City regularly read newspapers. By 1836, penny-paper circulation alone was rivaling the number of households in New York City.

Imitators made important changes and improvements. Of prime importance among these was James Gordon Bennett, who founded the *New York Herald* in May, 1835. Within six months, the *Herald* was close to the *Sun* and the *Transcript* in circulation. It passed the 20,000 mark in 1836 and pressed the *Sun* hard until the Civil War, when it finally took over first place. Among innovations credited to Bennett are the beginnings of the financial page, wider "beat-type" coverage of the city, and a forerunner of the society page. He bypassed the humorous police-court approach to concentrate on more exciting aspects of crime. Bennett even played detective in covering the case of a young clerk, Richard Robinson, charged with murdering a prostitute, Helen Jewett. The Robinson-Jewett murder case was the first one of wide interest—thanks to the penny press—involving principals of no social status. Bennett's own investigation convinced him of Robinson's innocence, and he hailed the latter's acquittal as a *Herald* triumph. Probably because Bennett had been a widely experienced newspaperman (Washington correspondent, editorial writer, and editor) before he started the *Herald,* he created a paper which appealed to both the penny-paper masses and people of

Figure 3.1. Replacement of small, cheaply produced journals by much larger newspapers—packed with expensive news and features—has made impossible the kind of competition which flourished 100 years ago. (Courtesy, **Dubuque Telegraph-Herald**)

Despite changes in mechanical and business aspects, putting out a newspaper still hinges basically on reporting and editing. A **reporter (upper, left)**, sent on assignment by the city desk, telephones his findings to a **rewrite man (upper, right).** The reporter may provide only bare facts from which the rewrite man will fashion the story, or he may dictate a finished story. **News editors (lower, left)** choose the small fraction of available staff and press-association stories and pictures which can be used, indicating on layout sheets how major elements will be positioned in the next edition. **Copy editors (lower, right)** do the final shaping. Everything from factual accuracy, through grammar and spelling, to stylebook conformity is checked within the limits of time. Conciseness and clarity are polished; trimming to fit a particular space, if necessary, is done here; directions on type styles and sizes are entered; headlines are written to news editors' specifications. [Omitted from this series are the supportive advertising and circulation operations.]

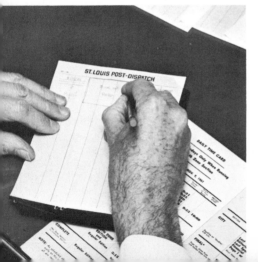
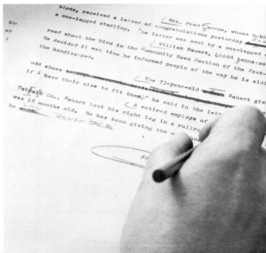

Copy reaches the composing room by pneumatic tubes. There a **copy cutter (upper, left)** divides big pieces into smaller "takes," parceling work out to **linotypists (upper, right)**. Identified by "slugs," the parts are assembled in **galleys (lower, left)** under headlines also set in the composing room. Printed on long strips, galleys are then checked against edited copy by proofreaders; printers replace lines containing errors with corrected lines in the galleys. Meanwhile, **engravers (lower, right)** process art work as cropped by editors. Photographs and line drawings are rephotographed and etched on zinc plates, which are mounted on type-high blocks. [Smaller newspapers use simpler engraving methods; many skip the stereotyping process—shown on the next page—and print directly from the type and engravings off a flatbed press. More and more newspapers are shifting from this letterpress method to offset printing. That involves photographic reproduction of pasted-up dummies and use of rubber-blanketed cylinders for transferring ink to the pages.]

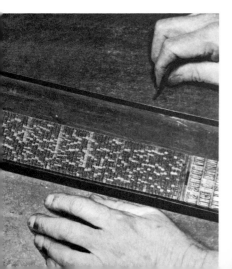

Printers fit type and engravings into **page forms (upper, left),** following layout sheets under makeup editor's guidance. **Stereotypers (upper, right)** place moist papier-mâché matrix in molder where extreme pressure forms the "page mat." Another **stereotyper (lower, left)** trims the mat, which then goes into the casting box to make a curved type-metal plate of the page. A **pressman (lower, left, below)** anchors the plate onto the press cylinder. Finally, the **presses (lower, right)** roll, turning out 96-page newspapers—folded, cut, and counted—at the rate of 160,000 per hour.

circumstance. His pioneering coverage of Wall Street made the *Herald* a banker's paper. His good handling of foreign news appealed to the best educated. His unusual treatment of crime news probably appealed to all. Bennett employed regular theater coverage, used more woodcut illustrations, and improved on the *Transcript's* pioneering sports coverage. His enterprise in arranging European correspondence, setting up a Washington bureau, hiring correspondents in other cities, and operating his own fleet of boats to beat others to news from incoming ships marked him as a newsman above all. He raised the *Herald's* price to two cents in 1836 so he could enlarge his page size and finance more news-gathering efforts. His attacks on the established six-penny papers earned him several beatings and finally helped make him the target of a boycott in 1840. The "moral war" against Bennett hurt him. Before it started, he was claiming 17,000 daily circulation and 19,000 for his weekly edition; five years later his sworn statements listed 12,000 for each. But enterprising news coverage, particularly during the Mexican War of 1846-1848, brought the *Herald* back to more than 30,000 by 1850 and to national leadership at 60,000 by 1860.

The most important imitator-innovator was Horace Greeley, who founded the *New York Tribune* in April, 1841. He proved that a penny paper could succeed without either frivolous humor from the police courts or more sophisticated concentration on crime and scandal. Greeley mixed good news coverage by an excellent staff with probably the most influential newspaper editorial policy ever created to lift American journalism out of the gutter. He proved dramatically that mass circulation could be achieved on a high moral plane and that newspapers could lead nobly while turning a good profit.

The daily *Tribune* reached 11,000 within seven weeks and climbed to 45,000 by 1860. Its weekly edition, as cleverly promoted as it was brilliantly edited, attained the fantastic level of 200,000 by 1860. It exercised "the greatest single journalistic influence" in the 1850s, according to historian James Ford Rhodes. One traveler from the East wrote back that the *Tribune* "comes next to the Bible all through the West." In *Main Currents in the History of Journalism*, Professor Willard G. Bleyer declared that Greeley's influence "has never been exceeded by that of any other American journalist."

The *Tribune* went after the news with twelve editors and reporters in its New York office, three Washington correspondents, five other national correspondents from Boston to California, and nine foreign correspondents—four in Europe, two in Canada, and one each in Mexico, Central America, and Cuba. What Bleyer described as the ablest staff then operating processed this news. It included Henry J. Raymond, who left to found the *New York Times* in 1851; Charles A. Dana, who gained fame as editor of the *New York Sun* after 1868; and Whitelaw Reid, who took over the *Tribune* after Greeley's death in 1872. The first woman to gain distinction in newspaper work, Margaret Fuller, worked for the *Tribune*. Typical of the high *Tribune* journalistic-literary level was a series on how the less fortunate lived in New York City, reprinted in a best seller, *Hot Corn: Life Scenes in New York Illustrated*. (The title was from an article about a street waif who sold boiled sweet corn near the *Tribune* office.)

Abolition of slavery was among Greeley's burning passions. An ardent Whig, Greeley had read himself out of the party in 1852, declaring that he could not give up his antislavery position. He joined the Republicans in 1854 and played a part in Abraham Lincoln's nomination in 1860. He vigorously opposed capital punishment and backed equal suffrage for women. Fascinated by Fourierism (a communistic concept), Greeley organized the *Tribune* as a stock company so that employees could own shares in the paper. He promoted labor unions to advance the workingman's lot and supported the ten-hour day. His quickness to embrace radical proposals got him frequently into trouble, but his sincerity and editorial skill maintained the *Tribune* through every crisis. He narrowly escaped when a mob attacked his office during the New York draft riots in 1863. He was among the most reviled by rival editors, particularly Bennett, during his stormy career. His courage in signing Jefferson Davis's bail bond in 1867 (to back the *Tribune*'s cry for "Universal amnesty—Impartial suffrage") typified the boldness that made him the greatest editor of his time.

Among the great newspapers of this period, Raymond's *New York Times* offered another important step forward after 1851. The *Times* offered both the broadest news coverage and the best advance in nonpartisanship, helping lead the American press toward its ideal of political independence. Edwin Lawrence Godkin's editorship of the weekly *Nation* (1865-1899) and the daily *New York Evening Post* (1881-1899) demonstrated the power of small, select circulations—both in the 10,000-20,000 range. Others important to the period include Samuel Bowles of the *Springfield Republican*, William Rockhill Nelson of the *Kansas City Star*, Henry Watterson of the *Louisville Courier-Journal*, Henry W. Grady of the *Atlanta Constitution*, Melville E. Stone of the *Chicago Daily News*, and Joseph Medill of the *Chicago Tribune*.

Faster communication and travel combined with the forward thrust of the penny press to change the news concept radically in this period. Transatlantic steamship service in 1838 cut the time for news from Europe to three weeks. By 1840, stretches of rail lines provided fast links with pony express from New Hampshire to North Carolina. Carrier pigeons and boats intercepting steamers at sea were used to speed news transmission. A Baltimore paper first used telegraphed news from Washington in May, 1845. By the next year, New York dailies were carrying a regular column of "Telegraph" news, and by 1848, the telegraph linked the eastern seaboard—from Portland to Charleston—with Milwaukee, Chicago, and St. Louis. Newspapers increasingly shared expenses in relaying news during this period, and this led ultimately to the Associated Press and other press associations.

More than 3,000 newspapers, including about 400 dailies, were on the scene when the Civil War started in April, 1861. The four years of bloody conflict tested every aspect of the press, from ingenuity to responsibility. Early fumbling with censorship by both the government and newspapers caused serious trouble for the Union. The South's 40-odd dailies caused fewer problems because of the Confederacy's greater unity and because a cooperative news association dealt more effectively with military censors than could the disorganized, highly competitive Northern newspapers. Telegraphic reporting of Union Army movements produced military security problems, with which no one knew how to deal. Generals, never kindly disposed toward reporters, and Washington officials sometimes used a heavy hand and sometimes just fumed ineffectively. Probably no war has been so completely covered by correspondents on the scene. The *New York Herald* (which reached 135,000 circulation after Fort Sumter) had 40 correspondents covering the battles. The typical eight-page paper devoted a third of its 48 columns to war coverage. Bennett estimated that he spent a half million dollars covering the Civil War. In addition to brilliant and enterprising reporting, newspapers employed maps and woodcuts to give their customers full accounts. Lincoln and his generals were freely second-guessed and otherwise criticized by editors as the conflict stretched on. A few newspapers openly opposed the war in sympathy with those Northern Democrats known as "Copperheads." British sentiment with the South led to a ban on British correspondents from battle areas after the first year. General Ambrose Burnside closed the Copperhead *Chicago Times* in 1864, but Lincoln rescinded the order after three days. General John A. Dix closed New York's *World* and *Journal of Commerce* for two days after they published a false report that Lincoln had ordered the drafting of an additional 400,000 men—an extremely incendiary story in light of the earlier draft riots. Samuel Medary, editor of the *Columbus Ohio Statesman* and the *Crisis*, a Copperhead magazine, was indicted for subversive activity but died while free on bond before he could be brought to trial.

The pressures of war coverage speeded the steady advance of production and news-gathering mechanics. The new stereotyping process of 1861, for example, enabled editors to use multicolumn cuts and headlines. Previously, column rules helped lock the type in place on the cylindrical surface of the revolving presses. It was risky to eliminate even part of a column rule until the paper could be cast into solid sheets for the press run. Heavy use of the telegraph probably contributed to both the inverted-pyramid story structure and reduction in opinionated writing. The per-word expense encouraged conciseness, and facts without opinion require fewer words. Frequent breakdowns in the telegraph inspired reporters to put the most important points first so that they would have the best chance to get through. Headlines were a natural outgrowth of the exciting bulletins used for up-to-the-hour coverage of the great war.

After the war, mechanical advances changed newspapers still more. Completion of the transatlantic cable in 1866 put a new meaning on timeliness for European news. The *New York Herald* paid $7,000 for cabling the text of a speech made by the king of Prussia when the war with Austria ended in 1867. Efforts to conquer the problems of hand-set type speeded up. (Mark Twain lost a fortune investing in automatic typesetting devices.) Variations of these were in use by the late 1880s, and Ottmar Mergenthaler perfected his "Linotype" machine in 1890. The telephone, invented in 1875, began showing up in news rooms in the 1880s. Typewriters were used in the 1880s and became common in the 1890s. Halftone photoengravings added to newspaper content in the last decade of the century. Meanwhile, improvements in stereotyping and creation of the web perfecting press had made possible high-speed printing of newspapers many times the size of the six-column eight-pagers of the Civil War era.

These advances were sounding the death knell for editors as newspaper proprietors in the old sense. Already, the capital required for starting a newspaper had leaped from the few hundreds with which Day, Greeley, and Bennett had started to hundreds of thousands—for equipment not even available fifty years earlier.

Onto this stage in the closing years of the period moved two giants of American journalism—Joseph Pulitzer and William Randolph Hearst. Their struggle for dominance of the New York market was epochal.

Pulitzer, a penniless immigrant, had risen by genius and hard work to newspaper prominence in St. Louis after serving briefly in the Civil War. Political associations led to his part ownership in a German newspaper in St. Louis, which he sold for $30,000. In 1878, he bought the *St. Louis Dispatch* at a sheriff's sale for $2,500 and combined it with John Dillon's *Post* to create the *Post-Dispatch*. After buying out Dillon, he steered the *Post-Dispatch* to evening-newspaper dominance in St. Louis. He moved to New York and bought the *World* from Jay Gould for $346,000 in May, 1883. The *World* was then an eight-page paper selling 15,000 to 20,000 copies at two cents, far behind the *Sun, Herald,*

Tribune, and *Times.* Pulitzer brought his assistant, John A. Cockerill, from St. Louis as managing editor and began changing the *World*'s news and editorial policies. He moved toward human-interest stories, gossip, scandals, and crusades in the news columns and dedicated what was to become the greatest editorial page of its time to battling for the people. Within four months, circulation had climbed to 40,000, whereupon the *Tribune* dropped to three cents and the *Times* and *Herald* to two cents. The *Herald* ran a full-page ad for six days in Pulitzer's *World* to announce its new price. *World* circulation passed 100,000 in the fall of 1884 and the *Sunday World* reached 250,000 in 1886. In 1887, Pulitzer launched the *Evening World* at one cent, and within five years the combined sworn circulation of 375,000 was more than double the nearest competitor's unsworn claim.

Pulitzer's improvements on established techniques, plus some original devices, set a newspaper pattern as revolutionary as that of the penny press. *World* news coverage pandered to the masses with crime and scandal and appealed to serious citizens with courageous exposés of bad government and predatory business tycoons. Reporter Elizabeth Cochran ("Nellie Bly") feigned insanity to get committed to Blackwell's Island, then wrote a stunning exposé series. *World* reporters ripped into lobbying at Albany and inhumane prison conditions. Cheating tenement builders, railroad robber barons, greedy monopolists, and aldermen who traded streetcar franchises for bribes were mercilessly exposed. The *World* took a cue from stunts like the *Herald*'s 1871 feat of sending Henry M. Stanley to find Dr. David Livingston in equatorial Africa. "Nellie Bly" circled the world in 72 days in 1889, beating the fictional record of Jules Verne's hero in *Around the World in Eighty Days,* which had been published seventeen years earlier. In 1885, the *World* collected small donations from its readers to build the $100,000 pedestal for the Statue of Liberty, after Congress and a private committee had failed to provide for the gift from France's people. Pulitzer challenged the *Herald*'s sports-coverage leadership by creating the first sports section. Enterprising use of illustrations—diagrams of crime scenes, frequent one-column portraits, regular editorial cartoons—also distinguished the *World* from its competitors. R. F. Outcault added the first cartoon comics with his "Yellow Kid." By the early 1890s, the *World* was printing sixteen pages daily and double that on Sundays. An important secret of Pulitzer's success was paying higher salaries for more and better reporters and editors.

Not the least important was the *World*'s outstanding editorial page, Pulitzer's first love. President Grover Cleveland and others attributed Cleveland's narrow victory in 1884—the Democrats' first in twenty-eight years—to the *World*'s support in delivering a crucial New York City

margin. Distinguishing characteristics of *World* editorial policy, however, were its quickness to criticize mistakes by those it had supported
and its willingness to stand against popular tides. Thus, in 1895, Pulitzer
vigorously attacked Cleveland's bellicose warning to Great Britain in a
dispute over the boundary between Venezuela and British Guiana.
Against a strong tide supported by most other big newspapers and
against the man he had just helped elect to a second term, Pulitzer
denounced the proposed "application of a false Monroe Doctrine" as "a
colossal crime." He cabled prominent English and Irish leaders for their
opinions and had them published under a banner headline. Secretary
of State Richard Olney threatened prosecution under a 1799 statute barring citizens from such unauthorized correspondence with foreign governments, but Pulitzer fired back a defiant reply. The war fever subsided.
That same year, the *World* singlehandedly stopped a multimillion-dollar
government-bond deal with J. P. Morgan and other financiers. Offering
to buy $1,000,000 worth itself, the *World* telegraphed thousands of banks
and obtained enough pledges to provide double the amount sought by
the U. S. Treasury. By forcing a public sale, the *World* struck a blow
at secret deals while saving the Treasury millions.

Pulitzer's profitable and inspiring journalism attracted young Hearst
to the scene. As a Harvard student, Hearst had been fascinated by
Pulitzer's sensational success. Having imitated it successfully on his
father's *San Francisco Examiner*, he moved into New York and bought
the *Morning Journal* for $180,000 in the fall of 1895. Leaning heavily
on $7,500,000 from his late father's silver-mining fortune, Hearst em-
barked on a wild spending spree to overtake the *World*. Cutting the
Journal's price to one cent, hiring an all-star staff, and out-Pulitzering
Pulitzer in the sensation department, Hearst quickly raised circulation
from around 75,000 to 150,000. Pulitzer's morning and evening papers
totaled over half a million, and his *Sunday World* stood close to that
—all yielding tremendous advertising profits. Hearst's fast rise made
Pulitzer nervous, however, and the invader's raids on his *World* staff
drove him to panic. At one swoop, Hearst hired Pulitzer's entire Sunday
staff, and the next month Pulitzer tried to strike back. Pulitzer's counterattack boomeranged, however. After he cut the morning *World* to one
cent, circulation rose only 40 per cent without hurting the *Journal*'s, and
advertisers balked at Pulitzer's rate increase. With Arthur Brisbane now
operating the *Sunday World,* the two Sunday papers fought a bitter
battle.

The *World* hired a new artist to draw its version of "The Yellow
Kid of Hogan's Alley" while Outcault drew his original for the *Journal*.
Posters promoting the feature for both newspapers led to the term
"yellow journalism," representing the sensationalism practiced by the

two newspapers. Brisbane, like his predecessor, filled the Sunday paper with pseudoscience and sex and drove it to 600,000 by the end of 1896. Then Hearst hired Brisbane away to edit his *Evening Journal,* and the second "Yellow Kid" artist went with him. (Brisbane, angered by a Pulitzer order to tone down the *Sunday World,* had asked Hearst for $150 a week plus $1 for every thousand circulation the *Evening Journal* gained. The gamble, in giving up his $200 a week on the *Sunday World,* paid off as Brisbane's salary reached $1,000 a week during the Spanish-American War.) The *World's* success with color printing inspired Hearst to install larger color presses, so he could print an eight-page colored-comics section on Sunday. By the end of 1896, his daily circulation was past 400,000. *Sunday Journal* circulation neared 400,000, and within another year matched the *World's* 600,000. Both dailies sold 1,500,000 copies November 4, 1896, reporting William McKinley's victory over William Jennings Bryan.

Made to order for the desperate circulation war was the Cuban insurrection against Spanish colonial authority, which had flared anew in 1895. Both papers, and Hearst's *Journal* in particular, have been given major blame for what may have been America's most unnecessary war. Sensational reporting of Spanish atrocities, real and alleged, fanned American sympathies for the oppressed Cubans. The *World* and *Journal* had top correspondents in Cuba, and numerous papers drew heavily on reports by Cuban refugees at Key West, Florida, and other points. Hearst sent Richard Harding Davis and the artist Frederic Remington to the scene. Typical of such coverage was a page-1 display under a two-line banner asking whether the American flag protected womanhood. A Remington sketch, covering half the front page, showed a naked Cuban girl surrounded by leering Spanish officers searching her clothing after the officers had boarded a ship flying the American flag. The *World* later revealed that no such outrage had occurred, but the flurry of other stories and demands for war drowned out the occasional bits of objectivity. Perhaps the most dramatic newspaper effort was *Journal* reporter Karl Decker's thrilling rescue of Evangelina Cisneros, a rebel beauty, from a Havana jail and her triumphal delivery to New York. Hearst's *Journal* set the pace in building war fever, but the *World* contributed mightily. Newspapers across the United States largely followed suit. Two months after the battleship Maine mysteriously exploded and sank with the loss of 266 Americans in Havana harbor in February, 1898, war came. Coverage of the four-month war was even wilder, with the *Journal* issuing as many as forty extras in a single day. Hearst took a personal hand, on one occasion capturing a group of Spanish sailors himself.

The Hearst-Pulitzer circulation war had served as a catalyst in developing big-business newspapering. Readers had learned to expect large omnibus newspapers—with expensively obtained news reports, sports sections, comics (colored on Sunday), photographs and lots of other art work. The era of editors starting newspapers with modest capital investments was buried deep by the turn of the century.

BUSINESS ENTERPRISE: 1900-PRESENT

By 1900, perhaps two dozen dailies had passed the 100,000 circulation mark. Starting a metropolitan newspaper required millions, and opportunities like that of Adolph S. Ochs in obtaining the *New York Times* in 1896 had almost disappeared. Ochs's publishing career typifies the changes. In 1878, he had bought a half interest in the four-page daily *Chattanooga Times* with a borrowed $250. Having paid off its $1,500 in debts and moved it forward, he was able to invest $75,000 in the faltering New York paper eighteen years later and establish a controlling interest by 1900. Meanwhile, his superb management and editorial foresight had multiplied its 9,000 circulation several times. Placing his *Times* squarely against the yellow journalism of that period, he adopted the slogan "All the News That's Fit to Print." He arranged exchanges with the *London Times* in starting toward his paper's eventual eminence in foreign coverage and began the practice of carrying full texts of important documents and speeches. The rise of the *Times* to top respect among America's dailies was steady in the early twentieth century.

The century's first decade saw the rapid rise of chain publishing as newspapering came more under the dominance of businessmen-publishers. E. W. Scripps and several associates had started large-scale chain efforts in the late 1890s, and the holdings were tripled to fifteen papers between 1900 and 1910. Meanwhile, Scripps built up another chain of a dozen dailies along the West Coast. The Scripps formula was to publish cheap but bright dailies dedicated to the working man—attacking capitalists' excesses, taking the side of strikers. He had interests in dozens of newspapers during the century's first quarter, and the surviving Scripps-Howard group attests to his success. Hearst invaded Chicago with an evening *American* and morning *Examiner* and Boston with an evening *Examiner* between 1900 and 1904, bringing his total to six papers in four cities. In the next three decades, Hearst added more than thirty papers, his chain crisscrossing the country from Boston to Los Angeles and from Atlanta to Seattle, before it began shrinking a few years after his death in 1951. Frank A. Munsey, who had made a fortune by pricing his *Munsey's Magazine* at ten cents, bought papers in five eastern metropolises during twenty-five years of sporadically trying to promote "efficiency" in newspapering. He succeeded mostly in establishing a record for closing down famous newspapers, however.

Reorganization of the Associated Press and the formation of United Press (by Scripps) and International News Service (by Hearst) marked the century's first decade also. In 1958, the latter two were merged into United Press International.

With the aforementioned special boost by Munsey, the number of daily newspapers began declining in the twentieth century. Depending upon which historian you choose, the high-water mark reached between 2,200 and 2,600 somewhere between 1909 and 1914. Consolidation for efficiency's sake marked most big businesses, and newspapers were no exception. Advertisers began focusing more intently on leading circulators; readers' demands for expensive features raised the stakes too high for marginal competitors; ruthless competition among publishers reduced the survival time of those who trailed the leaders; capital-gains tax provisions later on combined with the enormous resources of wealthier publishers to encourage consolidations and sell-outs. The rise of radio as a mass medium in the 1930s and of television in the 1950s provided competition that made multiple purchase of newspapers less attractive to customers and cut heavily into the growth of advertising revenue for print media.

Meanwhile, yellow journalism began yielding to better efforts early in the 1900s, though it had a limited revival during the war of the tabloids in the 1920s. Although motives have been questioned and excesses charged, crusades against governmental and societal ills in the century's first decade underlined an important press power for good. Magazines like *Collier's, McClure's, Cosmopolitan,* and *Everybody's* led telling campaigns against patent medicine abuses, municipal graft, and excesses of the robber barons. Star writers included Lincoln Steffens, Ida M. Tarbell, and Samuel Hopkins Adams. If crusades were effective promotional devices for Pulitzer's *World* and Hearst's *Journal,* they were also beneficial to society.

World War I, 1914-1918, provided another crisis for responsible press freedom—one not admirably handled by the press, the people, or the government. Anti-German propaganda created a war fever exceeding that generated against the Spanish two decades earlier. Immediately after America's entry into the war in April, 1917, President Woodrow Wilson appointed a newspaperman, George Creel, to head a Committee on Public Information. Creel's brilliant promotion of the "War to End Wars" was generously used by most of the press. Minority opposition was suppressed by both government edict and popular disapproval. The public, hoodwinked by some gross Allied propaganda (e. g., reports of German soldiers' cutting off Belgian children's hands) and less irresponsibly encouraged by Creel's modern public-relations campaign, dedicated itself spiritually to a war as never before or since. Towns changed their German names, the German language was removed from school curricula, and there were even reports of dachshunds' being stoned by mobs. In *The Rise of American Civilization*, the Beards called the Sedition Act of 1918 worse than the Sedition Act of 1798, but no important protest was stirred.

Creel's sin, if any, may have been in setting the stage for disillusionment which followed "The War to Make the World Safe for Democracy." Some historians believe that the "Jazz Age" of the 1920s can be blamed partly on the American people's disappointment in what followed the Great War.

In any event, a contributor to, or outgrowth from, the mood of the Roaring Twenties was another spate of journalism like that of the penny press and the yellow journalism of the nineteenth century. The *New York Daily News* appeared as a 16-page tabloid in June, 1919, under direction of Captain Joseph M. Patterson, co-manager of the *Chicago Tribune* with Colonel Robert R. McCormick. Crowds riding the twelve-year-old subway found it—at half a regular newspaper's size—convenient, and its emphasis on sex and crime appealed as had Day's police-court coverage eighty-six years earlier. Its heavy use of photographs also appealed to the masses. Beauty and other contests and innumerable coupon offers attracted circulation, and by 1924 it led American dailies with 750,000 circulation, a lead it has never relinquished. It passed the 1,000,000 mark in 1926 and the 2,000,000 mark in the 1940s. Patterson, like Scripps and Pulitzer, tuned the serious-news coverage to the working man in the *Daily News's* early years. Tabloids had been tried prior to Patterson's experiment, but none had found the formula as effectively as he had. He had taken his cue from the *London Daily Mirror*, and he made it a practice to watch readership habits in the streets. Patterson's success drew imitators, the first of whom was Hearst, whose morning *American* was being pressed by the new *Daily News*. In 1924, he brought out the tabloid *New York Daily Mirror*, hired a key performer from the *Daily News*, and frequently outsensationalized the original. Bernarr Macfadden, the physical culturist who had created the fabulously successful *True Story* magazine in 1919, started the *New York Daily Graphic* also in 1924. His editor, Emile Gauvreau, tried to outdo the other two with such innovations as the "composograph." When the *Graphic* could not get pictures at the scene, it posed scantily-clad models in reconstructed settings and dubbed in the appropriate faces. Murders provided the main fare in the battle of the tabloids. The most famous was the Hall-Mills case, which Hearst's *Mirror* staff exhumed from four-year-old files in 1926. The New Brunswick, New Jersey, police had assumed that the Reverend Edward Hall and Eleanor Mills, a church-choir singer, had been suicides. The *Mirror* brought forth new evidence, and the minister's widow was arrested. During an eleven-day trial, 200 reporters filed 5,000,000 words on the story. Rivaling the *Daily Graphic*'s photographic shenanigans was the *Daily News*'s sneaked photograph of Ruth Snyder's death in the electric chair in January, 1928. She and a corset salesman, Judd Gray, had been convicted in a sensational trial of having murdered her husband, Albert.

Generally, however, the *Daily News* left the worst excesses to its competitors. Hearst sold his unprofitable *Mirror* in 1928, but took it back two years later, and it eventually did better under Arthur Brisbane's editorship, ultimately reaching No. 2 in United States circulation before dying in 1963. Macfadden's "Porno Graphic," as it was disparagingly called, folded in 1932, partly because advertisers shied away from its scandalous columns. The tabloid format was copied in various cities, but many observers have remarked its failure to catch on more widely. In any event, the major tabloids made some worthwhile contributions along with their "gutter journalism" disgraces. They brought in more newspaper readers and inspired some worthwhile conciseness in respectable columns. They taught the value of pictures and showed through example that radical changes in old procedures could be successful.

The Great Depression, which followed the stock market crash of 1929, struck American newspapers a double blow. Radio's emergence as a mass medium during the 1930s took away business in addition to losses from the plummeting economy. Industrial production dropped 50 per cent in little more than two years; unemployment climbed to 15,000,000, and millions with jobs worked part time at reduced wages. National income dropped from $82,000,000 in 1928 to $40,000,000 in 1932, and bank failures averaged nearly 1,700 a year. Meanwhile, radio offered a new and relatively cheap attraction to poverty-plagued masses and a fresh hope for desperate advertisers. Comparisons of the 1919-1929 and 1929-1939 decades tell the story.

During the 1919-1929 period, United States population rose 16 per cent and daily newspaper circulation climbed 50 per cent. During the next decade, population rose 7 per cent, but circulation ended up at the 40,000,000 with which it had started. In 1929, Americans owned 14,000,000 radio receivers, and national advertising on radio totaled less than $19,000,000. By 1939, Americans owned 44,000,000 receivers, and radio's national advertising totaled $83,000,000. But while radio gained in "circulation" and advertising revenues, newspapers just maintained the former and suffered heavy losses in the latter. From a national-advertising peak of $260,000,000 in 1929, newspapers tumbled to $163,000,000 by 1934. Not until 1946 did newspapers' national-advertising revenue return to the 1929 level.

Newspapers launched a short, unsuccessful war against news broadcasting in the early 1930s. Members of the Associated Press voted not to furnish reports to radio networks and to limit members with radio stations to 35-word bulletins. United Press and International News Service accepted their newspaper clients' requests to stop serving radio. When radio stations pirated news from the papers, suits brought rulings that news had several hours' property rights. But radio networks set up their own news-gathering agencies, and a truce was soon sought by both sides. A compromise allowed two unsponsored five-minute newscasts a day from the Press-Radio Bureau after late 1933. However, several new services emerged to give radio stations something more than those tidbits. Most prominent was Transradio Press Service, which had signed up a third of America's 600 stations by the late 1930s. This new competition inspired UP and INS to negotiate their way back into radio news, and by 1940 AP and UP both were supplying special radio-news reports. Newspapers learned, painfully, that radio newscasts could not be suppressed and, happily, that newscasts tended to whet more appetites for newspapers.

Radio's instant relay of President Franklin D. Roosevelt's "fireside chats" and such momentous events as King Edward VIII's abdication in the 1930s clearly carried journalism into a whole new era. Newspapers turned more to specialization and depth reporting, though their response in that direction was much greater with competition from television in the 1950s and 1960s. The old newspaper "extra" slowly died away, ending both a promotional device and a great expense. A greater need for accuracy and completeness, now that citizens could compare reports with broadcasts of actual events, added practicality to the ideal of responsibility. Radio provided a substitute for the newspaper competition which had been disappearing since the century's first decade. Radio commentators stirred new activity on the editorial pages, mostly in the form of adding syndicated columnists—often including some with opposing views.

Magazine journalism went through several upheavals during the twentieth century. Typical of the industry's revolution is the story of the *Saturday Evening Post*, an undisputed leader of 2,000,000 circulation in the first third of the century. In this last third, it ranked in the top ten with a circulation of 6,700,000, but operating losses moved Curtis Publishing Company to kill the *Post* in 1969. Advertisers have demanded selective audiences rather than just millions of subscribers, and the per-unit cost of circulating copies has become a losing proposition for a majority in the multimillion range. Those not at the very top in their particular field cannot attract the advertising revenue on which their profits depend. The deaths of prominent leaders like *American, Collier's,* and *Woman's Home Companion*—all with circulations in the millions—attest to this economic phenomenon since the 1950s. Successive increases in postal rates and other mail-circulation expenses led *Cosmopolitan* to concentrate on newsstand sales in the 1950s, despite the long-time dominance of subscription circulation. The use of "split-run" ads has helped some magazines; by providing one advertiser with a less expensive coverage of a limited area and another advertiser the same chance in a different area, magazines have moved back into better competition with other media. Revolutionary changes in types of magazines have marked the century—the *Reader's Digest* introduced pocket-sized packets of condensed articles from other magazines in 1922; *Time* introduced the important news weekly in 1923; *Life* and *Look* attracted new audiences with picture magazines in the 1930s. Magazines had a brief flurry of yellow journalism on a massive scale with the emergence of *Confidental* in the 1950s, but the fad subsided quickly. Quality magazines like *Harper's* and *Atlantic Monthly* found a place with their limited, selective audiences.

World War II's impact on press freedom was relatively less than that of World War I. A small isolationist minority—led by the Hearst papers and the *Chicago Tribune*, tried vigorously to discourage America's drift toward war without either private or government harassment of serious note. ("HOUSE PASSES DICTATOR BILL," the *Chicago Tribune's* page-1 banner shouted as the interventionist Lend-Lease measure moved America toward war.) Radio's enterprising coverage of war's approach in Europe—and the two years before Pearl Harbor forced America's entry—will stand as one of journalistic history's grand achievements. Wartime newsprint shortages and phenomenal listenership during World War II increased radio's share of the total advertising dollar nearly 4 percentage points while that of newspapers dipped 7 points (magazines picked up the balance) between 1940 and 1945. By 1950, newspapers had gained back more than 4 points and radio had dropped back 4 points (magazines lost their 3-point gain, and television had picked up its first 3 points). More than 1,000 American correspondents covered the far-flung war fronts, and 37 lost their lives. Normal censorship troubles prevailed, from the Navy's long hold on losses at Pearl Harbor in 1941 to the final defeat of Japan in 1945. However, Americans edged a little closer to the revolutionary thought that bad war news might be helpful for a democratic society on occasion. One notable example was the 1944 release of a photograph showing American soldiers dead on the Anzio beachhead in Italy.

The Cold War Era following World War II provided new tests for American press freedom. A strong trend against open government was partially checked by strong press efforts to overcome growing secrecy. That battle continues in the last third of the twentieth century.

Coverage of the Korean War (1950-1953) and the Vietnam War's escalation in the 1960s brought new levels of critical reporting and editorial discussion by all arms of the nation's press. General Douglas

Mass communication's youngest journalistic medium, television, depends as heavily on good news-gathering and editing as does the newspaper. A **newsman (upper, left)** radios directions on covering a story to a mobile unit. At the scene, a **reporter and camera man (upper, right)** interview principals and record the news scene. Film, rushed to the station, is processed by a **technician (lower, left).** [In the case of a story breaking during newscast time, pictures can be transmitted for live broadcast.] Developed film is screened by **news editors (lower, right),** who make basic choices from total footage. The rigidities of newscast formats require more rapid decisions within less flexible limits than is the case with planning space allotments in a newspaper. TV news editors can handle only a fraction of the newspaper's volume, and the pieces to make their thirty-minute or sixty-minute packages must be trimmed and proportioned much more carefully than are their counterparts in print.

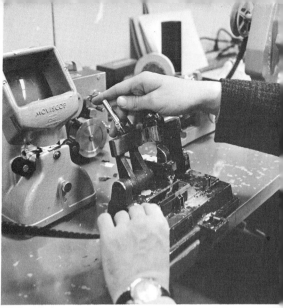

Moving pictures supply an unmatched attraction for customers but threaten news-judgment. Exciting film can help a weak story crowd out a more important one or warp the viewers' grasp of the total story. Basic choices made, a **reporter (upper, left)** edits film, checking frames through a viewfinder and listening with a sound reader to locate the best segments. The **reporter (upper, right)** then splices film, removing extraneous bits and noting precise timing for broadcast. Other **newsmen (lower, left)** check press-association Teletype copy to select major stories not covered by the staff. **Flip cards (lower, right)** are made with wirephotos—like those on table at left—and still shots from station files; heat and pressure are used to mount the pictures on cardboard. A thirty-minute newscast's two dozen stories with accompanying pictures and diagrams are chosen from several times that many, provided by the staff, the network, press associations, and other sources.

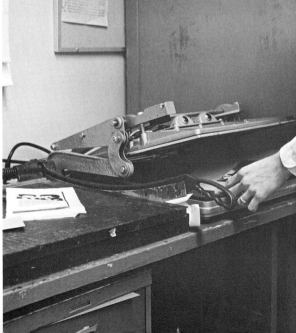

Special needs in writing for the ear and coordinating copy with film, combined with demands for extreme conciseness, make the tasks of the **writer (upper, left)** unusually demanding. [Although "readers" still flourish on small stations, most major newscasters rewrite their own final copy for broadcast.] The **newscaster (upper, right)** goes on the air with a production distilled from hours of work behind the scenes; the map projected behind him illustrates the kind of graphics that have marked the best TV news shows. The **program director (below)** and his control-room crew check the monitors, showing what's on the air and what's coming up, against the news producer's script. They project news film, signal camera switches, and key in flip cards and "supers"—namelines accompanying film. Last-minute bulletins or live camera coverage of a breaking story would be engineered from here.

—Photographs by Dick Williams, WBNS-TV (Columbus, Ohio)

MacArthur's imposition of strong censorship measures on the heels of Korean War reverses brought protests from newsmen, rather than complacent acquiescence. And South Vietnamese government moves against American reporters failed to stop coverage embarrassing to the American side. Television news films of American soldiers' burning Vietnamese huts shocked the people back home, but a new level of sophistication tolerated this departure from atrocities-by-the-other-side-only war reporting.

The race is between sophistication born of exposure to so much more news delivered so much faster and fears born of that same increasing onrush. The instant, overwhelming truths of television newscasting have both toughened and challenged America's commitment to free-flowing information. Citizens were shocked when a mother first learned of her son's being wounded in Vietnam by watching a telecast battle sequence. Millions were stunned when they saw Jack Ruby kill President John F. Kennedy's accused assassin, Lee Harvey Oswald, on a live telecast from Dallas, Texas, in 1963. Magazine and newspaper reports of American-aided preparations for the ill-fated 1961 attack on Fidel Castro's Cuba alarmed Americans. Many blamed the press for irresponsibly alerting Castro and thus contributing to the Bay of Pigs fiasco; others realized that Castro had known more than Americans were told by their press and recognized their need to carry heavier informational burdens if democracy was to function in this nuclear age. Questionable government-policy decisions involve larger citizens' stakes now than they did when the Theodore Roosevelt Administration took Panama Canal Zone property from Colombia in 1903. Mere pangs of conscience after the fact are too little and too late in this age of intercontinental missiles.

But the press's margin for error has shrunk as the people's need to know has mushroomed in both volume and speed. Scholars like Professor Raymond B. Nixon of Minnesota believe that the American press is headed toward, or already moving into, a new era—some kind of "Social Scientists' Press." Proponents say that modern America cannot risk exposure to the jingoism of a Hearst bent on winning circulation contests and public office. They argue that even press concentration on trivia—like that of the New York tabloids in the 1920s—presents a grave danger by diverting public attention from substantive issues. The idea is that owners will yield much of their editorial control to acknowledged experts in sociology and political science, who can better tune the mass media to citizens' needs. Whether this is happening or can happen on any significant scale, or whether it should happen, is a subject for endless debate among practicing journalists and students of the press.

FOR FURTHER STUDY

1. Browse through the bound volumes (or microfilm files) of your local newspaper—or any in a convenient library—to compare news columns, editorial pages, entertainment, and advertising then with now. Compare any feature, from language style to use of art, for differences and similarities.

2. Study radio logs (in newspapers or at stations) for changes in program diets between the 1930s and 1940s and today.

3. With what historical developments could today's "underground press" be compared?

4. Do the files of the "good, gray" *New York Times* reflect any influences of the tabloids during the 1920s?

5. After each of newspapering's massive-circulation surges—in the 1830s, 1890s, and 1920s—content turned more serious within a decade. Compare that trait with network television's programming. Has it adjusted in like fashion? If not, why not?

SUGGESTED READING

BEARD, CHARLES A., and BEARD, MARY R., *The Rise of American Civilization*, New York: The Macmillan Company, 1947. Check "Press" listings in the index for general historians' view of press's role in America's development.

BLEYER, WILLARD G., *Main Currents in the History of American Journalism*, Boston: Houghton Mifflin Company, 1927. Bleyer's treatment of colonial history and English background is especially good.

EMERY, EDWIN, *The Press and America*, Englewood Cliffs, N. J.: Prentice-Hall, Inc., 1962 (2nd ed.). Probably the most interesting complete history, this offers the best treatment of electronic journalism in a general text.

HALE, WILLIAM HARLAN, *Horace Greeley: Voice of the People*, New York: Harper & Row, Publishers, 1950. [Available in Collier paperback.] An inspiring biography of the man who led America's first mass press toward useful pursuits.

LEVY, LEONARD W., editor, *Freedom of the Press from Zenger to Jefferson*, Indianapolis: The Bobbs-Merrill Co., Inc., 1966. [Available in Liberal Arts paperback.] (See Nelson's book below.)

MOTT, FRANK LUTHER, *American Journalism*, New York: The Macmillan Company, 1962 (3rd ed.). This successor to Bleyer's work long stood as the standard journalism history. It is still the most detailed and offers the best inclusion of magazines among general journalism histories.

NELSON, HAROLD L., editor, *Freedom of the Press from Hamilton to the Warren Court*, Indianapolis: The Bobbs-Merrill Co., Inc., 1966. [Available in Liberal Arts paperback.] Levy's and Nelson's books reprint and comment upon the significant documents in American journalistic history, from letters and speeches to laws and court decisions, covering press freedom from colonial times to the mid-1960s.

POLLARD, JAMES E., *The Presidents and the Press*, New York: The Macmillan Company, 1947. Every President's relations with the press, from Washington to Franklin D. Roosevelt, are covered. (Pollard has updated the series with additional articles on Harry Truman, Dwight D. Eisenhower, and John F. Kennedy in *Journalism Quarterly*.)

SWANBERG, W. A., *Pulitzer*, New York: Charles Scribner's Sons, 1967. This is the most inspiring biography of the great journalist, who shaped modern newspaper journalism in America. Swanberg's earlier *Citizen Hearst* [available in Bantam paperback] offers a good account of Pulitzer's younger rival.

TALESE, GAY, *The Kingdom and the Power*, New York: The World Publishing Company, 1969. This behind-the-scenes story of those who run the *New York Times* is journalism at its best.

[For additional readings, see: PRICE, WARREN C., *The Literature of Journalism*, Minneapolis: University of Minnesota Press, 1960 (2nd printing). Pages 3-43 list various histories; Pages 44-215 list biographies; several more are listed on pp xi-xiv.]

Part Two

How Journalism Functions

Part Two

How Journalism Functions

CHAPTER 4

Journalistic Writing

The same rules of grammar applying to all literate communication hold for journalistic writing. Observed lapses into "journalese" and strings of clichés should not even inspire imitation, let alone draw the inference that basic grammar can be ignored along with any effort toward superior writing. So fundamental is good grammar and so valued is superior writing that no one should pursue an editorial career without loving language. Beyond that truth lie some structural techniques special to the four media. Both consumers and would-be practitioners should understand these.

American newspaper-reading habits, restrictions of the format, and the many pressures of speed have dictated peculiarities in the news-story form. Effective news-writing for radio operates under even more technique restrictions. The television newscast, requiring synchronization with film clips, demands still more attention to mechanics. Fact-writing for most magazines is least restricted of the four in terms of story-structure mechanics.

What is written, of course, is infinitely more important than how well the structure follows any medium's style. Accuracy and its close ally, completeness, are news-reporting's primary concerns. The most beautifully written, perfectly structured news story is worthless if it omits essential details. And a complete, but badly written, story, violating all the rules of its medium, offers something of value for dedicated consumers who can sift the significance from the journalistic rubble. Unfortunately, only a minority have the intelligence and background to sift for themselves. And few of those have either the time or patience for the task these days. They are more likely to turn the page, pick up another journal, flip the dial, or go fiddle with the hi-fi.

Our limited look at techniques is concerned with how they affect news communication, not with any goal of mastering them. A "buried lead," for example, may suggest bias rather than a mere journalistic failing.

NEWS DETERMINANTS

Several lists of news determinants (or news values) have been concocted by textbook authors, and all are equally unimportant. They serve as handy temporary labels for discussing news judgment, as between competing stories and among elements within a given story. Working newsmen do not check against such a list, and if they did, their widely differing evaluations of the list would kill its usefulness as a common denominator of news. Therefore, we present our list of four and one-half determinants for discussion purposes only:

1. *Timeliness*: All other factors being equal, today is greater than yesterday. Today's decision against trying to override a presidential veto probably tops yesterday's actual veto—providing your readers or listeners got the veto story. When the time differential involves only hours (a matter of the opposition's having gotten the break on the story), this determinant can be overworked in structuring the new story. It can be dangerous when it rules out both the "old" story and a new version of it.

2. *Proximity*: All other factors being equal, here is greater than there. A race riot in Chicago tops a race riot in London on a national network newscast, and a small race riot in Denver tops a bigger one in Cleveland for the *Denver Post*. Few big dailies focus on this to the point of provincial extremism, as when a 100,000-plus Ohio paper played a local $289 burglary ahead of Brazilian President Getulio Vargas's suicide in August, 1954. But old-fashioned tendencies toward local emphasis at any cost handicap news judgment for a Jet Age generation.

3. *Magnitude*: All other factors being equal, the bigger (i. e., the bloodier, the more unusual, the more exciting) event is greater than the little (routine) event. A traffic accident killing eight persons calls for stronger treatment than a single-fatality accident. (Prominence of the story's principals is a factor in magnitude: movie star Jayne Mansfield's 1967 highway death was front-paged across the nation.) Charles A. Lindbergh's solo flight across the Atlantic in May, 1927, is probably unrivaled among "positive" stories accorded press attention for magnitude in the twentieth century. Unhappily, negative events seem to dominate in magnitude. Critics blame the press, but people are more often fascinated by disaster, crime, and violence than by happy moments of achievement. A 12-inch account of the United Appeals Drive's going over the top cannot rival a 12-inch story of the UA treasurer's absconding with the funds. Unless public interest can be built up to the climax of achievement—as with Lindbergh's flight, John H. Glenn's first Ameri-

can space orbit, or Neil Armstrong's historic first steps on the moon —positive events develop little magnitude potential. Obeying the law, not being injured or arrested in race riots, and not getting killed by tornadoes are too commonplace (thank goodness) to win news coverage —or attention—for magnitude.

4. *Significance*: All other factors being equal, an event directly affecting 100 per cent of the audience is greater than an event directly affecting 10 per cent. A proposed sales-tax increase from 3 per cent to 4 per cent outranks a proposed one-cent-per-pack cigarette tax. The big joker in applying this determinant is the danger of stopping with surface significance, failing to find or point out a greater significance than the apparent one, or the one suggested by an interested party. In the hypothetical example, for instance, extending the sales tax to previously exempted purchases could be more important than the rate increase. If another plan had called for a 5 per cent sales tax maintaining exemptions on food, for example, the true significance belonged on the average-cost-per-family rather than the simple difference in rates. Abuse of this news indicator comes mostly in the form of attaching false importance— through the reporter's ignorance or laziness or through prejudiced application of company policy. ("Major relief for the nation's newsroom manpower shortage is promised by a jump in college journalism enrollments" when more journalism majors are bypassing the newsroom would illustrate the former. The latter is demonstrated by a procurfew newspaper's story: "Nearby Mudville has suffered little teen-age crime since enacting a curfew last month"—overlooking the fact that it had "little teen-age crime" before the curfew was imposed.) Neglect, rather than abuse, is the largest failing with significance as a news determinant. This problem is dealt with in Chapter 5.

4½. *Company Policy*: Regardless of other factors, an event of special interest to the boss is greater than other events of equal consequence and many of larger consequence. Owners and editors are only human, and some degree of this quasi-determinant operates in most newsrooms. It ranges from a relatively harmless overemphasis on news about the boss's alma mater to vicious slanting of news concerning politics and government. A small Western paper printed not a word about the opening and operation of the city's first commercial radio station until some former employees sued the station for overtime pay. Then it departed from an old policy against publicizing such "assaults on management" to exaggerate the suit's importance. Occasionally, company policy can be valuable in the total information stream. Stubborn emphasis on worthwhile, but relatively unnewsworthy, subjects like the United Fund wins some public attention. Better, however, than annually listing goals and officers (only the names are changed to reward the dutiful), reporters might work on real news angles that would win wider reader-ship. They could dig out and report why the Boy Scouts get more than the Girl Scouts and explain the relative shares of the YMCA and CYO. (United Fund officers probably would not appreciate such attention.)

Note the all-other-factors-being-equal qualifier on each of the four real determinants. Does the fact that a community leader died on the morning newspaper's time justify downgrading the afternoon newspaper's report twelve hours later? Did the local Future Farmers banquet deserve two minutes with film against only a sentence noting Russian Premier Joseph Stalin's death on a March 5, 1953, eleven o'clock newscast? Should an Illinois daily consider the story magnitude of a berserk New Jersey clerk's shooting ten persons greater than the significance factor of Con-gress's killing an income-tax surcharge? (If so, does the slaughter story need a banner line, pictures, diagrams, and sidebars in a largely home-delivered paper?) Can the surface significance of the School Board vice-president's routine elevation to the presidency really outweigh the mag-nitude of the board's firing ten first-year teachers? (Magnitude, especially when neglected close to home, often has significance buried beside it. Were the dismissals for incompetence or insubordination, or for union-organizing or for circulating *The Catcher in the Rye?*)

As do the four functions listed in Chapter 1, the four determinants overlap. Magnitude is magnified by proximity and so is significance. A shootout downtown has greater impact than a shootout fifty miles away, and the significance of open-housing bills is greater for residents and neighbors of the black ghettos than for rural dwellers.

NEWS-WRITING RULES

Good news-writing has two important characteristics which generally distinguish it from other kinds of good writing. Both are relatively young in terms of American journalistic history, and both are under heavy attack. One—*objectivity*—has been openly demoted by America's leading news magazine, badly mangled by a few journalists who still profess to observe it, and denounced by many who reluctantly but faithfully try to practice it. The other—*inverted-pyramid* story structure—appears to be safely ensconced in most newspaper columns, but its rigidities are regularly assailed, and it has yielded somewhat below the lead para-graph since World War II.

OBJECTIVITY

Objectivity, as a widespread news-story characteristic, probably dates from the turn of the century. Most, though not all, of the arguments about it hinge on definition. Objectivity-purists insist that reporters must not go beyond the facts which obtrude into the news. Here is a hypothetical example:

> A: Sen. J. M. Rail charged today that "at least 50" State University professors are "traitors to America." The Winnemucca Democrat said he would start naming them on the Senate floor if University President Johnson Smith "fails to clean house within the next month."

Extreme "interpretationists," on the other hand, might value-judge Rail's charge out of hand:

> B-1: Sen. J. M. Rail was at it again today, irresponsibly demanding that State University President Johnson Smith fire 50 "traitors to America" from the faculty. . . .

Or, they might shortcut in the other direction:

> B-2: Sen. J. M. Rail carried his courageous fight against Communism's stranglehold on the state university to SU President Johnson Smith's door today. . . .

Proponents of Example A argue that any journalistic interpretation of Rail's Senate speech belongs to editorial writers and commentators. Not only is it wrong for newsmen to "play God" by interpreting events, they insist, but also public confidence in news-believability is shaken. Any bending in the direction of Example B-1 may alienate Senator Rail's fans and others suspicious of professors, the purists say. And any tendency toward Example B-2 threatens the trust of those who fear witch-hunting. Extreme objectivists believe that reporters must pass on "the news as it comes" without searching for rebuttals or supporting facts, let alone decreeing who is right and who is wrong in the news report.

Interpretationists, on the other hand, reply that choosing to report Senator Rail's speech—instead of other events—is a value judgment in itself. Having judged what is important, they contend, newsmen must finish the job by telling how it is important: Is Rail's charge important because professor-traitors threaten students' loyalty or because Rail is behaving irresponsibly as a senator? Interpretationists dismiss editorials and commentaries on grounds that they reach too few in the news audience. Nor does Example A's being followed next day by a rebuttal satisfy them. Results, they say, range from mind-set favoritism of Tuesday's first report to discouragement with trying to follow the news, which tells them one thing Tuesday and the opposite Wednesday. Extreme interpretationists argue that presenting both sides in the same news story only confuses laymen, who need clear guidance from reporters and editors who "know the truth."

American journalism seems to have focused on what might unimaginatively be called an objective-interpretive treatment of news. It is interpretive in that good reporters do seek related facts and opinions beyond those which merely obtrude at a given moment. It is objective in that opinions are attributed to sources, not stated as facts. Such a rendition of our hypothetical story might go something like this:

> Sen. J. M. Rail's charge of "at least 50 traitors" on the state university faculty drew angry denials and counter charges today.
>
> SU President Johnson Smith challenged Rail "to produce one single name now—right now" or withdraw the charge.
>
> Rail made the charge during Senate Education Committee hearings this morning. The Winnemucca Democrat said then that he would start naming the 50 if Smith "fails to clean house within the next month."
>
> Rail left town right after the hearings and could not be reached for comment on Smith's reply. A staff aide said, "We have the names, but only the senator can release them."
>
> Governor Jones said he was "shocked" by Rail's charge but would withhold further comment until he could talk with Rail.
>
> SU Academic Dean Follensby Doe labeled Rail's charge "bloody nonsense" and declared Rail was "hiding behind legislative immunity to slander intellectuals who are a threat to his demagoguery."

Such a story will displease extremists on both sides of the Rail controversy. Pro-Rail readers will say it is stacked against the senator and count lines to prove it. Those who fear witch-hunting with as much panic as the pro-Rail people fear a Communist threat will decry the story's damage to professors in general and to State University in particular. Both would be correct in part, but the alternatives—A, B-1, B-2, or suppression of the story—range from worse to unthinkable in a democratic society.

INVERTED-PYRAMID STORY FORM

News-writing's other clearly distinctive characteristic, the upside-down story structure, raises both literary and ethical questions. At its best, the inverted pyramid is awkward; at its worst, it is almost impossible to understand. The following United Press International roundup is bad, but not an extreme sample:

> A vice-president took charge of San Francisco State College today hours after the abrupt resignation of the president. He immediately canceled his predecessor's "open campus" policy and had 35 demonstrators arrested.
>
> Students who forced the resignation of the University of Hawaii president earlier this week continued their so-far successful sit-in while holding out for one last demand.
>
> Dr. John Summerskill caught San Francisco State protesters off guard Friday night by flying to Ethiopia to look for another job after

announcing his immediate resignation. He had been scheduled to resign Sept. 1.

Dr. Donald Garrity, vice-president for academic affairs, took over as acting president, adopted a hard line and ordered the administration building closed. It had been left open 24 hours daily by Dr. Summerskill as part of his "open campus" policy in the face of demonstrations aimed at canceling a Reserve Officers Training Corps program.

Thirty-five persons, including three faculty members, were arrested when they refused to leave.

Out in the Pacific, students continued their week-long sit-in at the University of Hawaii, demanding amnesty for the 153 persons arrested last Tuesday night during an administration building sit-in. . . .

Trouble for the reader begins with the writer's clumsiness in trying to tell two hours-apart incidents in the lead paragraph. Since that college's troubles had been page-1 news, he could easily have begun: "San Francisco State College's new acting president canceled the 'open campus' policy today and had 35 demonstrators arrested." The "new" and "acting" could hold readers until a second sentence backed up to cover Summerskill's abrupt resignation.

The reader's troubles are compounded by the second paragraph's sudden departure for Hawaii. The reader is seven words into the paragraph before he discovers that it is talking about a different resignation. A simple transition, such as "Meanwhile, University of Hawaii students continued . . . ," would have helped. But the third paragraph's switchback to San Francisco, again without transition, would drive many readers to less frustrating pursuits. If he starts the fourth paragraph, an alert reader should wonder whether Garrity will be Hawaii's ex-president or Hawaii's new president or the victim of a third collegiate coup.

Perhaps the strongest critic of the inverted pyramid was the late Carl Lindstrom, distinguished editor of the *Hartford Times* before his retirement in 1960: "It destroys suspense by trying to tell all the facts at the very outset; it also leads to repetitiousness in that it is usually followed by a succession of inverted pyramids." (The foregoing UPI sample illustrates both of those faults—and so does the other half of that story not reproduced here.)

Lindstrom cites another, more serious, danger: "It causes misquotation of speakers or quotation out of context because the reader's mind is not prepared, as the listener's mind is, for the nub of the message." The distorted-quotation fault is but one example of reaching too far for a striking lead. Undeniably, the temptation to exaggerate the climax is greater when the climax is told first than when the writer builds toward his conclusion with simple facts. Take the example of a reporter checking statistics on marriages among local high school students. Telling the story chronologically, he could not whomp up much excitement with the facts that 25 out of 2,100 dropped out for weddings last year as against 20 out of 2,000 the year before. But the inverted-pyramid, exciting-lead syndrome can inspire some half-truth whoppers—e. g., "Marriages among local high school students jumped 25 per cent last year. . . ." or "The high school marriage rate skyrocketed last year. . . ."

Readers (and, to a lesser extent, listeners) may undo the damage by analyzing the facts in context when those are given, but the lead's impact usually sticks. (Headline scanners and inattentive listeners are doomed to be misinformed.)

When vital facts are omitted, even the minority of careful news consumers have no chance. Here is an example from the author's own bitter experience as a news subject:

> DES MOINES, Iowa, May 7—(UPI)—A journalism professor who said newspapers are pursuing circulation instead of "truth" is the first prize winner in the Sigma Delta Chi Foundation's writing awards competition, it was announced today. . . .

The essay in question criticized editorial-writing, not total newspaper effort as implied in that story's lead. Calling for use of by-lined dissents by editorial writers, it actully praised newspapers for "balanced news coverage"! Yet its author incurred the undeserved wrath of working newsmen and, worse, became an unwilling ally of unreasonable press critics.

Despite its handicaps, the inverted pyramid is here to stay in the news columns and—in specially adapted form—in newscasts. Departures from it may occur more frequently, but two factors make the climax-first approach almost mandatory for most news stories:

1. Newspaper readers demand to know the latest or most important development immediately—to decide whether the story warrants full reading, or to get the gist of the news in a hurry. This factor has grown with increasing demands on the reader's time. For several decades after the practice started as a kind of accident during the Civil War, it was principally a printing convenience. Leisure-time activities other than newspaper-reading grew with the shorter work week, increased ownership of automobiles, development of radio and television, and the spread of family boating and extended traveling. Reporting the day's news does not permit the literary polishing possible in books and magazines; hence "cover-to-cover" attention is neither expected nor given with daily newspapers. Broadcast news faces a different attention problem, and writers often delay crucial details past the first sentence. The brevity of newscast stories, however, obviates need for much pyramid analysis.

2. Mechanical and time limitations make end-of-the-story climaxes dangerous. Page makeup problems and last-minute news breaks require

trimming stories. The last-paragraph climax could be lost. Even if the makeup editor notices the deviation, he may have trouble cutting other paragraphs because of transitional approaches to the climax. The first three paragraphs of a six-paragraph inverted-pyramid story can deliver the main points, and they inevitably will make better sense than either half of a chronological rendition. (*New Yorker's* "Most Fascinating News Story of the Week" feature thrives on chronological stories chopped off in the composing room.) Rigid newscast timing by the writers precludes most such dangers on the air, where little more than the story's climax is told anyway.

Programs aimed at getting away from upside-down stories include one launched by United Press International in 1960. Here is a sample of the lead from one of its "Blue Ribbon" stories:

> NEW YORK (UPI)—The King's domain covered a vast area—as large as all the United States and then some—and he was dearly loved by his people, especially the children.

As it appeared in an Ohio evening daily, under the headline "King's Domain/Covered U. S.," this probably missed its mark. The story continued for two more paragraphs and another sentence before telling that "The King" was dead, instead of retired or merely displaced, and that he was a circus clown. Preoccupied with his prose, the writer forgot to mention the king's age (a prime item in any death report) or anything about survivors in his eleven paragraphs.

Compare it with the lead on the Associated Press version, as carried by another Ohio evening paper:

> NEW YORK (AP)—Felix Adler, 62, who tickled five decades of circus audiences by waddling around the rings in a droopy clown's suit followed by oinking piglets, died yesterday.

This is a contest of suspended interest (UPI) versus interest in Felix Adler or circus clowns or death-at-62 (AP). In terms of informing large numbers of readers, AP's version is the clear winner. The first copy editor might have evened things a bit by digging down for his headline: "Death Claims/ King of Clowns" (it will fit)—or would that have spoiled the package for true devotees of suspended interest?

COMPLETENESS

Completeness is not a special characteristic of news stories, but a special kind of completeness may be. News executives at all levels, in overwhelming numbers, list failure to get complete stories as the No. 1 fault of novice reporters. News experts disagree on how many points are needed in a given story, but there exists an impressive accord that goes

Figure 4.1. The copy desk staff (foreground) takes a rare breather as a city room full of reporters and rewrite staffers (background) work on stories that will flow through the news desk, just in front of copy desk, to the copy editors. (**Toledo Blade** photograph)

something like this: City Editor 1 may choose to use only Points A, B, and C, while City Editor 2 wants those plus Points D, E, and F; it is the complete handling of each point mentioned on which both editors would agree. Examine this story from the weekly student newspaper of a modestly endowed private college (points are lettered for discussion):

Ⓐ Student Senate tabled the proposed mandatory student cultural fee and Ⓑ approved the Student Government 1967-68 budget last week.

Ⓒ Senate tabled the cultural fee until senators can take a straw vote on it in their respective groups. The bill, which originally called for

Ⓓ a student fee to finance the Lecture-Movie Series and Artist Series, was amended by Senate to read that the "University subsidize" the two series.

Ⓔ According to Senate Chairman Rich Cunningham, if the bill is passed, Senate will suggest three means of subsidy: to extract the entire sum from University funds, to add the fee to student tuition costs, or to combine the first two methods.

Ⓕ The bill was originally proposed by the service honoraries Mortar Board and Omicron Delta Kappa because the two series need financial assistance to assure their continuation.

The Student Government's $26,809 budget was passed unanimously by Senate with no major discussion.

Failure to develop Point Ⓔ wrecks the entire story. How much is "the entire sum"? (If no one knows, the newspaper should alert the citizens it serves to the fact that their governing agency is asking them to vote a blank check. This the reader could deduce from the facts—if he had them.) Is there a surplus in the college's operating budget to provide all or part of the mysterious "entire sum"? (Again, if neither the college treasurer nor student government treasurer knows, the readers should be so informed.) If no surplus exists, what college services might be dispensed with to provide this proposed new budget item? (Readers ought to know at least the amount so they could estimate whether it would cost half a professor or the baseball squad's spring trip south.)

Proper development of Point Ⓔ might have caused the reporter to see the contradiction between its middle choice (student fee) and Point Ⓓ. Are the senators polling their constituencies on a "University" subsidy which the Senate can then convert to a partial-subsidy or a no-subsidy-at-all deal? Point Ⓐ is at best incomplete and at worst in error because the senators, according to Point Ⓓ, at least amended "the proposed . . . fee" before they tabled it. (Incidentally, "tabled" suggests "killed for now" in most contexts; in any event, the lead sentence could have said what it meant—"sent an amended cultural-fee proposal back to the students. . . ")

Point Ⓕ demands a qualifier (who says they "need financial assistance"?), if not more complete information on costs versus revenues in recent years.

Point Ⓑ clutters the story's lead. It could have been covered with a transitional phrase ("In other business") in the last paragraph. Told more completely (comparison with previous totals, round amounts delegated to major categories), it belongs in a separate story.

Let us apply the time-honored (and textbook-worn) "5 Ws and H" test to the story and its lead: *Who*—Student Senate. *What*—tabled the cultural fee (or did it?). *When*—last week. [Actually, timeliness might shift attention to what the senators have done since last week (polled their groups) or what they will do this week (vote on the amended bill).] *Where*—understood (and wisely omitted here). *Why*—overlooked by the reporter (this could have led the reporter to unravel the problems of Points Ⓔ, Ⓓ, and Ⓐ). *How*—overlooked (was the bill "tabled" by unanimous or split vote or by consensus?).

MISCELLANEOUS "RULES"

Arbitrarily short paragraphs are a peculiarity of news stories. They horrify English-composition teachers who revere good paragraphing, but they are typographically essential. Restoring one word in a galley-proof correction may necessitate resetting all remaining lines in the paragraph. Obviously, eight-line paragraphs can be fixed more quickly than 16-line paragraphs, to say nothing of the relative chances for new errors in the reset lines. (True, the proofreader might cut something from lines following the restoration, but that presents another danger, and proofreaders lack editing powers.) Late-breaking developments and corrections can be handled between short paragraphs but not in the middle of long ones. In addition, most newspaper columns are only a fraction of most book or magazine page widths and shorter paragraphs are therefore needed for better appearance.

Adherence to a stylebook is perhaps the least important special concern in reporting, but it warrants some attention here. Following style is important to the publication. It can be important in terms of fairness—if John Doe becomes Mr. Doe in the second reference, there should be a reason for John Smith's becoming only Smith. It is important in terms of clarity—Romania one time and Rumania the next may confuse readers geographically. It helps with efficiency—reporters, copy editors, and proofreaders can waste time and money changing spellings and capitalizations back and forth. It can contribute to the publication's personality—the *New York Times* differs markedly from most newspapers in its capitalization and tendency-not-to-abbreviate styles; the *Chicago Tribune's* modernized spelling is distinctive. [The adoption of a joint AP-UPI news-wire stylebook since 1960 has inspired many papers to abandon individuality in this department. Installation of automatic typesetters for wire copy in effect forced uniform mechanical style on hundreds of dailies.] Appendix C contains samplings from a stylebook.

READABILITY

Successful writers have always, at least unconsciously, been concerned with reader understanding. After World War II, Rudolf Flesch's *The Art of Plain Talk* (1946) sparked considerable research and practice in the art of writing for readability. Robert Gunning's *The Technique of Clear Writing* was prominent among following efforts. Several "exact formulas" to score a given piece's understandability have been devised. They are imperfect, but attention to their principles can be valuable guides toward clearer writing. Three chief factors are measured:

1. *Sentence Difficulty.* For handy counting, average sentence length is used. Complexity is obviously important, but length tends to parallel that condition.
2. *Word Difficulty.* Again for handy measuring, some form of syllable-counting is usually employed. Flesch uses the number of syllables per 100 words. Edgar Dale and Jeanne S. Chall of Ohio State University produced a list of 3,000 easy words and assigned negative weight to words outside that list.

   [Gunning's Fog Index[1] uses the percentage of uncapitalized words with three or more syllables, not counting easy combinations like beekeeper or verbs where the third syllable is a suffix—as in *debated.* The six-sentence "Student Senate" story on pp. 110-111 has 17 such words. Its Fog Index is computed by adding 11.5 (percentage of such words—17 out of 148) and 24.7 (average sentence length) and multiplying the total by the constant 0.4. Its score is 14.48—college sophomore level; 13 is rated difficult.]
3. *Degree of Abstraction.* This is the factor most difficult to measure. Flesch devised a positive weighting system—counting the percentage of personal words (pronouns, "people," and names) and the percentage of personal sentences (questions, direct quotations).

Two things about readability formulas should be remembered: (1) They provide only striking approximations of readability. With a bit of effort, you can construct two passages in which the more difficult will have a better readability score. (2) Nevertheless, the experts have focused attention on factors which most writers can improve. But rigid adherence to any writing formula ruins the writing and, more important, can interfere with the reporter's main job—telling the story. Ruthless shortening of sentences produces rough prose, and stringent limiting of vocabulary can muffle good reporting.

Abstraction presents the biggest challenge. And it looms largest in stories where significance is the key determinant (as in reporting on the Truth-in-Lending Law). Readers and listeners find such stories difficult to understand. Worse, few are tempted to try. Hence journalists, recognizing the significant dangers and promises of abstract news developments, as in city planning, must translate proposals into concrete examples of what they mean. The press's cry for "freedom of informa-

[1]Robert Gunning, *The Technique of Clear Writing,* New York: McGraw-Hill Book Company, 1968 (Rev.).

tion" is an abstraction largely lost on an uncomprehending public. Only when concrete examples, involving real people, are reported is there any chance that the lay public will become interested. An Associated Press series did that effectively. Among examples it cited was a secret kept for fifteen years in a Midwestern city of 68,000: City officials had suppressed a U. S. Public Health Service report that the city's water had a dangerous bacterial count because they "didn't want to alarm the people." At the very least, reporters can leaven the language of abstraction with personal words and direct quotations.

Rules for good composition, except those on paragraphing, apply to news-writing. Worthy of special mention here (as other ways of saying "Make it readable") are:

1. Be concise. Omit needless words. ("*He* likes to fish" is better than "*He is a man who* likes to fish.") Avoid negative structures. ("They *forgot* to register" is usually better than "They *did not remember* to register.") Avoid the passive voice. ("Jones *recalled* Smith's 1966 defeat" is usually better than "Smith's 1966 defeat *was recalled by* Jones.") Beware of overusing there-were and it-is phrases. ("*Neither camp was inclined* to dispute the poll" is better than "*There was no inclination in either camp* to dispute the poll.") Eliminate strings of prepositional phrases. ("Thousands were homeless today in Southern Ohio's worst flooding since 1913" is three phrases and eight words better than "Thousands of Ohioans were homeless today in the worst flooding in the southern areas of the state since 1913.")

2. Be specific. Generalizations contribute to abstraction. They often appear to deviate from objectivity; sometimes they are wrong—at least from different perspectives. ("Snow fell on 20 days during November" is better than "November was an unusually snowy month.") A basketball coach may not regard a six-footer as "tall." If a generalization ("a narrow victory") is interesting, specifics usually improve its interest ("the narrowest victory in 20 elections").

Good grammar is, as we said, the first essential of effective reporting. Errors in number agreement and pronoun reference can confuse or misinform the audience. Incorrect word usage and faulty syntax also can destroy respect for journalists, at least among their most important customers. Spelling is important to newspapers. Pronunciation is important to newscasts. Whether they take an exceptionally liberal view (accepting such horrors as ". . . tastes good like I knew it would") or an extreme purist position (condemning *Webster's Third* for yielding on so many fine points), most dedicated journalists care mightily about language. The enthusiastic modernist wants to use "the people's language" so that masses will be tuned in on his stories; the hard-nosed purist worries lest "disinterested" will be interpreted as "uninterested" by one block of readers and as "unbiased" by another. Typographical errors and other slips in speedily produced newspapers lead some casual observers to the erroneous conclusion that newsmen care little about language. A closer look, and some understanding of operations, would reveal quite the opposite. Factual accuracy, delivered in good language, is the hard-sought goal of every effective news medium.

News-writing's two primary distinctions—objectivity and inverted-pyramid story structure—place immediate handicaps on it as a literary form. Sentences are complicated and lengthened by the requirement that opinions be attributed. ("Sen. Rail's charge is nonsense" is more read-able than "Sen. Rail's charge was called 'nonsense' by SU Academic Dean Follensby Doe.") Traditional objectivity requires an impersonal tone, robbing newsmen of chances to sprinkle in more personal words. ("Our delegation asked for a recess" is more readable than "The American delegation asked for a recess.") Trying to tell the climax and enough situation-identifying details (most of the 5 Ws and H) in the lead tends to lengthen and complicate sentences. That process is repeated as report-ers fight to keep the story short and pack prime material into the top of the story, where it is safer from last-minute cutting.

Considering the handicaps, one wonders how newsmen produce as much good prose as they do.

Rigid timing restricts broadcast news-writing in several ways. Spe-cific examples of script directions illustrate. A radio news-writer may figure on the basis of something like fifteen normal typewritten lines (sixty units per line) to fill one minute. Since a five-minute newscast may lose one and one-half minutes to commercials and station identifica-tion, he often has to work in terms of thirty-second stories (seven or eight lines) or even briefer. (A thirty-second story is equivalent to a two-inch-long story in a regular newspaper column.) The television news-writer handles an even trickier format. He usually works with twenty-five-unit lines on the right side of his copy paper, leaving five and one-half inches on the left for video cues and timing notes. He computes on the basis of one and one-half seconds per line, and his writing must be keyed to film spots as well as to different announcers' speaking paces. Writing for broadcast must be simpler than that for print. (Appositional phrases, for example, can result in terrible con-fusion among listeners who have no chance to "reread" the sentence.) Both broadcast newsmen and their listeners must carefully evaluate such limitations. Extreme brevity is the primary concern. Richard R. Clark, a WCBS-TV news producer and former newspaperman, put it this way in a 1969 letter to his old journalism teacher:

> When you used to hammer into us, "Write tight," you really didn't
> know what a tight story was . . . and I don't mean just brief. I mean
> getting the whole nuts of the story into 30 seconds. And there's no dead-

line like a television deadline. I've had several old newspaper people who have suffered the demise of the NYC newspaper industry working for me and the thing that hits them first is the conciseness with which they have to write. It's difficult at first, but it can be done.

Of course, the real challenge is that this business is just a baby. Every day, it seems, we come up with a new and better way of getting a story across, and far-reaching imagination certainly has a home in television news.

Whether on the air or in print, good journalism starts with good writing.

FOR FURTHER STUDY

1. "Inverting the pyramid" is easier to understand than it is to perform. Compare these 16-word leads on the same story:

HORRIBLE	WEAK	BEST
City Council met last night. Seven members were present to discuss an agenda of five items. . . .	City Council discussed traffic problems last night. Congestion on Main Street was the No. 1 topic. . . .	City Council refused to ban parking on Main Street in a 5-2 vote last night. . . .

Check some news-story leads in college or small-town newspapers to see if you could have gotten to the climax faster as on the right above.

2. Cover a TV program like "Meet the Press" or some local meeting and compare your account with those of professionals in the next day's newspapers.

3. Scoring each determinant by whatever weighting you choose, compare the play of stories against each other in a newspaper or newscast. Do the same for elements within a several-paragraph newspaper story. Do you agree with the professionals' apparent ratings ("pyramiding") within the story? Are any stories shortchanged with a paragraph only in a news roundup?

4. Compare morning and evening newspaper treatment of the same story. How different is the later lead from the earlier version's? Compare AP and UPI versions of the same story in two different morning newspapers, or two different afternoon newspapers. Do the leads emphasize the same angle?

5. Apply Gunning's Fog Index to a piece of your own writing. Measure comparable segments in *Atlantic Monthly* and *Reader's Digest*.

6. Compare a newspaper story's structure with that of a broadcast version, by listening carefully or visiting a station to examine a script or piece of radio news copy from the teletype.

7. Compare a *Time* magazine account of some controversial issue (e. g., a political appointment) with that of a newspaper. Do *Time's* rejections of objectivity and the inverted pyramid give its version an advantage in readability?

SUGGESTED READING

BERNSTEIN, THEODORE M., *The Careful Writer*, New York: Atheneum Publishers, 1965. Among comprehensive reference volumes, this is particularly useful to journalists.

BROWN, CHARLES H., *Informing the People*, New York: Holt, Rinehart & Winston, Inc., 1957. Dating is a minor handicap in this otherwise good treatment of news-writing.

CBS News, *Television News Reporting*, New York: McGraw-Hill, 1958. Technical differences in news-handling for TV are clearly spelled out. Chapter 15 explains "Writing for Television."

FLESCH, RUDOLF, *The Art of Readable Writing*. New York: Harper and Brothers, 1949. [Available in Collier paperback.] This revision of Flesch's pioneering readability work treats all three factors.

GUNNING, ROBERT, *The Technique of Clear Writing*, New York: McGraw-Hill Book Company, 1968 (Rev.). Easiest of readability works, this explains the Fog Index.

MacDOUGALL, CURTIS D., *Interpretative Reporting*, New York: The Macmillan Company, 1968 (5th ed.). Part one of this bible among reporting textbooks provides excellent detail on how to write news stories.

STRUNK, WILLIAM, JR., and WHITE, E. B., *The Elements of Style*, New York: The Macmillan Company, 1959. [Available in paperback.] Probably the best brief guide to good composition. Rules 10, 11, 12, 13, and 16, pp. 13 to 25, are especially valuable for news-writing.

[For other references, see: PRICE, WARREN C., *The Literature of Journalism*, Minneapolis: University of Minnesota Press, 1960 (2nd printing). Books on writing for newspapers and magazines are included in lists on pages 316-331, and some on radio and TV news-writing are included in lists on pages 387-393. Pages xi-xiv list a few more.]

CHAPTER 5

Reporting the News

Reporting the news involves more than journalistic writing technique. Responsibilities for informing the American people have multiplied decade by decade in the twentieth century. Mere recording of "happenings" is criminally inadequate, as every competent newsman knows. Today's citizen is infinitely more dependent upon forces and institutions outside his direct control than was his counterpart 200, or even 50, years ago. Local government zones him more restrictively, curbs his driving and parking freedoms, and takes more of his income to provide more expensive services; state government impinges more on his pocketbook and even second-guesses his local government's intrusions; and the federal government crowds closer as it grows bigger. All three levels of government "interfere" with his life—from how long and where he shall attend school to how he provides for his retirement—in a degree not even dreamed of fifty years ago. Meanwhile, his dependence on nongovernmental institutions has also mushroomed. The modern citizen depends heavily on the reliability and competence of gas, electric, and telephone companies; his well-being can be improved or damaged by trade unions and professional societies. As the United States population has grown from 4,000,000 in 1790 to well past 200,000,000 today, his comfort and even his survival depend ever more on how his neighbors behave. Problems ranging from birth-rate pressures to polluting the atmosphere threaten individual freedoms.

All arms of the press have moved toward meeting today's larger demands, some more than others. Staff specialists in science, politics, education, religion, and urban affairs are common in both print and electronic media. Newspapers and magazines devote more columns to backgrounding the news. Television specials, some in prime time, probe society's problems in ways no medium could prior to the twentieth century's second half. Channel-switching and page-flipping restrict many of these "blockbuster" efforts to a minority, but an important one.

Something of a revolution is stirring in the total flow of news. Good editing is essential, but reporting provides the first key. With more people depending upon fewer newspapers, the room for error has shrunk as has the time it takes to get from here to there. The subsidiary information media—television, magazines, and radio—have both aided the quest for accuracy and provided checkpoints that have raised the accuracy requirements. Shallow treatment of significant news poses two dangers. Bored by trivia, modern man can turn from the news to a myriad of leisure-time lures in and out of the media. Or, led astray by inaccurate and confusing news reports, he can become a dangerously misguided citizen, prey to demagogues of the political right and left.

DIGGING FOR ACCURACY

News accounts necessarily carry incidents and quotations out of their original context. The reporter's challenge is to restore a proper semblance of the context in his abbreviation and rearrangement of the event's details. Failure to do that produces "false alarm" stories, destructive of the medium's overall power to inform the people. Take this example of a March, 1953, story under the headline "May Ask Draft for Civil Defense":

> WASHINGTON—(AP)—The Nation's new civil defense administrator says an effort will be made to recruit millions more volunteer workers, and if that fails "I wouldn't hesitate to ask for a draft." He is Val Peterson, former governor of Nebraska. He spoke on a television program Sunday.

During that Cold War "crisis," civil defense was a major issue. Appearing on NBC's "Meet the Press," Peterson had said repeatedly that he believed volunteers would come forward. Near the end of the 30-minute show, he was cornered. Asked whether he would drop his civil-defense plans or turn to a draft if too few volunteered, he chose the latter. His main point had been the need to inform Americans of air-war dangers, and he had emphatically rejected the idea of a draft. A more honest lead might have gone something like this:

> WASHINGTON—Civil defense units can be brought to full strength only if Americans are told the truth, Val Peterson, new civil defense administrator, told a televised *press conference* Sunday. He *admitted* he "wouldn't hesitate" to use the draft if voluntary measures failed, *but he insisted*: "I'd like to think we can get the volunteers."

The italicized words mark special efforts to place Peterson's words in perspective. The *press conference* is important to the circumstances;

admitted qualifies the tone; *but he insisted* adjusts the emphasis. The result is less exciting, but excitement should be saved for legitimate usage. The AP original provided qualifications, but several papers ran only the first paragraph.

At about that same time, controversy was swirling around the eight-year-old United Nations and possible UN admission of Red China. Trygve Lie, who had just resigned as UN secretary-general, made an American lecture tour. In his efforts to promote the UN, Lie avoided referring to Red China's possible admission. At a press conference following one Midwestern appearance, an alert reporter pressed Lie for his feelings on the issue. Lie finally admitted that Red China's membership might be necessary someday. The reporter's paper presented a story giving readers the clear impression that Lie was touring the United States in behalf of Red China's admission to the UN. The story's text did not even distinguish between Lie's prepared remarks before an audience of hundreds and his obviously reluctant reply to a question at a small press conference. Going after the former secretary-general's opinion was good reporting, but the final product sounded a false alarm and damaged the newspaper's credibility for all those who had heard Lie's lecture. (Ironically, Russia—then Red China's chief ally—had vetoed Lie's re-election as UN head. Had that reporter and his editors done their homework, the story might have avoided the infection caused by such surface-scratching.) Even a newspaper opposed to the United Nations should have been interested in Lie's hesitancy about the subject of admitting Red China.

Late in 1967 when the Vietnam war was going especially badly, a former U.S. ambassador to Saigon spoke "off the record" at a World Affairs Council luncheon in an Eastern city. A reporter questioned him after the speech and elicited from him the opinion that America should carry the ground war into North Vietnam. The reporter's paper shouted the news under an eight-column banner, triggering national and international reactions. During the ensuing shock waves, the ambassador was reported as having said he had been misunderstood, then misquoted, and finally that he had not even talked with the reporter. Believers in a watchdog press could sympathize with the editor's having challenged an "off-the-record" speech before 500 citizens. And they could commend the reporter for uncovering such hawkish views in such high places. But the editor's later explanation too lightly dismissed his paper's failure to identify the context: "Unfortunately, the story in the last edition, written under deadline duress, did not make clear the exact circumstances under which it was developed." The war-escalation proposal of that ambassador —who still held an important diplomatic post—was worth top news play. His having ventured the opinion in a man-to-man interview reflected significant thinking in high places. However, the story's erroneous indication that he had delivered the opinion in a prepared address before 500 leading citizens could have suggested that Washington was floating a trial balloon. Both truth and effective press freedom suffered. The hundreds who heard the formal address—and those to whom they talked— lost confidence in newspaper reliability.

Unlike the out-of-context error mentioned in Chapter 4, the examples here stem from failure at a higher level. None exemplified a misunderstanding of basic meaning. Rather, they occurred because the reporter or his paper was trying to make a nugget of news shine more brightly by removing its wrappings, or the reporter was neglecting his homework. Speed, as the apologetic editor said, contributes to this kind of error. The root cause, however, is more likely to be the journalist's failure to understand the significance of what he is covering. In the three foregoing examples, questions like these should have been processed: How likely was a new civil-defense administrator to threaten a draft before his volunteer program had been fully tested? What was his deadline for filling his quota with volunteers? If Trygve Lie favored eventual admission of Red China, why was he reluctant to admit it? If the ambassador favored new escalation in Vietnam, had that anything to do with his having left Saigon? Why did he not present that view in his off-the-record speech to the World Affairs Council?

It takes only a few minutes with the *New York Times Index* or with clippings in his own paper's library, and with sources like the *World Almanac, Who's Who in America,* or the *Reader's Guide to Periodical Literature* to prepare for many assignments—providing the reporter keeps abreast of current events. Too many reporters approach stories with preconceived certainties about what they will bring back and a woeful lack of background. Added to this failing is the modern "handout" pitfall— whereby the reporter acquires an apparently complete story which he need only "rewrite"—i. e., rearrange a few phrases and paragraphs. Finally, there is the tendency to handle certain kinds of stories the way they have always been handled, without giving them a fresh look. Here are a few paragraphs of a typical perennial cluttering news columns and newscasts:

> More than 4,000 Ohio Veterans of Foreign Wars meeting at the Neil House Hotel Saturday were to name Joe Byers of Akron as the outstanding post commander of 1968.
>
> The award is presented to the post having the highest membership gain. By Sunday night the Ohio organization will have more than 70,000 members, according to State Commander Myron Young of Ellsworth, Ohio.
>
> Young said this year's convention is the largest the Ohio VFW had held. He added that Ohio will be the fourth largest VFW organization in the U.S. when the 70,000 goal is reached.

The story includes seven more paragraphs, all but one of which are similarly written for VFW-insiders. More important than the wordiness throughout ten of its eleven paragraphs is the element of interest to both VFW members and outsiders buried in paragraph 5:

> Members urged the U. S. to take whatever measures necessary to win the Vietnam war in a resolution approved to resist communism. It also recommended a permanent U. S. fleet be stationed in the Indian Ocean, and for this country to withdraw from the United Nations in the event Red China is admitted.

Were these repetitions of past resolutions or new ones? Were they unanimously endorsed? What cross section of veterans—Vietnam, Korea, World War II, and World War I—was represented in the voting? What percentage of eligible veterans belong to the VFW? Did "whatever measures" include invasion of North Vietnam or use of nuclear weapons?

Without answers to such questions, the story is less interesting and, what is worse, potentially misleading. The resolutions reference might better have been omitted. The total story and thirty-two column inches of pictures consumed 58 per cent of the nonadvertising space on page 3. Doubtless that pleased the sixteen persons who saw their names in print or could recognize their pictures, but it constitutes a questionable space expenditure for a daily over 200,000 in circulation.

A 1968 article in *Time* magazine reported: "U. S. journalism schools are improving these days. . . . Many . . . try to deal with the broad spectrum of human dialogue. Stanford's Department of Communication, for example, has added courses called 'Government and the Mass Media' and 'Ethics in the Mass Media' to stimulate students' thinking about their work in the wider context of society." Unless "these days" covers several decades, that observation was about as appropriate for a 1968 news weekly as noting the spread of "talking pictures." A telephone call to any of five journalism schools within the metropolitan New York City area might have uncovered the fact that courses in government and the press and ethics in the press were not new. Thus, if journalism schools were "improving these days," other factors were responsible.

Interpretation of facts often involves explaining what they do not mean. In 1939, the U. S. Justice Department secured an indictment of the American Medical Association and others for conspiracy in restraint of trade. A Federal District Court ruled the indictment was improper. The Justice Department appealed, and the U. S. Supreme Court refused to consider the appeal, whereupon it was reported that the high court had "upheld" the district court. Actually, the refusal involved a procedural technicality—the necessity for prior action by a U. S. Court of Appeals. As it turned out, the latter ruled for the prosecution, and the case was tried in district court. The AMA was convicted, and its appeal of the conviction eventually reached the U. S. Supreme Court, which unanimously upheld the conviction—demonstrating how wrong the earlier story's upholding-the-defense interpretation had been.

An elected representative may vote against strengthening a bill he favors only because he fears the stronger bill has less chance of being enacted. Another representative of similar sentiments may vote against the unamended bill because he considers it a dishonest half-a-loaf. Unless the reporter digs out such background and explains it, his readers or listeners will be either misinformed or uninformed.

EDUCATING THE CUSTOMERS

An often-forgotten axiom in the news business warns: "Never overestimate the public's knowledge and never underestimate the public's intelligence." Among other things, this suggests that hard news can be understood by large numbers if newsmen supply enough background material. Citizens may lack the knowledge to understand why, in a given election year, the minority party can hope to capture the House when it has no chance to take the Senate—unless the story "reminds" them that senators serve for six years and House members for only two. The Roper Poll reported a few years ago that 70 per cent of the American people did not know the length of a U. S. senator's term. Lacking such knowledge, they can neither understand nor be interested in the story. Any story involving geography calls for special effort. George Gallup told the Center for the Study of Democratic Institutions in 1962 that half of a test group of college graduates could not find the state of Illinois on an outline map of the United States. Nor could they identify the shortest route from England to India. Reporters dealing with an Illinois senator's interest in the Great Lakes Seaway and those covering the 1956 Suez crisis could report more effectively if they recognized such reasons for never overestimating educated readers' knowledge. Televised network newscasts have done well with map usage, but more newspaprs should follow the example of the *New York Times* and the *St. Petersburg Times*.

Newspapers might profitably expand on *Congressional Quarterly's* "Congressional Boxscore"—diagraming the status of major bills before Congress. Readers with special interest in a given bill often quit trying to untangle sporadic stories headlined "House Unit OKs VISTA," "Senate Cuts VISTA Funds," "VISTA Goes to Conference." If each installment carried a small box score on that bill's overall status, some readers might develop the kind of interest baseball fans exhibit in following their box scores and league standings.

All news media could profit from a public-service campaign aimed at educating more citizens. In a report to the Center for the Study of

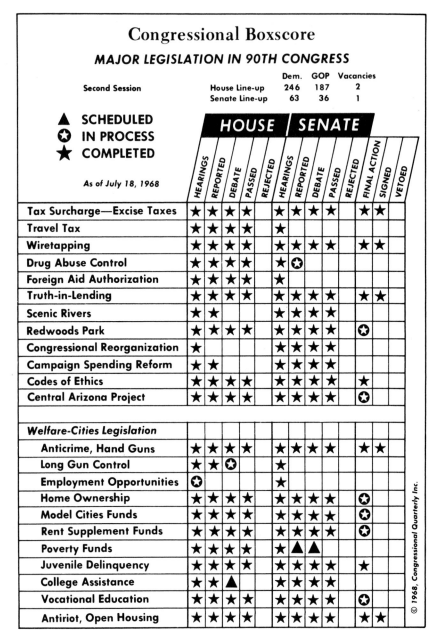

Figure 5.1. Diagraming complicated news developments helps readers become interested in affairs of significance. Citizens should ask for more such aids, and newsmen should supply them. (Courtesy, **Congressional Quarterly**)

Democratic Institutions, Elmo Roper said that only 10 per cent of American citizens were politically active. Another 20 per cent reported some participation in civic affairs. But, Roper said, 70 per cent would have to be called "dormant." His research indicated that only a few more than two out of five Americans could identify either of their two United States senators. Broadcast and printed interviews with their state's senators on major current proposals could reduce citizen ignorance and attract more news interest at the same time. The media themselves could undertake studies of their publics to determine attitudes and measure interests with a view to more effective communication.

Philip E. Meyer, a *Detroit Free Press* reporter, told of just such a project by the Knight newspapers in Detroit and Miami. In the June, 1968, *Nieman Reports,* Meyer reviewed a complex, computer-measured study of attitudes among ghetto dwellers that indicated previously unrecognized groupings. By identifying the size of the "conventional militants" and the "violent militants"—and what dominates the attitudes of each—newsmen found new news sources and better ways to report the news effectively.

Supreme Court Justice Abe Fortas, in his 1968 book *Concerning Dissent and Civil Disobedience,* maintained that the First Amendment was designed to preclude law-breaking as a means of influencing the United States government. But exponents of civil disobedience argue that the modern press has blocked proper circulation of minority viewpoints. A typical charge is that the press refuses to report illegal discrimination by an employer until the victims break some other law to win public attention. They contend that freedom of speech and the press can be effectively employed by dissidents only through sit-ins, riots, and other breaches of the law, which force mass-media attention to their complaints. Radical changes in the laws and their enforcement during the 1960s—after both nonviolent and violent demonstrations—suggest there has been some truth to their arguments. The larger truth in the ex-justice's contention should be heeded by newspapers, magazines, radio, and television. By expanding its Fourth Estate role, the press can enlarge its serious audience and make the First Amendment fulfill the function explained by Fortas.

An excellent example of how the press can do more than "support the status quo" by serving as democracy's watchdog is offered by the experience of a weekly-newspaper editor in Western North Carolina. His attention to a single citizen's complaint, his early battle without help from other media, and the later entry into the fight by fellow journalists provide a kaleidoscopic picture of what is right and what is wrong with the American press at this point in history. The story is best told by the editor himself. Ted Smiley, who had become financial editor of the

Honolulu Advertiser after leaving North Carolina, wrote it this way for the May 25, 1968, *Editor & Publisher*:

PUBLIC TELEPHONE

BY TED SMILEY

It started off almost by accident, but it led to eight conspiracy indictments, the humbling of a giant U. S. corporation, and the planned spending of $5,500,000 to bring modern telephone service to the people of 11 rural counties in the Great Smokies of Western North Carolina.

I was in the post office of Bryson City, N. C. (Pop. 1,082) one July morning in 1966 when Col. H. H. H. "Hap" Clark (USAF, Ret.), thrust an envelope at me.

"Read this," he said. "Just read it, then let me tell you the story."

The envelope contained a colorful brochure from the Western Carolina Telephone Co. Inc., citing the advantages of having a second telephone in the house.

"A second telephone! Hell and damnation, I've been trying for two years to get even a first telephone!"

The colonel had bought a mountain just outside Bryson City, and had built an expensive retirement home.

"They promised me phone service as soon as the house was built. They've been promising ever since, but I can't pin 'em down. Two years, now. Going on three.

"Check this out, Mr. Editor. You'll find plenty of people getting the same treatment, or worse."

Into a Mess

I then was editor and owner of the *Smoky Mountain Times*, a 3,000-circulation weekly newspaper in Bryson City. I also owned the 1,150-circulation *Andrews Journal* in a neighboring county.

As Hap Clark suggested, I did check out the telephone situation. That first check led to more than a year of investigation, of news stories and editorials which blew the lid off a scandal involving the top officers of two telephone companies and two other corporations.

As soon as I printed the first editorial blast, information poured in.

Western Carolina Telephone Co., Inc. had:

● Taken over one local telephone company, and had been granted a franchise by the state upon its promise to bring the local company into its service. Five years later the local subscribers had no telephone service.

● The company had collected deposits as much as seven years previously from residents of another area, but had failed to install service.

● Western Carolina Telephone Co., and its affiliate, Westco Telephone Co., had been "paying" premium prices for equipment which Southern Bell Telephone Co. engineers described as "worthless."

● In defiance of Rural Electrification Administration rules, the companies had borrowed REA money and had bought shoddy equipment without bids, on a contract basis.

- REA regulations about the number of parties on a line had been ignored.
- Business firms wishing to do business with Western Carolina or Westco had to pay a 10 per cent kickback to an intermediary designated by an official of the affiliated companies.
- Telephones throughout the 11-county mountain region where the companies held a state-granted monopoly were out of order as much as they were working.
- One local business—a hotel-restaurant-recreation complex, valued at more than $1,000,000—had to try to do business with only a pay telephone connecting it with the outside world, and had to pay $37 a month for that privilege.
- In my home county alone, the annual income from telephones was more than $300,000, and the total annual expense for upkeep was less than $25,000.
- Virtually every subscriber was billed for long distance calls never made. This was documented a hundred times over.

Residents sent more than 500 letters of protest, by actual count, to the North Carolina Utilities Commission, and were promised a "thorough investigation."

The "investigator" came into the area, was provided with two body-guards by Western Carolina Telephone Co., spent 20 minutes telling Mayor Ted Hyams of Bryson City what wonderful service the region was receiving, and vanished.

As the evidence piled up, and was printed in the *Smoky Mountain Times* and *Andrews Journal,* along with vigorous editorial comment, the telephone companies began to feel the heat.

The news exposés and editorials helped win me the North Carolina Press Association award for best editorials of 1966.

The presentation was made by Governor Dan Moore, who asked to be kept abreast of developments.

When he felt the time was right, the governor fired two members of the utilities commission, and "suggested" that the state attorney general look into the situation.

At the same time, I informed the parent corporation, Continental Telephone Co. Inc., of the evidence in my possession, and sent the regional manager copies of my news stories and editorials.

This resulted in sending of 13 Continental investigators into the Great Smokies region. These investigators filed a 180-page report saying they could find no evidence of wrong-doing.

Public Hearings

However, the governor, the attorney general and the revamped utilities commission thought differently.

Public hearings were held at which hundreds of area businessmen and residents told their stories.

Continental sent a top executive to the hearings. He listened for a day, then interrupted to confess that conditions were intolerable and would be corrected.

I pointed out editorially that these promises had been made before, and called for revocation of the franchise.

For reasons best known to themselves, the region's television stations and other newspapers sided with the telephone combine.

Television commentators called the hearings "comic" and "unbelievable."

I was called "an unsophisticated hillbilly" and a "crackpot country editor."

Roger Tatarian, editor of United Press International, advised his North Carolina bureau to take a look at what was happening.

After UPI broke the story statewide, including my printed charges of flagrant thievery, payoffs and kickbacks, the region's dailies felt obliged to print my charges.

The State Bureau of Investigation, the district solicitor (prosecutor) and a special assistant attorney general began to probe in depth.

I sold my papers on October 1, 1967, and, after winding up my affairs in North Carolina, moved to Hawaii.

On February 1, 1968, a grand jury returned eight conspiracy indictments. It named the vice president of the two telephone subsidiaries to Continental; the former president, who had been forced to resign as a result of my charges; the former chief engineer, who also had been forced to resign for the same reason; the intermediary in the kickback deal, who was president of a "front" corporation; that corporation and another "front," of which the president was the former telephone firm chief engineer, and the vice president, the former telephone company president.

Every count in the indictments was a paraphrase of charges my newspapers had printed. There was not one new item.

Late in March, the individual defendants were convicted on the conspiracy charges and the court imposed a penalty of six months in jail (suspended) and a fine of $1,500 on each. The charges against the companies were dismissed.

The week after the indictments were handed up by the grand jury, Continental announced improvements would be made in the mountain region at a total cost of more than $5,500,000.

Although I now am some 6,000 miles away, I am proud that the governor of North Carolina saw fit to write my new employer commenting on my work in that state.

(Used by permission of Editor & Publisher © 1968.)

INFORMING OPINION LEADERS

Dependence on telephones and the excitement of conflict (Editor Smiley versus the telephone company and public utilities commission) produce good readership for a campaign like the foregoing. The popularity of "Action Line" operations by many dailies in recent years illustrates—at a lesser level—the salability of helping citizens "fight City

Hall." However, less dramatic undertakings—like CBS-TV's "Hunger in America" in 1968 and news columns on urban renewal—often attract relatively small audiences. Surface readings of readership studies and audience ratings suggest that such efforts are largely wasted. But wise, dedicated journalists know better.

They recognize that reaching an elite of decision-makers is important both idealistically and practically. That small audience has to be weighted, as advertisers weight the clientele of a class publication, in terms of importance. It includes government officials and politicians, influential ministers and teachers. It also includes what *Louisville Courier-Journal* Managing Editor George N. Gill calls "people who don't necessarily hold the titles . . . people who devote a great deal of attention to the present and future course of their communities." The idealistic justification for reporting on pollution, traffic problems, urban blight, crowded schools, and bad government is obvious. Less so are the practical benefits. These range from prestige, filtered to the masses by their leaders, to esprit de corps among staff members. Managing editors and broadcast-news directors testify repeatedly that a major attraction for getting and holding good reporters is journalism's chance to help make this a better world. The positive correlation between journalistic longevity and attention to significant issues is undeniable. It is true that noble journalistic institutions like the *New York World* have died and noble efforts like the late Edward R. Murrow's televised "See It Now" have been shunted aside. Nevertheless, the tombstones in journalism's graveyard record shorter average life spans for frivolous endeavors like the *New York Daily Graphic* than for serious contenders in the free-press marketplace.

Television's attention to depth reports will remain more limited than that of the printed media because of TV-programming policy and time's inflexibility. Most advertisers shy away from controversial programs, and prime-time deviations from pure entertainment invite channel-switching on a level that is suicidal under the TV-advertiser "numbers game" rules. Using space flexibility, newspapers and magazines can offer the usual diet of lovelorn advice, sports, and comics and still make room for pioneering explorations of complex problems.

Such an exploration was offered in a widely used United Press International series by Louis Cassels in 1967. A note accompanying the series as it was reprinted in UPI's *Selections 1967* explained:

> On Aug. 4, 1967, UPI's main news wires were cleared to make room for this dispatch by Louis Cassels. It reflected his findings in the course of a 2,000-mile tour that took him from the still-raging Detroit riots to New York, Newark, Toledo and Rochester. It was transmitted for publication on Aug. 9.

This article was a journalistic departure for a news agency because it not only reported but presented the writer's personal views and engaged in urgent advocacy.

"This is unusual for UPI," Editor Roger Tatarian advised subscribers. "But the racial situation facing the country also is unusual, and we felt that a writer of Cassels' experience and stature should not be restrained from going in whatever direction his own judgment and experience led him."

Several hundred newspaper editors from coast to coast endorsed UPI's feelings on the importance and significance of Cassels' report. Rarely has a single article been read by such a large national audience.

Cassels, senior editor in Washington, is a veteran of 26 years with UPI. His special field is religion.

THE NEGRO IN REVOLT: WHAT NOW?
By Louis Cassels
United Press International

The black uprising in America's cities is far more extensive and far more serious than most white people like to believe.

It is not a passing phenomenon, stirred by "outside agitators."

It is not a mere outburst of hooliganism by a "small minority of lawless people."

It is not a new phase of the civil rights movement—although it may disrupt indefinitely that attempt to gain equality for Negroes by non-violent means.

What, then, is going on?

And what can be done to wipe out the root cause?

The answer to the first question is so obvious that it can be missed only by those who dislike or fear reality. As to the second, there is a solution. But it is going to require something more in the nature of a crusade than a program. And the cost is going to be enormous even for a nation accustomed to thinking in terms of billions.

The cost of not doing it could be greater still.

After visiting riot areas in Detroit, Newark, Rochester, Toledo, Harlem and other cities and talking to hundreds of Negroes, public officials, social scientists and law enforcement officers, I am convinced that we were all hasty in the earlier 1960s in describing as a revolution the Negro's struggle for equal rights before the law. This is the revolution. That was just a preliminary.

To deal with it will require political courage and leadership of the highest order, higher even than in wartime because of the complexity of the problem. It also requires understanding and good will on the part of whites far beyond anything they have been called upon to demonstrate so far.

But the alternative is spreading bloodshed, massive property destruction and bitterness that could poison race relations for more decades to come.

Only the relatively few whose judgment is warped by passion can seriously doubt this nation's ability—and determination—to put down revolution. But the price of armed repression would be incalculable.

Whether the Negro revolution can be stilled depends in large part on the reaction of white society, which thus far has been characterized by an almost total lack of understanding.

At this moment, the revolution is unorganized. There is no strategic plan, no central guidance. The only clear objective which the revolutionaries have at present is a determination to give "whitey" a bad time. They want to shake him up and make him realize that Negroes are fed up with overcrowded, overpriced, rat-infested ghetto housing . . . with menial jobs that won't pay for any of the luxuries which an affluent society constantly flaunts in their faces . . . with rude and sometimes abusive treatment by police . . . with irregular garbage collection . . . with inferior public schools that no white neighborhood would tolerate. Most of all, perhaps, they want an end to the constant, day-to-day humiliation that white people inflict on black people by little insults and condescensions, such as calling a grown man "boy."

Black power agitators such as Stokely Carmichael and H. Rap Brown and Communists are trying to move in and capture control of the revolution. Their strident incitements to riot doubtless have contributed to a heightening of tension in many areas, and may even have supplied the sparks which touched off one or two of the riots which have spread terror and destruction through U. S. cities this summer. But professional troublemakers did not create the revolutionary situation, and so far they are not calling the shots.

This is not merely my opinion. It is also the conviction of FBI agents and military intelligence officials who have made exhaustive but futile attempts to find evidence that the urban rioting is being stage-managed by outside elements.

In nearly every instance to date, rioting has been triggered by some relatively minor incident. In Detroit, it was a police raid on an after-hours drinking spot in the Negro section. In Newark, it was the arrest of a Negro cab driver. Usually, it is not the incident itself but the wild rumors which accompany it that strike fire into the tinder of the ghetto's pent-up resentments. Thus, in Detroit, the false report got around that police had seriously injured one of the women arrested in a "blind pig" raid, by shoving her downstairs. In Newark, the rumor (also false) was that an arrested cab driver had been beaten to death.

The fact that such rumors can spread like wildfire, and be believed by Negroes, is a measure of the deep distrust of "whitey's government" —and particularly its police department—which pervades the black districts of most American cities.

The myth that riots are carried out entirely by a tiny minority of hoodlums has been propagated by both whites and Negroes who are reluctant to acknowledge the scope of Negro disenchantment with American society.

There is some basis for the myth. The most conspicuous participants in ghetto riots, particularly in the early stages, are roving gangs of young

Negroes, ranging in age from early teens to the late twenties, who are totally alienated from society and hostile to all forms of authority.

They hate white people (whom they call "hunkies") with a consuming passion. They also hate black people who have "made it" in whitey's world; these are invariably labeled "Uncle Toms." They are not concerned with voting rights, or desegregated schools, or job opportunities. They don't want to work, or go to school. They'd much rather roam the streets, talking tough and blaming whitey for cheating them out of the abundant life they see advertised on TV. They are eager to believe any black power propagandist who tells them they are only taking what is rightfully theirs when they loot stores.

I heard the pure gospel expounded by a 14-year-old boy in a dirty t-shirt, who was part of a gang that surrounded me and another UPI reporter outside a stripped appliance store on Detroit's 12th Street.

"Whitey got it all," he said, thumping my chest. "And now we gonna take our share."

But all of the rock-throwing, window smashing, looting and fire-setting is not done by young toughs. Once a riot starts to get out of hand, an anything-goes atmosphere seems to spread through a ghetto. The opportunity to express pent-up resentments, and at the same time pick up a TV set or a case of whiskey, is irresistible to some older Negroes, including many who have responsible jobs and ordinarily would not think of stealing.

"They looked like they was doin' it just for kicks," said a Negro woman, who identified herself as the minister of a small store-front church on Detroit's West Side. "I was shocked when I saw some of the respectable, God-fearin' people who was running out of stores with their arms full."

In the past, Negro merchants were usually able to protect their stores by writing "soul brother" on the windows. But this device doesn't always work any more, for two reasons. First, white people now know the password and may use it; and second, some of the "soul brothers" who were spared in Detroit showed their gratitude by tripling prices on milk and bread when the Negro community was faced with an acute food shortage after the riot.

It is doubtless more than coincidence that a very large proportion of the burned-out stores in Newark, Detroit, Rochester, Toledo, Harlem and Milwaukee bear Jewish names.

"There's a lot of anti-Semitism as well as general anti-white feeling in this rioting," said Albert Demayo, manager of Rabin's Quality Clothing store on Joseph Avenue in Rochester. He said his store had been fire-bombed both in Rochester's big 1964 riot, and again in a small-scale disturbance this summer.

"We've been in this neighborhood for 28 years," said Demayo. "But we've had it. We're going to close down and move out."

Even when you count the older Negroes who join in briefly during the early "carnival" stage, the number of active participants in a ghetto riot is usually a small percentage of the total Negro community. The best estimates indicate that the figure rarely exceeds 10 per cent.

What about the remaining 90 per cent?

Many of them will tell you, with obvious sincerity and even vehemence, that they are more bitterly opposed to rioting than any white person can be.

"It's our neighborhood that's being destroyed, our families who are being caught in the gunfire," a Negro bus driver told me in Detroit. "I've got a pretty nice home. I don't want these damn fools to burn it down."

That is the "voice of reason" that white people want to hear but it is not necessarily the authentic voice of the ghetto. That voice is far more angry and impatient.

Interviews with scores of white collar, job-holding, middle-class Negroes revealed that their dominant attitude is strikingly similar to that which prevailed among the better-educated white people of Little Rock, Ark., Oxford, Miss., New Orleans, La., and other southern cities a few years ago when whites rather than Negroes were rebelling against law and order.

Every reporter who covered white riots in the early days of the civil rights movement remembers the eagerness of respectable white folk to have the world know that the disorders were being carried out by a minority of rednecks and toughs. But if you continued the conversation, many of them would reveal that while they disapproved of the "excesses" of the rioters, they sympathized with their basic objective of showing the government that the South would not accept integration.

Today one encounters the same split reaction among middle-class Negroes. They cannot condone looting, arson, and sniper warfare—they are genuinely shocked by such things. But a great many think that rioting may be the only way in which Negroes can finally convince white people that something must be done about slum housing, unemployment, and discrimination.

PART TWO: WHY NEGROES ARE ANGRY

The Negroes who are rioting in urban ghettos have specific grievances which they're eager to spell out to anyone who'll really listen.

I've listened to hundreds of them in the past two weeks. And whether the scene was 12th Street in Detroit, or Dorr Avenue in Toledo, or the Central Ward in Newark, or 125th Street in Harlem, the words were strikingly similar.

The ghetto Negro's number one complaint against white society is his difficulty in getting a job—not just menial work sweeping out a warehouse or picking tomatoes, but a good job that pays him enough to live in reasonable comfort. If you explain that he's not qualified for a skilled job because he has inadequate education, he'll remind you that it was whitey who kept him, until recently at least, in segregated and second-rate schools.

Recent studies by the U. S. Department of Labor indicate that fewer than half the Negro men in a typical urban ghetto have full-time jobs paying as much as $60 a week. Four out of ten have no regular jobs of any kind. Unemployment is particularly severe among younger males—

the group that is supplying most of the manpower for riots. Two years before Newark exploded in rioting, an unofficial commission warned the city fathers that 10,000 unemployed youngsters between the ages of 16 and 21 were walking the streets.

Housing is the second great grievance. "Despite all of the government programs that we hear about, the actual housing conditions of most urban Negroes are still deplorable," said Loftus Carson, executive director of the Monroe County Human Relations Commission in Rochester, N.Y.

"Slum landlords are getting outrageous rentals for crumbling, rat-infested dwellings that are unfit for human habitation."

The UCLA study showed that dilapidated housing leads all other grievances among Negroes in the Watts area of Los Angeles. The Brandeis University survey, covering six other major cities, revealed that three out of every four Negroes are highly incensed about the quality and price of the housing available to them.

Having walked through more slum streets in the past two weeks than ever before in my life, I can see why. Any white American who wonders what the rioting is all about can get a leg up on the answer by just driving through a Negro section of the inner city and asking himself: "How would I like to raise my children in this environment?"

"Police brutality" is a third complaint frequently heard in the ghetto. If you pin them down to specifics, you find that a relatively small number of Negroes have personally experienced, or witnessed, actual brutality in the sense of police beating helpless people in custody. But a much larger percentage say that they, or people whom they know, have been insulted or treated with a degree of rudeness which white people rarely experience at the hands of law enforcement officers.

Outside a pool hall on Dorr Avenue in Toledo, Ohio, a 24-year-old Negro spat in disgust when he was asked about the black community's relations with police.

"Whenever they come down here, they call us (obscenities)," he said, employing one of the more revolting terms in our language. "If you're just standing on the street corner, talking to a friend about your date last night, they come along and shout for you to bust it up and move on."

Another young Negro, wearing a thin fringe of beard, chimed in:

"And if you don't trot fast enough to suit them, they get out and stick-whip you."

Toledo officials deny this and say that the city's police have displayed wisdom and restraint in coping with racial incidents.

Which version is closer to the truth? I can only report that in every ghetto I visited, a majority of Negroes seemed to regard the police as their enemy.

Often, the complaint is not that police are too aggressive, but that they are indifferent to crimes in which Negroes are victims. "We get lousy protection in this area, nothing like the white neighborhoods get," said a Newark Negro. "Sometimes they don't even bother to respond when you call in about a robbery or street assault."

It is also widely believed in the ghetto—with what justice it is difficult to tell—that Negro residential areas are discriminated against in other municipal services, including garbage collection, welfare programs, recreational facilities and fire protection.

Next to police and landlords, the favorite villains of ghetto residents are white storekeepers.

"They know we have to buy from them, because it's too hard to take a bus out to the big supermarkets in the white neighborhoods, and the downtown stores won't give us credit anyway," said a Negro auto worker who lives on Detroit's West Side.

"So they jack up prices and sell stale food and factory-reject clothes and other junk. And if you have to buy on time, the carrying charges just eat you up."

PART THREE: WHAT CAN BE DONE?

The immediate necessity is to maintain public order. However deep the grievances which inspire it, rioting is a destructive act which hurts innocent people of both races, and jeopardizes the very fabric of civilization. As President Johnson said in his television address to the nation July 28, "There is no American right to loot stores or to burn buildings or to fire rifles from rooftops . . . that is crime and crime must be dealt with forcefully and swiftly and certainly, under law."

Law enforcement officials have learned some painful lessons from past riots. One is that it takes a very finely balanced mixture of firmness and restraint to cope with a racial incident in the ghetto tinderbox.

If police get too tough too soon, it's like throwing gasoline on a fire. But if they lean too far in the opposite direction—as they did in Detroit, when they watched looters without trying to stop them—they invite a swift spread of disorder.

It has also been made clear that calling out the National Guard is not always an adequate solution. In some places, such as Cambridge, Md., Guard units have handled riot situations with great skill. In others, such as Newark and Detroit, it has been all too obvious that many Guardsmen have had very little military experience and no riot training whatever.

Untrained youths do not turn into battle-wise soldiers merely by putting on a pair of fatigues and a helmet. Skittish under fire, they are apt to respond to a single sniper shot—or even a firecracker—by spraying rifle and machine gun bullets at everything that moves. I feel strongly about this because I nearly got shot one night in Detroit when police and Guardsmen began shooting at a sniper or snipers whom they couldn't locate. Other bystanders, including a four-year-old child in an apartment and a woman tourist standing at a motel window, were killed.

There was a striking contrast between the West Side of Detroit patrolled by the National Guard and the East Side in which the seasoned paratroopers of the regular Army were posted. The paratroopers never fired wildly. When a sniper opened up, they located the building he was in, surrounded it, went in and dug him out the hard way—without jeopardizing all the other residents by spattering the windows with bullets.

Pacification came very quickly in areas occupied by paratroopers.

The lesson that Detroit Mayor Jerome Cavanagh drew was that there should be a force of trained federal troops available to big cities as soon as a riot begins. While President Johnson has not endorsed that idea, he has ordered the National Guard to begin training its men in riot control.

The Federal Bureau of Investigation also is distributing to police departments around the country a manual on riot control which includes badly needed advice on how to handle snipers.

Another measure which many law enforcement officials consider essential to future riot control is the legislation which has been pending in Congress ever since President Kennedy's assassination, to impose curbs on the sale of guns and pistols.

"This country has to act to control firearms," Atty. Gen. Ramsey Clark said. "If Newark and Detroit don't demonstrate that necessity, nothing can."

If armed repression, however efficient, is America's only response to the Negro uprising, its cities may be in for an indefinite siege of guerrilla warfare.

"The aimless violence and destruction can be contained through military means, but only drastic changes in the life of the poor will provide the kind of order and stability that Americans desire," said Martin Luther King Jr.

President Johnson expressed a similar view in his TV address on the rioting:

"The only genuine, long-range solution lies in an attack upon the conditions that breed despair and violence."

Although no one can now envision all of the details of the solution that will be required, it is already evident that it will involve a mammoth commitment of national resources, vastly exceeding anything that the administration or Congress has yet dared to propose.

Vice President Hubert H. Humphrey, trying to suggest the magnitude of the response that is needed, speaks of a "Marshall Plan" for urban America. The Marshall Plan for postwar rebuilding of Western Europe involved a U. S. outlay of $13.5 billion over four years. It saved Britain, France, Italy, West Germany, Greece, Turkey and several other nations from communism, or chaos.

The cost of the Marshall Plan will be very modest compared to the sums which the United States will need to expend if it seriously intends to seek a "genuine, long-range solution" of the ghetto's problems. But the cost of not solving those problems would be incalculably greater, solely in financial terms, not to mention lives.

The urban coalition, a group of business, labor, religious and civic leaders headed by Mayor John V. Lindsay of New York and Mayor Joseph M. Barr of Pittsburgh, has called a national conference in Washington late this month to formulate specific proposals for a vastly increased government assault on the ghetto's job, housing and poverty problems.

"We call upon the nation and the Congress to reorder our national priorities, with a commitment of national resources equal to the dimensions of the problem we face," said the coalition in announcing the conference.

Mayor Ivan Allen Jr. of Atlanta, Ga., has urged an increase of $30 billion a year in federal spending for housing programs, job training, improvement of slum schools, and anti-poverty projects which are directly beneficial to ghetto residents.

There are no signs that Congress, in its present mood, will vote even a fraction of the funds proposed by Mayor Allen and others. On the contrary, Congress seems bent on curtailing even the "war on poverty" that is now under way. While the ruins of Newark were still smouldering, the House rejected—with jocular debate and whoops of laughter—an administration bill that would have allocated $40 million to control the infestations of rats which are an important source of ghetto misery.

"Only a mammoth program can head off the developing trend toward revolution," Dr. Jack E. Dodson, associate professor of sociology at the University of Houston, told UPI. "But in the current context of American politics, I don't seriously think changes on the necessary scale will be made.

"The United States is on the verge of being ripped apart. If we continue on our present course, I foresee a time when Negro slum areas will become reservations encircled by para-military police forces to maintain order."

Dr. Dodson hopes he will be proved wrong. And in that hope he is not alone.

(Reprinted by permission of United Press International.)

Careful reading of Smiley's article and the series by Cassels will reveal how widely reporters should interview and what kinds of government agencies, books, and reference materials can provide background to make stories meaningful. News-gatherers must seek real truths with much the same discipline employed by scientific researchers. News consumers must read, listen, and watch critically to separate the shallow messages from those with rewarding depth. Not until the late 1960s did some news media begin to learn that their standard ghetto news sources were inadequate. They learned it the hard way as unexpected violence ripped the black communities of Los Angeles, Cleveland, Newark, and Detroit. Sometimes the best service is performed by information that leaves the public uncertain about conditions, because those conditions are uncertain. Certainly, the age of simple cops-and-robbers stories and other accounts of "good guys versus bad guys" is fast fading. Media offering only that kind of fare survive because of their entertainment. Failure to produce their primary excuse for existing will doom all of them to third-rate status and most to eventual extinction.

Meanwhile, facing up to the escalating challenges of the 1960s and 1970s has placed practicing journalists on ever higher levels of prestige. Journalism has always helped produce great authors like Charles Dickens, Mark Twain, and Ernest Hemingway. Lately, increasing num-

bers of persons distinguished in letters and the social sciences have
been moving into journalism, where so much of the action is. The
benefits for discriminating users of the mass media have been multiplying apace.

FOR FURTHER STUDY

1. If Americans ever knew more about the governments geographically closest to them, journalistic practice has reversed that for most of
the nation. A senior editor of *Time* demonstrated this to a journalism
class during President Dwight D. Eisenhower's Administration. Students
contrasted Eisenhower's spending "so much time" golfing with their
governor's nose-to-the-grindstone regimen. The visiting journalist stunned
them by revealing that their governor golfed every day the weather
allowed, a fact which the state-capital press corps had agreed to suppress
in behalf of the governor's image. Such a gentlemen-journalists' agreement would be impossible in Washington's better talented, more sophisticated press corps. Is the government-closest-to-the-people concept a myth
or a reality in your community?

2. Clip several stories from a local newspaper. Ask persons mentioned and others who should know to evaluate factual accuracy. How
many errors are alleged? Do any of the sources disagree with each other?
Are any out-of-context charges reasonable, or do they reflect the source's
discomfort at being exposed to the public prints?

3. Take careful notes at a speech or meeting involving matters about
which you are informed. Compare your impressions with what professional journalists report. Are their omissions reasonable? Evaluate the
stories' emphases.

4. From conversations with friends or conversations overheard in
public, list some ideas for investigative reporting like the Ted Smiley
and Louis Cassels examples in this chapter. Consider grumbling about
a school cafeteria or health service or complaints about radio programming or "unfair" government.

5. Using the *World Almanac*, outline a story project on presidential
succession. Check the Twenty-Fifth Amendment to the Constitution,
and look under "President of the U. S." to find the order of succession,
how many years the nation has been without a vice-president, and other
related facts.

6. Outline background on the senior U. S. senator from your state.
Start with *Who's Who in America* and check sources like the *New York
Times Index* and *Reader's Guide to Periodical Literature* for articles
about or by him.

SUGGESTED READING

CHARNLEY, MITCHELL V., *Reporting*, New York: Holt, Rinehart & Winston, Inc., 1959. Chapters 16 and 17 deal with "investigative" and "interpretive" reporting.

Columbia Journalism Review (602 Journalism Building, Columbia University, New York, N.Y. 10027). This quarterly regularly offers superior analysis of news performance by all media.

COPPLE, NEALE, *Depth Reporting*, Englewood Cliffs, N. J.: Prentice-Hall, Inc., 1964. Chapter 5 is especially valuable in this book, which deals with the need to go beyond surface reporting.

MACDOUGALL, CURTIS D., *Interpretative Reporting*, New York: The Macmillan Company, 1968 (5th ed.). Chapters 9-19 offer guidance, from elementary to sophisticated, in specialized coverage.

MEYER, PHILIP E., "A Newspaper's Role Between the Riots," *Nieman Reports*, June, 1968 (Vol. 22, No. 2). Meyer explains how two newspapers employed sociological research methods on ghetto problems.

STEFFENS, LINCOLN, *The Autobiography of Lincoln Steffens*, New York: Harcourt, Brace & World, Inc., 1931. Parts II and III offer inspirational (although sometimes cynical) examples of good muckracking journalism.

CHAPTER 6

Editing the News

A young journalist in the West thrilled his family in announcing that one of America's best newspapers had just hired him. But faces fell when he said he was to be a copy editor. "I suppose you have to start someplace," a kindly uncle sympathized. Their reaction typifies public ignorance of editing's critical importance to journalism. Some laymen believe that news media have to hunt for enough material to fill their columns or newscasts, and some assume that all newspaper reporters write the headlines over their stories. A few working newsmen share part of the public ignorance, as was demonstrated on New York's experimental newspaper *PM* in 1940. *PM* started without a copydesk, but added a large one within its first week. A few small papers and more small radio stations function without real editing operations, but their news offerings are generally feeble.

The fact is, of course, that copy editors (called "sub-editors" in Europe) at least equal reporters in importance on good newspapers. Most copy editors are "graduate reporters," and minimum pay-scale differentials usually favor copy editors over reporters. (The old-fashioned term "copyreader" is often confused with "proofreader"—one who corrects galley proofs, rather than edits.) Any good reporter with experience can tell of editors' having spoiled good stories by tampering with his original prose, by cutting important parts, by attaching misleading headlines, or by running other stories instead of his. Occasionally a good, experienced reporter will admit that editors have improved on his original efforts—by eliminating errors, by filling story holes, or (rarest of all) by tightening his writing.

Readers and listeners cannot benefit from good reporting if poor editors choose not to put the best stories into the pages and newscasts which finally reach the public. News value is ruined when editors change accurate reports into erroneous stories or miswrite the headlines on which scanners depend. Badly edited TV film can distort a reporter's otherwise balanced account of a campus demonstration. On the other hand, good editing—from wise choice of stories to improved phraseology —enhances good reporting. Reporting and editing overlap each other. An editor assigns the reporter; the reporter "edits" by choosing which story elements he will report; the editor may "report" on his own—from file material or by telephoning additional sources.

SELECTING THE DAY'S NEWS

Today's tremendous news flow subjects conscientious editors to more than an embarrassment of riches. Studies have indicated that a typical metropolitan daily's news hole can carry as little as one-tenth of what is available to editors. During World War II's newsprint scarcity, when news transmission was slower than now, the *New York Times* collected 1,000,000 words daily, but it could print only about 200,000. (By 1969, it was collecting 2,000,000 words a day.) Either the Associated Press or United Press International alone supplies more copy than an average daily can print—to say nothing of copy from its own local reporters, news bureaus, and correspondents, and subsidiary news and feature services. Considering that a half-hour newscast carries less than half of a regular-size newspaper's front-page total, broadcast news directors face even larger selection problems.

WNBC-TV's "Sixth Hour News" in New York City illustrated the time squeeze on a quiet news day in 1968. With time taken for commercials and sports, the remainder of the program's sixty minutes carried nineteen stories plus the weather. About one-third of the nineteen were local. That same day the Associated Press's A wire for evening newspapers pumped out sixty-one stories and seven sets of thirty-six shorts (obituaries, "People in the News," brighteners). [That twelve-hour A-wire cycle also carried two story precedes and forty-nine new leads, adds, inserts, and corrections, in addition to six advisories to telegraph editors.] A 52-page Illinois daily of just under 50,000 circulation ran fewer than half those national and international stories. A 28-page Ohio daily, in the 100,000 range, ran only nineteen as it devoted two-thirds of its news space to local copy.

Major newspapers and broadcast units supplement the basic worldwide coverage by AP and UPI with one or more other syndicated news services. Important ones available to newspapers include the New York Times, Chicago Tribune-New York Daily News, Los Angeles Times-Washington Post, and Chicago Daily News services. Dow Jones (financial) and North American Newspaper Alliance (features and news) are

start new paragraph:	in only six states. [The Republican
spell out:	carried ④ states, including (Ala)
abbreviate; use numerals:	won in Moline, (Illinois), by (sixteen) votes
indent on left:	(United Press International listed six.)
indent on both sides:	(United Press International listed six.)
center the line:	] By Associated Press [
delete, leave space:	less than 15 percent
delete, close up:	spent the weekend.
set lower case:	William Rogers, Secretary of State, said
capitalize:	secretary of state William Rogers
transpose elements:	Ambassador (Bunker) Ellsworth
follow unusual spelling:	Loyd Easton or: Dick Gordin
insert apostrophe:	He was the Giants leading hitter.
insert comma:	secretary of health education and welfare
insert period:	He was the Giants' leading hitter
insert space:	increased by 27 percent
eliminate space:	He left for the week end.
opening quotation mark:	I will vote for him every time."
closing quotation mark:	"I will vote for him every time.
insert hyphen:	It will cost $15=million.
delete within paragraph:	Smith issued a statement Tuesday:
(and move colon)	declaring he opposed such a new tax
	and promising to vote against it:
	"I will oppose this tax to the end."
delete between paragraphs:	Smith issued a statement Tuesday:
(and move colon)	declaring he opposed such a new tax
	and promising to vote against it:
	"I will oppose this tax to the end."

Figure 6.1. Typical Copy Editing Symbols (made right on the copy).

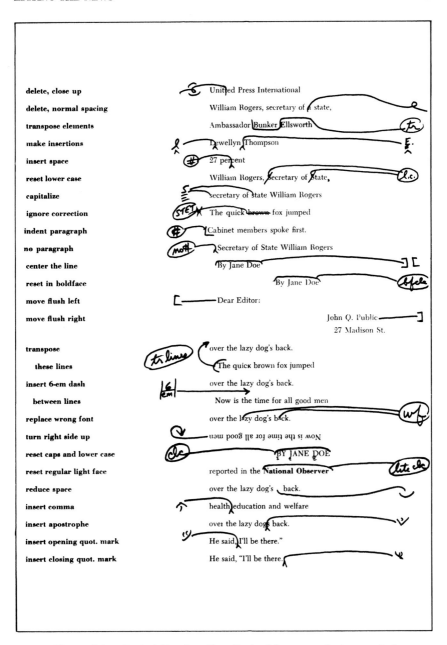

Figure 6.2. Typical Proofreading Marks (always made in margins).

among specialized agencies. Foreign news service is supplied by Reuters, Canadian Press, and several others. Altogether, *Editor & Publisher Year Book* lists more than 150 "News and Picture Services"—ranging from city bureaus through specialists like Religious News Service to the AP and UPI. *Broadcasting Yearbook* lists three dozen "Radio and TV News" services, including AP and UPI.

Step Number One in news selection, then, is investment in reporters, correspondents, and news services. No daily newspaper or broadcasting outlet can perform its full journalistic duty without a minimum AP or UPI service, although some pretend to. Some fail even with a major news service. Radio stations which neglect local reporting and editing, assigning just any employee to "rip and read" five-minute press-association summaries, are the worst offenders. They offer, as CBS Correspondent Eric Sevareid told the Massachusetts State Legislature in 1967, "non-news programs." Sevareid observed: "People tune in to them, I think, not to know what has happened, but what has *not* happened—to make sure that the atomic bomb has not fallen, that bubonic plague is not sweeping the nation. It would be as useful just to ring a bell every hour on the hour and have someone cry, 'All's well.' "

Emphasis rivals selection in editing importance. Whether a story gets two minutes early in the newscast or thirty seconds on the tag end declares "This is important" or "This is unimportant." Presenting a political accusation under a four-column headline on page 1 delivers a great deal more impact than the very same words under a one-column head on page 14. (In some cases, the latter treatment more effectively deflates a story than would its omission.) The problem of judging news is complicated by considerations of fair play. If the Kiwanis convention, in a dull news week, got film coverage, do the Rotarians "deserve the same" in a busy news week? If page 2 carried a judge's demand that Lawyer A be disbarred last July, should not Lawyer A's "acquittal" six months later get equal attention?

Table 6 presents an interesting comparison of how eleven major morning newspapers covered two stories on Vietnam-war policy in the late summer of 1967. On a Thursday, Senator John Stennis's Preparedness Investigating Subcommittee issued a report calling for escalation in the bombing of North Vietnam. The next day, President Lyndon B. Johnson held a press conference, during which he rebutted major contentions in the Stennis report. The American Institute for Political Communication in Washington, D. C., analyzed the handling of stories about these events. Table 6 is based on the AIPC findings.

Three of the eleven "played" only the Stennis report, four only Johnson's reply, and two did it with both. Interestingly, differences did not necessarily reflect the newspapers' editorial views. For example, the

TABLE 6

COMPARATIVE NEWS PLAY

	STENNIS REPORT			JOHNSON'S REPLY		
	Page	Space★	(source)	Page	Space★	(source)
New York Times[a]	1	36.5	(staff)	1*	30	(staff)
Philadelphia Inquirer	1	31.5	(staff)	1*	27	(staff)
Washington Post[a]	1*	33	(staff)	1*	22	(staff)
Atlanta Constitution	1*	31	(AP)	5	8	(UPI)
Miami Herald	1*	27.5	(staff)	1*	12	(AP)
Detroit Free Press	1	24.5	(AP)	1	19.5	(UPI, AP)
Chicago Tribune	10	23	(staff)	1	43	(staff)
Kansas City Times	1*	22.5	(staff)	7A	6[b]	(N.Y. Times)
Houston Post	1*	36.5	(AP)	1	24	(UPI, AP)
Los Angeles Times	1	38	(staff)	1*	29	(staff)
Seattle Post-Intelligencer	A	8	(AP)	A*	11	(AP)

★Column inches exclusive of headlines.
*Indicates use as lead story for the day.
[a]Both the *New York Times* and *Washington Post* also carried texts of the statements.
[b]The *Kansas City Times* omitted Johnson's reply in its report of the press conference. Managing Editor John S. Chandley explained that full coverage in the *Kansas City Star*, sister paper, the preceding day precluded repetition next morning. Similar policy, relating to the *Atlanta Journal*, may have affected the *Constitution's* coverage.

—Table based on research conducted by the American Institute for Political Communication. Reprinted by permission from AIPC SPECIAL REPORT, November, 1967.

hawkish *Chicago Tribune* gave better position to Johnson's reply than it had given to the Stennis report's call for more bombing. The dovish *Miami Herald* gave 27.5 column inches and staff coverage to the pro-hawk story but used only 12 inches of the AP report for the rebuttal.

The role of news-judgment editing is clear here. No other explanation accounts for the *Kansas City Times*'s running Johnson's press conference on page 7A and omitting his reply to the Stennis report at that. The omission is explained in the Table 6 footnotes. [The 25 per cent less space given to the reply overall was probably caused in part by the smaller news holes in Saturday papers.]

FINAL ACCURACY CHECK

An important factor in selection and emphasis of news involves total accuracy. Simple facts do not necessarily add up to truth because news stories seldom carry all the facts. *The Autobiography of Lincoln Steffens* recounts Steffens's creation of a "crime wave" by the simple process of reporting stories previously ignored by men on the police beat. A contest among reporters led to what looked like an upsurge in

New York City crime. Such a distortion by facts is less likely today than it was when Steffens competed in the Yellow Journalism of the 1890s.

Eric Sevareid, in his speech before the Massachusetts Legislature, explained how he had seen facts collected by a TV camera twist the truth when he visited Vietnam in 1966: "Buddhists staged some riots in Saigon and Da Nang. The TV cameras wheeled up. They focus, of course, on whatever is most dramatically in motion. They act like a flashlight beam in the darkness. Everything else around, however vital to the full story, is lost in the darkness and ceases to exist. The pictures could not show you that a block away from the Saigon riots the populace was shopping, chatting, sitting in restaurants in total normalcy. The riots involved a tiny proportion of the people in either city; yet the effect of the pictures in this country, including in the Congress, was explosive. People here thought Vietnam was tearing itself apart, that civil war was raging. Nothing of the sort was happening."

Editors with access to varied reports and a background of experience serve as the final checkpoints against such mangling of the truth. If News Service A reports that a former President referred to a famous general as "squirrel-headed" and News Service B denies it, editors taking both services must decide whether to print A's report, heed B's report, or temper A with B. They must measure every news story's context against as much of the original event's context as they can learn. Good reporters deserve to be trusted, of course, and only stupid editors make substantive changes on the basis of their own prejudices or without clear bases for contradiction. But even a good reporter can stand too close to a story sometimes.

Figure 6.3. The "slot" man directs six copy editors on the rim of this traditional U-shaped copydesk. He checks their work and sends it to the composing room via pneumatic tube at his right. Conveniently located library is just behind copydesk. (Courtesy, **Toledo Blade**)

Public opinion polling offers an example of how editors should weigh more than a single expert's account. Within the same week in February, 1968, two major polls reported sharply different findings on American voters' opinions. Comparing President Lyndon B. Johnson (before he announced he would not run) with Richard M. Nixon and Nelson A. Rockefeller in two-way races and in a three-way race with George C. Wallace, this is what they reported:

	LBJ	NIXON	(UND.)	LBJ	NIXON	WALLACE	(UND.)
Poll X	42	42	(16)	39	39	11	(11)
Poll Y	48	43	(9)	47	38	10	(5)

	LBJ	ROCKY	(UND.)	LBJ	ROCKY	WALLACE	(UND.)
Poll X	41	46	(13)	37	40	13	(10)
Poll Y	46	41	(13)	44	37	12	(7)

Thus, Poll X showed Rockefeller clearly ahead of Johnson in two-way and three-way races, with Nixon able only to tie. Poll Y showed Johnson comfortably ahead of both candidates, with Rockefeller only negligibly closer than Nixon in the three-way tests. Yet some news media presented one or the other poll with no qualification, let alone any reference to the contradictions.

Earlier, within a day of each other, Poll X had reported that the President's "popularity has risen from its October low point" to 48 per cent voter approval, and Poll Y had said it had "sunk to an all-time low" of 43 per cent approval. One network news show reported only the "all-time-low" finding; another, more responsibly, gave both results. Some newspapers used headlines like "LBJ's Ratings Touch Bottom" and "LBJ Popularity Bounds Upward." At least one of those had to be wrong. The danger of misinforming the public is closely followed by the danger of losing credibility among customers perceptive enough to note such errors.

Responsible editors consider the factor of timing. How long might readers or listeners have to live with a story about which doubts loom large? Millions could react to an erroneous story on an early-evening network newscast for critical hours before a correction could reach most of them. Yet withholding significant facts can damage public trust, thereby weakening the mass media's ability to keep wild rumormongers at bay.

The problem was well illustrated—and well handled—by the Louisville newspapers in a Memorial Day, 1968, edition. The last edition of

The Courier-Journal & TIMES

VOL. 226, NO. 151   ******   LOUISVILLE, THURSDAY MORNING, MAY 30, 1968   68 PAGES   10 CENTS

Guard Leaves Trouble Area; Curfew Is Lifted by Schmied

Mayor Kenneth A. Schmied, in a meeting yesterday with Negro militants, agreed to have National Guardsmen withdrawn from guard duty in Louisville's West End and said he would not impose a third night of curfew on the city.

And Schmied consented to a plan whereby city police and a group of some 30 special Negro marshals would take over in the 25-block area patrolled by Guardsmen since the trouble broke out Monday night.

At 10:30 p.m.—nearly six hours later apparently had been successful in keeping trouble down, although looting had been

more serious than the previous two nights.

"I know there are some minor incidents which look bad, but over-all—to this point—I think it was a good idea," Hyde said.

There were no confirmed reports of shooting or sniping in the area, he said.

More stories and pictures, Pages A 8, 13, 14 and 16, and B 1.

and fewer state and county police were being used than on previous nights.

One man wearing a white armband, the

identification used by the marshals, was arrested and charged with looting, but Hyde said that "95 or 40 (marshals) are doing a good job. Generally, speaking, the marshals—after they got organized—have been doing a good job up to now."

In accordance with the plan, Guardsmen were withdrawn shortly after Schmied met with a delegation of Negroes in late afternoon. Twice the Guardsmen returned briefly to the trouble area from their headquarters, but were withdrawn both times after Negro leaders and the marshals convinced crowds to disperse.

In the later hours, Negro community leaders cruised through the area asking

cooperation, and their efforts apparently met with success.

The plan was worked out by Schmied and Negro leaders and announced by the Mayor at a meeting with the Negro delegation in a parking lot adjacent to police headquarters at Seventh and Jefferson in late afternoon.

But even as Schmied announced that police patrols in the West End would return to normal, the restraint of city officials was being tested.

New reports of looting and disorder in the area of 38th and Dumesnil came

See GUARD
Back page, col. 3, this section

TIRED GUARDSMEN take time out for a smoke and to catch up on the news they were a part of yesterday in the schoolyard of Brandeis Elementary School, 26th and Date, Guard command post. These men returned to the school with the general withdrawal of National Guardsmen from trouble area in the West End yesterday.

De Gaulle Goes Home; Rumors Say He'll Quit

By LOUIS NEVIN

PARIS (AP)—President Charles de Gaulle left Paris secretly yesterday for a visit to his country home, setting off published speculation that he plans to resign as chief of state of this strike-crippled nation.

Workers and students shouted for De Gaulle's resignation and the ouster of Premier Georges Pompidou in a massive march from the Place de la Bastille to the Place de la Republique, an anti-government demonstration that police estimated drew 100,000. Other estimates said more than 200,000 marched. The Communist-led General Confederation of Labor organized it.

Cries went up for early national elec-

Radio Message Heard; May Be Missing N-Sub

WASHINGTON (AP)—The Navy announced last night that patrol aircraft flying about 110 miles east of Norfolk, Va., heard a radio message identifying the sender with the code word for the missing nuclear submarine Scorpion.

The message said:

"Any station. This net network. This is," and then the Navy code word for the Scorpion.

The search commander has ordered ships and aircraft to investigate, the Navy said. The message, picked up at 8:28 p.m. EDT, was monitored by six other Navy stations and a bearing was obtained to the source of the signal.

This was the first message heard

Kennedy Dealt a Blow

Oregon Gives Nixon,

The Courier-Journal & TIMES

VOL. 226, NO. 151   ******   LOUISVILLE, THURSDAY MORNING, MAY 30, 1968   68 PAGES   10 CENTS

Two Shooting Deaths Follow Calmer Evening in West End

Two Negro youths were shot and killed in Louisville's West End about midnight last night after a period of comparative calm.

One of the two was shot by police and the other apparently by a liquor store owner, police said.

Police said both of the dead youths were shot in the act of looting.

The shootings marred a day in which tensions seemed to ease after Mayor Kenneth A. Schmied agreed to have National Guardsmen withdrawn from the trouble area, decided not to impose a third night of curfew and sent special Negro marshals into the West End to try to restore order.

The actions brought a marked easing of the widespread disorders that broke out Monday night.

Police identified one of the dead youths as Matthias Washington Browder, 19, of 722 S. 38th. He was pronounced dead on

More stories and pictures, Pages A 8, 13, 14 and 16, and B 1.

arrival at General Hospital shortly after midnight.

Police said W. J. Berger, owner of Vermont Liquors, 509 S. 34th St., told them he shot the youth when he tried to break

into the store. Deputy Coroner Charles Proctor said Browder was shot once in the neck.

The other youth, identified as James Groves, 14, of 846 S. 32nd, was hit twice in the right side by two shotgun blasts fired by Patrolman Charles Noe. He said he fired when the youth, his arms loaded with loot from a store at 32nd and Garland, refused to obey an order to halt.

Groves also was dead on arrival at General Hospital about midnight.

Lt. Col. Bert Hawkins said Noe and his partner went to the store at 32nd and Garland in response to a trouble call

and three youths, Groves one of them, fled with their arms full.

Hawkins said the officers fired one shot in the air in warning, and then, when the youths fled into a dark lot nearby, Noe fired in that direction and apparently hit Groves.

Investigation showed the boys had broken through a window to enter the store, Hawkins said, and additional loot was found hidden in weeds nearby. The window had been covered by a metal grill and plywood, Hawkins said.

In the other shooting, Berger told

See TWO YOUTHS
Back page, col. 3, this section

TIRED GUARDSMEN take time out for a smoke and to catch up on the news they were a part of yesterday in the schoolyard of Brandeis Elementary School, 26th and Date, Guard command post. These men returned to the school with the general withdrawal of National Guardsmen from trouble area in the West End yesterday.

De Gaulle Goes Home; Rumors Say He'll Quit

By LOUIS NEVIN

PARIS (AP)—President Charles de Gaulle left Paris secretly yesterday for a visit to his country home, setting off published speculation that he plans to resign as chief of state of this strike-crippled nation.

Workers and students shouted for De Gaulle's resignation and the ouster of Premier Georges Pompidou in a massive march from the Place de la Bastille to the Place de la Republique, an anti-government demonstration that police estimated drew 100,000. Other estimates said more than 200,000 marched. The Communist-led General Confederation of Labor organized it.

Cries went up for early national elections to solve the crisis, set off by student rioters, that has paralyzed French industry and transport and left up to 10 million workers on strike.

Where Did He Step on the Way?

Premier Premier Pierre Mendes-France, renowned for once having tried to make milk drinkers out of wine-loving

POLICE TASK FORCE officers stand guard outside the Lucky Morris Pawn Shop at 28th and Greenwood, which was looted for the second time at 7:30 p.m. yesterday. It had been broken into during rioting Monday night.

Radio Message Heard; May Be Missing N-Sub

WASHINGTON (AP)—The Navy announced last night that patrol aircraft flying about 110 miles east of Norfolk, Va., heard a radio message identifying the sender with the code word for the missing nuclear submarine Scorpion.

The message said:

"Any station. This net (network). This is," and then the Navy code word for the Scorpion.

The search commander has ordered ships and aircraft to investigate, the Navy said. The message, picked up at 8:28 p.m. EDT, was monitored by six other Navy stations and a bearing was obtained to the source of the signal.

This was the first definite indication since the hunt for the Scorpion and its crew of 99 officers and men began Monday, shortly after the submarine failed to make radio contact as expected for docking at Norfolk.

Crew Listed as Missing

Earlier, the Navy officially declared the crew as missing.

Kennedy Dealt a Blow

Oregon Gives Nixon, Humphrey Major Boost

By WARREN WEAVER JR.
© New York Times News Service

PORTLAND, Ore.—About 575,000 Oregon voters have moved the nation perceptibly closer to a choice between Richard M. Nixon and Hubert H. Humphrey

voters gave another massive endorsement to former Vice President Nixon, rejecting free-spending campaigns for two absentee candidates, the anxious governor of New York and the reluctant governor of California.

Figure 6.4. Original and made-over editions of combined May 30, 1968 **Louisville Courier-Journal & Times** holiday issue illustrate responsible news-judgment decision. (Courtesy, Louisville Courier-Journal and Times Co.)

the combined holiday issue of the *Courier Journal* & *Times* was carrying a lead story on the apparent ending of serious racial disturbances in Louisville's West End. National Guard units had been pulled out of the trouble area, and the curfew had been lifted. Then, just past midnight, two Negro youths were shot and killed in looting incidents. Although those terrible facts did not reflect the general mood of cooperation between authorities and black leaders, the editors remade page 1 for good reasons—not without serious discussion of the alternatives, and certainly not to sell more newspapers. They recognized that no regular editions of the evening *Times* were scheduled for the holiday and that the make-over edition could deliver factual accounts of the tragedies to the West End. Figure 6.4 shows the tops of the original page 1 and the makeover. Note how the latter's headline and page makeup feature the bad news while trying to convey the significant factor of calmer overall relations.

PROBLEMS WITH HEADLINES

Peculiar to the print media are the problems of writing headlines. Newspapers especially have developed two reader dependencies on headlines, which have made them enormously important. Most readers choose stories on the basis of headlines. Thus, inadequate headlines—those lacking clarity or interesting points—deprive good stories of their deserved readership. Even more critical is the fact that readers get many of their facts from headlines alone. Inaccurate headlines are potentially more dangerous than inaccurate stories. When the *New York Journal* of February 17, 1898, carried the banner, DESTRUCTION OF THE WAR SHIP MAINE WAS THE WORK OF AN ENEMY, it committed a journalistic sin not adequately atoned for in the following decks or story text where the news was de-escalated to attributed opinions and "The *suspicion* that the Maine was deliberately blown up grows stronger every hour." (Italics added.)

Only those who have composed headlines appreciate how hard it is to fit interest and accuracy into allotted headline space. Type cannot be squeezed, and "headlinese" ("Hits" for Criticizes, "Seen" for Predicted) risks either misunderstanding or no understanding. Modern trends toward horizontal page makeup (multicolumn headlines with stories spread horizontally beneath them) have alleviated the problem on some newspapers. Standard-size papers which have changed from eight- to six-column format have added a third to one-column counts in a given type size. A majority of newspapers, however, still use formats and type sizes that demand great skill in writing headlines. The fitting difficulties are such that copydesks have devised elaborate counting systems to estimate whether lines will fit.

The "flit" system is most widely used: Half-units are allotted to *f, l, i, t; I;* spaces; and most punctuation marks. Full units are used for *a, b, c,* and most lowercase letters; figures; and *?, $,* and a dash. One and one-half units are allotted to *m, w; A, B, C,* and most uppercase letters; and to *%.* Two units are used for *M, W.*

All-capital headlines call for a simple variation: half-units for *I,* spaces, and most punctuation marks; full units for most letters, figures, *?,* and *$;* and one and one-half units for *M* and *W.*

Type styles require variations in accordance with a fat *O* or a thin *J,* for example. Newspapers using "stepline" heads, instead of the popular flush-left, sometimes employ more elaborate counting systems to balance lines more closely—so that left-side indentions on lines 2 and 3 match right-side indentions on lines 2 and 1, respectively. Loose flush-left heads can be counted on a simple one-unit basis, if the editor knows how to allow for preponderances of fat or thin letters in a given line. Note the count sizes of samples in the *Toledo Blade* head schedule in Appendix D.

With space-fitting limits in mind, let us return to the errant headlines mentioned in connection with opinion-polling stories. Below are examples of how headlines should qualify what they promote:

	BAD	BETTER
Story X	LBJ Popularity Bounds Upward	LBJ Popularity Rises, Poll Says
Story Y	LBJ's Ratings Touch Bottom	Poll Puts LBJ At Low Point

The improved headlines attribute the rise or fall to a source, instead of stating flatly that the President's popularity has risen or fallen.

TOTAL EDITING

Beyond their basic "gatekeeper" function of deciding which stories should reach their public and with what emphasis, editors have final responsibility for other elements of accuracy and clarity, ranging from stylebook conformity to understandability. For radio news, this might involve such small points as changing "The market was off" to "The market was down"—to avoid aural confusion of "off" with "up." Editing entails scrupulous attention to spelling and grammar—primarily for their part in accuracy, and secondarily for the medium's image as an accurate performer. (Pronunciation takes part of the place of spelling on newscasts, of course, particularly where news is read by a nonjournalist announcer.)

Unlike the proofreader, with whom he is often confused by laymen, the good copy editor is expected to improve phrasing—shortening or lengthening sentences, improving vocabulary, rearranging paragraphs, or adding explanations to make better stories. The best operations encourage second-guessing by copy editors on such matters as story emphasis. Having studied a story closely, a copy editor may detect flaws overlooked in the hasty perusal by a city editor or news editor, flaws warranting a "hold" on the story. Or he may spot a news gem buried in a hastily written roundup of School Board actions and get it pulled out for deserved separate treatment. The copydesk rim provides the last chance for repairing and improving the news package.

Note the copy-editing of the June 27, 1968, AP story (Figure 6.5). Look beyond the mere mechanics of paragraph markings and minor corrections. In paragraph 1, "constitutional" and "citizens" were inserted to clear the way for reducing wordage, including a prepositional phrase. The "all" was inserted because two states already allowed eighteen-year-olds to vote. The third line was cut as being of little value. The sixteen-word insertion brought higher the special-message aspect and used "the draft" to replace the stuffier "to bear arms." The original two paragraphs with sentences of thirty and thirty-five words have been reduced to one paragraph with sentences of nineteen and twenty words.

The original third paragraph, reduced by two prepositional phrases and six words, becomes the second. Paragraphs four and five, containing sentences of thirty-five and thirty-one words, respectively, become paragraph three with sentences of eighteen and twenty-eight words.

More important than any of those changes might be addition of background information on voting laws. The *World Almanac* would have revealed to the copy editor that Georgia and Kentucky already allowed voting at eighteen, that Alaska permitted it at nineteen, and Hawaii at twenty.

Automation has sharply reduced opportunities to edit AP and UPI copy used on hundreds of small and medium dailies since 1951. A tremendous boon to composing-room efficiency, the Teletypesetter (TTS) has unfortunately discouraged individualism in the total processing of wire copy on newspapers using the service. The Associated Press estimated that about half of its 1,236 newspaper subscribers used TTS in 1968, and United Press International said "slightly more than half" of its 1,200 newspaper customers did so. It is safe to assume that most of the AP-UPI overlap of about 700 American-newspaper customers occurs among the biggest, non-TTS subscribers, and therefore that about 1,000 of America's 1,752 dailies in 1969 were using TTS wire copy.

The Teletypesetter provides both teletype-printed copy and perforated tape. Running the perforated tape through a machine automatically sets galleys of type at high speed. If the copy editor does more than proofread the teletype copy, he forces time-consuming resetting by shop compositors. This would destroy the benefits of automatic typesetting

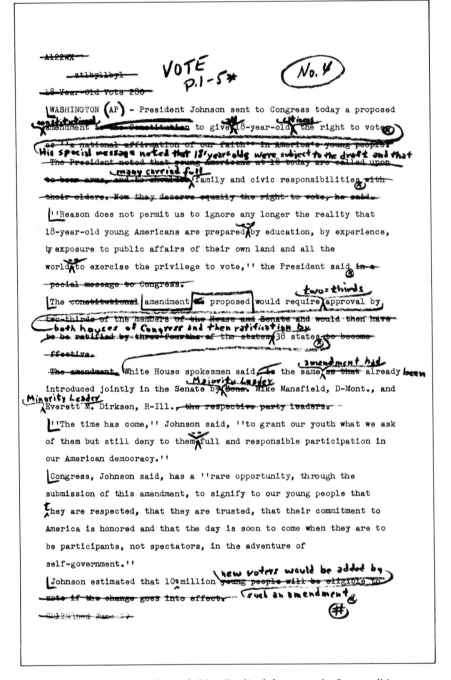

Figure 6.5. Story slugged "Vote" edited for page 1, 5-star edition.

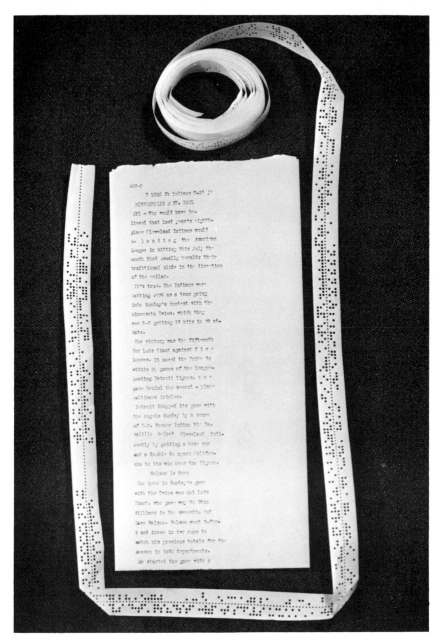

Figure 6.6. The roll of punched tape, spread around the teletyped UPI copy, will set the 82 justified lines of copy automatically when run through the Teletypesetter attachment on the Linotype machine. A big savings in the back shop, it precludes much editing of wire copy in smaller dailies.

and could wreck the entire composing-room schedule. Hence, editing the press-service copy in such newsrooms is largely confined to selecting stories and writing headlines. The editor can still trim out paragraphs, correct gross errors, and occasionally throw away the tape so he can have a story completely set from edited wire copy. But his most refined touches as an editor must be restricted to other copy.

The editing loss may not have been great on small, understaffed newspapers, where wire copy was railroaded prior to 1951 anyway. But it has dimmed the luster of some medium dailies, and tendencies to use more wire copy because it is cheaper have been detected in some dailies. One outgrowth of TTS's advent was creation of a joint AP-UPI style-book and its adoption by most dailies in the name of obvious efficiency.

However automated the transmission of news copy may become, the need for careful editing of good reporting will remain. Fundamental in the process is careful attention to language. Theodore M. Bernstein, assistant managing editor of the *New York Times*, offered excellent advice in his June 6, 1968, issue of *Winners & Sinners*:

> What language should The Times speak: stuffy and square or groovy and with it? The answer is neither. We certainly should not speak in forbidding and ponderous tones, alien to the modern world. But neither should we seize upon every latest bit of slang, every new misuse of words, every solecistic locution, and imagine that thereby we are being up to the minute and communicating better with today's restless generation. Are we really accomplishing anything if we say that "5 London Papers Up Price" (March 17) or speak of "every media" (May 16) or report that someone sought a "tax hike" (May 9) or refer to "phony" currency (April 12) or report that a party was "tossed" at Cape's Tavern in 1783 (April 6) or tell of rock music that was provided "for free" (May 6)? Are we communicating in any way better when we say that white-tie attire "isn't all that comfortable" (May 25) or "Everybody keep their fingers crossed" (May 1) or "No one need feel cheated if they see" one or another of the casts in a show (May 1)? There can be no doubt that written English is more informal now than at any time in the past and that the pace of change has quickened. When new words or new meanings of words prove needful—"in," "moonlighting," "kickback," "blast-off," "sit-in," "crackdown" and many more—the language enriches itself by welcoming them. Nor can there be any doubt that the light touch, the breezy touch, makes for interesting reading. But lightness or breeziness does not require slang, erroneous use of words or faulty grammar. The primary purpose of The Times, of course, is to inform, but a secondary, yet important, purpose is to educate. And at least part of that educational function is to hold up to those who are being educated a shining standard—in this context a shining standard of reputable English. Why not give the teachers a hand? Whatever you write, whatever you edit, keep in mind that it is going to be read by youngsters in school, youngsters who form a substantial part of the daily circulation. Dig?

FOR FURTHER STUDY

1. Minimum reference materials for any news copydesk should include an unabridged dictionary, a recent atlas, the current *World Almanac,* a city directory, the local telephone book, the state's Blue Book (and that of any neighboring state in the immediate audience or circulation territory), a large city map (posted for easy checking), and the current *Who's Who in America.* Examine news stories closely and list other references especially useful for careful editors. Large county and state maps? Other cities' telephone books? An encyclopedia?

2. Check reprint credits in a recent *Reader's Digest* and compare the original printed version with the condensation. Note how much and what was cut from the original.

3. Compare broadcast and printed versions of the same story by clipping a late-edition afternoon newspaper or early-morning edition and taking careful notes on an early-evening newscast.

4. Try writing a No. 4 *Toledo Blade* headline (see Appendix D) for the story slugged VOTE on page 152. The top two lines should count no more than 15 1/2 each, and the next two lines not more than 17 each.

5. The *New York Times*—using condensed, all-cap type—has an unusually large line count for its top-of-the-page one-column headlines. Compare its count maximum with those of other eight-column newspapers. What benefit does the *Times* reader get in return for his eyestrain?

6. Compare the news-gathering resources of newspapers and stations on which you depend. (For broadcasters, you may have to ask the station directly. Credit lines will produce a list for newspapers, and the current *Editor & Publisher Year Book* lists major services subscribed to by all daily newspapers.)

7. Compare editing of several evening or several morning newspapers—from where they place the same press-service stories to differences in length, phraseology, mechanical style.

SUGGESTED READING

BERNSTEIN, THEODORE M., *Watch Your Language,* Manhasset, N.Y.: Channel Press, 1958. [Available in Pocket Book edition.] A magnificent collection of meaningful rules on language and readability, especially for newspaper editors.

CBS News, *Television News Reporting,* New York: McGraw-Hill Book Company, 1958. The mechanics of editing and reporting blend more closely in broadcasting.

CHARNLEY, MITCHELL V., *News by Radio,* New York: The Macmillan Company, 1948. Despite its publication date, this book is still highly recommended by teachers in electronic journalism.

CROWELL, ALFRED A., *Creative News Editing*, Dubuque, Iowa: Wm. C. Brown Company Publishers, 1969. A profusely illustrated textbook with emphasis on trends for the future in newspaper editing.

GARST, ROBERT E., and BERNSTEIN, THEODORE M., *Headlines and Deadlines*, New York: Columbia University Press, 1961 (3rd ed.). [Available in paperback.] Not as comprehensive as Westley's book, mentioned below, but its recency gives it an advantage.

KALISH, STANLEY E., and EDOM, CLIFTON C., *Picture Editing*, New York: Holt, Rinehart & Winston, Inc., 1951.

Newswire Stylebook (Revised, 1968). Available from either Associated Press, 50 Rockefeller Plaza, New York, N.Y. 10020, or United Press International, 220 East 42nd Street, New York, N.Y. 10017.

RIVERS, WILLIAM C., *The Mass Media: Reporting, Writing, Editing*, New York: Harper & Row, Publishers, 1964. Newspaper, magazine, radio, and TV editing are covered—with examples—in Chapters 10, 12, 13, and 14, respectively.

WESTLEY, BRUCE, *News Editing*, Boston: Houghton Mifflin Company, 1953. Still the best how-it-should-be-done textbook on newspaper editing, despite its publication date.

World Almanac (published annually by Newspaper Enterprise Association, 230 Park Avenue, New York, N.Y. 10017. Available in both hardbound and paperback). Browsing through this volume offers an education in one kind of fact-checking editors should master.

CHAPTER 7

The Influence Function

The editor of a small daily once said he could "do more to influence local opinion" by the way he edited the news than by running editorials. That theory overlooks at least two factors. News does not break in accord with needs for thought-provoking presentations of major public problems. And good editorials can add direct punch to the indirect influence of news, however narrowly it may be edited. The editor later admitted that he neglected the influence function because his publisher disliked good—i. e., sometimes controversial—editorials. That excuse was almost, but not quite, adequate. Even namby-pamby editorials can make readers and listeners think by offering well-researched summaries of critical issues. The hodgepodge of daily news reports requires some sifting by those who watch the whole picture for the benefit of those who can watch only fragments.

The easy accessibility of Congressional Quarterly services enables any editor to provide solid editorial-page perspective on significant news. An *Editorial Research Reports* subscription provides five 550-word backgrounders every week on topics ranging from the arts to foreign affairs and four 6,000-word research pieces every month. The most overworked editor can occasionally run the 500-word digests of the latter or the backgrounders, credited to *Editorial Research Reports*. And most editorial writers can use the wealth of factual background to undergird their own expressed opinions. As of 1967, a total of 358 dailies—including America's best—were subscribers. [Weekly rates ranged from $4 for under-5,000 circulation to $45 for over-600,000.] Another 85 (plus 218 of the 358) subscribed to *Congressional Quarterly Weekly Report*, which provides detailed analyses of Congress and politics, including full texts of major statements and presidential press conferences. [Rates for that service ranged from $5 to $50 weekly, and both services were priced together at from $8 to $85.50 per week.]

Direct expression of opinion, as distinguished from attributed opinions incidental to news reports, is the second most important duty of a free press. Citizens in a democratic society need to be challenged by strong viewpoints which can jar the glut of information into more meaningful patterns. Every press unit should present its own staff opinion and provide for outsiders—experts and plain citizens, alike—to do the same. Traditionally, the print media have done a better rounded job with this than have radio and television.

THREE OPINION RESOURCES

Three opinion sources should be utilized:

1. *Local Staff.* Potentially most important of the local-staff devices is the editorial, dealt with later in the chapter. If no editorials, or only weak editorials, are offered, publishers and broadcasters can make their direct contributions by employing staff columnists or commentators. In fact, opinion offerings by individuals can add a valuable dimension to a program with effective editorials. Corporate reservations about what goes into *New York Times* editorials need not restrict, in the same degree, columnists like James Reston, C. L. Sulzberger, and Tom Wicker. Sydney J. Harris's column in the *Chicago Daily News* can have a wider range than can the anonymous offerings of editorial writers, hemmed in by committee interpretations of what the institution should say. Ideally, direct expressions of opinion should be provided by each of the more than 6,000 broadcast outlets, the more than 1,700 dailies, the hundreds of "general and farm" magazines, and the thousands of weekly newspapers. Whether the opinions are those of the publications and stations (editorials) or those of staff employees is not crucial.

What is crucial is that too much of the journalistic-opinion flow has been confined to commentators based in New York and Washington. If a staff commentator on KOTA-TV in Rapid City, South Dakota, cannot match Eric Sevareid's insights on federal-state relations, he should be able to match those of opinion leaders in Rapid City. And his views can reach larger audiences than can the nonjournalists' at regular, given times. No one on Wyoming's smallest daily knows as much about American foreign policy as a Walter Lippmann, but some staff member should know as much about it as whoever holds forth at the local coffee shops. And his printed opinion can serve as a local common denominator for wider community discussion. Controversy on national issues stirred by a local offering can outdraw equal efforts by a syndicated writer. The *Providence Journal* and *Bulletin* found that a staff writer's attacks on Vietnam-war policy produced many times the local reaction that any equally vehement syndicated offerings had. The object is to make citizens think about important issues, and local commentaries produce special psychological effects. If citizens only scoff at the "prophet without honor in his own country," that scoffing tends to move them from total apathy. And, of course, no Sevareids or Lippmanns can speak out on the purely local issues in all of America's 3,072 counties.

Editorial cartoonists (a third local-staff device) are maintained by only a minority of dailies. Publishers' penuriousness can be blamed in part, but skilled craftsmen in that medium are scarce. Senior editors can fix the efforts of fledgling writers, but editorial cartoons are stark and final as they come from the novice's pen. It is easier, cheaper, and safer to rely on the 50-odd syndicated cartoonists. That is regrettable because it restricts a peculiarly effective opinion-stimulator to too few sources. It also means that local issues in hundreds of cities with dailies cannot be touched by the editorial device with highest "readership." Although one great cartoonist predicted that television broadcasters might adapt the device, no evidence was forthcoming nearly a decade later. (Mayor Samuel W. Yorty did use them on his televised counterattacks against *Los Angeles Times* criticisms in the late 1960s.)

2. *Outside Journalists.* Syndicated and network-relayed opinion dominate American newspaper and broadcast influence efforts today. From their beginnings, radio and television have depended almost exclusively on nationally shared commentators, rather than on local performers. Two factors discourage broadcast editorials—a belief that broadcasting's "fairness image" will be injured and fears of shifting Federal Communications Commission rulings. The equal-time threat could wreak havoc with program schedules. Eight years after "outlawing" station editorials, the FCC reversed its policy in 1949, but wary broadcasters have held back. The *1969 Broadcasting Yearbook* reported that only about 11 per cent of radio and TV stations presented editorials daily. More than half the TV and FM-radio stations never editorialized. A third of the AM-radio stations presented editorials less often than weekly, and nearly one-half not at all. However, the impact of network commentators has been considerable—greater than their allotted time would suggest. Stretching from the 1930s to the present are names made great by varied mixing of news and opinion—H. V. Kaltenborn, Elmer Davis, Gabriel Heatter, Raymond Gram Swing, Fulton Lewis, Jr., Edward R. Murrow, Paul Harvey, David Brinkley, Howard K. Smith, Eric Sevareid, and others. Some have crossed the news line to the left and some to the right; some have stuck close to the news, a few have strayed far afield. Their stimulation of thinking—among those who agreed or disagreed, or who had held no views—has been as great as it would be difficult to calculate.

Syndicated newspaper columns got their modern start in the 1920s and mushroomed during the 1930s. Steady growth has made their dominance of journalistic opinion an American peculiarity. Major newspapers

Figure 7.1. One of the best balanced "influence diets" is offered by the **Los Angeles Times.** Local staff work dominates the editorial page with three editorials, Conrad's cartoon, and a foreign correspondent's backgrounder. Six letters-to-the-editor and a reprinted Herblock cartoon lend variety. (Courtesy, **Los Angeles Times**)

Figure 7.2. The "op editorial" page features work by outsiders. Three syndicated columns (Buchwald, Evans-Novak, Pearson), a special backgrounder by Isaac Don Levine, and a **Dallas Times Herald** cartoon are leavened with two of the **Los Angeles Times**'s own syndicated cartoons. (Courtesy, **Los Angeles Times**)

which do not regularly run outside political columnists (*New York Times, Chicago Tribune, Milwaukee Journal*) are exceptions. Generally, the larger the newspaper, the more syndicated columns it carries. The volume has reached such proportions that readers occasionally need special guides. For example, James Bassett, *Los Angeles Times* director of editorial pages, explained to subscribers in November, 1967, that fifteen syndicated columnists were providing an average of six to seven pieces a day—not all of which could be fitted into the space opposite the editorial page. (Columnists tend to attract followings, and irregular use can bring complaints. One Eastern newspaper, testing popularity of features, got almost as many calls on leaving out a Washington pundit as it did on omitting a comic strip. An omitted astrology column won the contest.) Bassett took the occasion to explain political balance in the syndicated offerings. Carefully noting that exact political labeling was risky, he arranged the *Los Angeles Times* stable this way:

"LIBERAL"	"MODERATE"	"CONSERVATIVE"
Drew Pearson	Joseph Alsop	William F. Buckley, Jr.
Max Lerner	Charles Bartlett	Barry Goldwater
Joseph Kraft	Boyd Lewis	Henry Hazlitt
Carl T. Rowan	Rowland Evans—	James J. Kilpatrick
Roy Wilkins	Robert D. Novak	Henry J. Taylor

These men produced from one to seven columns (500 to 1,000 words each) every week. Underlining Bassett's caution about labeling, we could add important names to each column: "liberals"—Walter Lippmann, Clayton Fritchey, Whitney Young; "moderates"—Marquis Childs, Roscoe Drummond, the syndicated *New York Times* columnists; "conservatives"—David Lawrence, Russell Kirk, Paul Harvey, Jenkin Lloyd Jones. The trend toward offering a balance of columnists has grown with the decline of newspaper competition. Significant commentary of a "neutral" type is carried to millions, coast to coast, in the humorous columns of Art Buchwald and Russell Baker.

More newspapers use syndicated editorial cartoonists than employ their own, and many of the latter supplement their own staff's work with that of others. Little effort at balancing cartoonists, as is practiced with columnists, has occurred, however. Somehow, editors reject the idea of balancing cartoons by the conservative Joseph Parrish with those of the liberal Herblock (Herbert Block), even though they are willing to offer a conservative David Lawrence and a liberal Carl T. Rowan side by side. Among widely syndicated cartoons are those of Bill Mauldin, Herblock, Paul Conrad, Pat Oliphant, Art Poinier, Dan Dowling, Don Hesse, Robert York, Hugh Haynie, and Parrish. Newspapers and magazines also pick

"We Can't Burden Our Children With Deficit Spending"

Figure 7.3. Editorial cartoons like this one by Herbert L. Block (Herblock) of the **Washington Post** have enormous impact on both hurried and more reflective readers. (From **Straight Herblock** [Simon and Schuster, 1964])

We have written a letter to your congressman about gun control.

All you have to do is sign it, and mail it.

Dear Congressman:

Please help stop the killing. Listen to the majority (85% according to a recent Gallup Poll) of your constituents - who want rigid gun control laws. Please work for legislation to:

1. restrict hand guns and ammunition to law
   enforcement and military use - and to
   private citizens who meet reasonable
   official qualifications.

2. require registration of all guns and
   ammunition sold.

3. forbid all mail order sales of guns
   and ammunition.

Nothing is more urgent. Please do something.

Sincerely,

Name _____

Address _____

WRITE YOUR CONGRESSMEN—% HOUSE OFFICE BUILDING OR SENATE OFFICE BUILDING, WASHINGTON, D.C. 20000

Figure 7.4. This "ad-itorial" was part of a campaign provided by North Advertising, Inc. of Chicago shortly after the 1968 assassination of Senator Robert F. Kennedy. Radio and television versions also were offered for small fees to corporations or media desiring to promote gun-control laws. Home-made versions of such commercials may yet broaden the voice of the people in the media. (Courtesy, North Advertising, Inc.)

up nonsyndicated cartoons, making still more names familiar. Humor without a special political slant has made Jim Berry's work popular across the land.

3. *Laymen.* With 20 per cent fewer dailies serving more than twice as many citizens as in 1910, the problem of providing adequate outlets for lay opinions has grown enormously. Efforts range from excellent on some newspapers to near zero on most broadcast units. Sins include too little attention and unfair editing practices (e. g., presenting only the worst letters on the other side). Conscientious editors of letters battle constantly against pressure groups, space-wasting by emotional cat-versus-dog proponents, faked signatures, and extremists who do not understand libel laws. Radio and television stations have toyed with man-on-the-street interviews and beepered telephone calls. Round-table and conversational shows have produced broadcasting's best success in airing lay citizens' views.

As journalism has become more sophisticated, the problems of presenting the people's opinions effectively have mounted. Both as an exercise in journalistic duty and as a salable commodity, better handling of nonjournalists' views remains a major challenge. One bright hope, the "ad-itorial," has emerged in recent years. Borrowed from political candidates, this involves purchasing space or time to present private views more impressively than media normally can permit. Amateur pundits can break out of the 300-word limits and employ pictures, tape recordings, and better positioning for their appeals. (For example, ten persons can buy a quarter page for $5 each in a small daily; two dozen can do it for $20 each in a daily of 225,000 circulation.)

EFFECTIVE OPINION WRITING

Two factors are essential to every editorial, and a third should be present in most. The three factors are:

1. *Be specific.* If this rule were observed, many editorials, mercifully, would never be printed or broadcast. An editorial should offer facts—if anything, more concrete than those in the news stories to which they relate. Generalized observations and opinions are as unimpressive as they are uninteresting. In commenting on results of the 1968 New Hampshire presidential primary, one editorial noted: "Sen. Eugene McCarthy polled a bigger vote than most people had expected." How many votes did McCarthy receive? What percentage did "most people" expect him to win? (Better still, what had the polls forecast?) The be-specific rule applies both to reviewing pertinent news-story facts and to facts dug out of files or original sources. A Midwestern editorial effectively struck down a congressman's defense of office nepotism by citing

statistics with care. The congressman had said his daughter mailed "between 2,000 and 3,000" letters congratulating new parents every month. Telephone calls to four county seats revealed an average of fewer than 1,000 births in the congressman's district over the period in question.

2. *Give the other side's best arguments.* An editorial supporting a school-bond issue gains in honesty-impact by conceding that retired property owners on fixed incomes will be hurt if voters do their duty. The concession demonstrates sincerity and deflates opposing arguments by showing clearly that the advocate sees both sides. (It also lays groundwork for another editorial topic.) Too many editorialists either ignore the other side or saddle it with "straw man" arguments easily unhorsed. Foes of loyalty oaths for teachers pretend not to see the strategy of being able to indict subversives ("who wouldn't hesitate to sign such oaths") for perjury. They thus miss a chance to influence intelligent, undecided persons, who could be impressed by their grasp of the real issues and their fairness. Foes of stricter gun-control laws should admit that such laws do provide another trap for criminals ("who would not obey the law anyway") just as concealed-weapons charges have worked that way. They and the loyalty-oath foes can then concentrate on whether the admitted advantages outweigh the price in either case.

3. *Take a forceful position.* Few issues warrant editorial comment until the commentator is in a position to give them meaning by taking sides. "This will bear watching" falls with a thud for the citizen seeking views with which he can agree or disagree, or about which he is still making up his own mind. Yet publishers and broadcasters, fearful of alienating any segment of their heterogeneous audiences, restrict a surprising number of editorial explorations to on-the-other-hand deadends. The author once sat in on a special editorial-page conference, called because a news executive feared a "bad appointment" was pending for police commissioner. A strong editorial warning the mayor away was agreed upon. It is a commentary on modern editorials that the resulting piece upset no one. The mayor made the appointment, totally unaware of any editorial disapproval.

Suppose that an editorial were to be written on the AP's proposed 18-year-old voting amendment story on page 152. Worried lest the teen-aged targets of their new circulation drive or the steady older customers might be annoyed, many an editorial staff would list points on both sides and conclude that "The idea deserves study" or "It will be interesting to watch. . . ." Aimed toward such a conclusion, the writer lacks any real inspiration either for research or literary effort. If, however, he is to support or oppose it, he faces a stimulating challenge which he can relay to his readers. The *World Almanac* will yield numbers of eligible voters and how many voted in recent elections. The 10,000,000 new eligibles would represent 9 per cent of those eligible in the election before President Johnson's plea to Congress. A proponent might cite that as a negligible addition and no threat of upheaval. An opponent might dig out statistics on the 1960 and other close elections to warn against an inexperienced "new balance of power." Further research on the average age of marriage ("to shoulder family . . . responsibilities"), voting-age limits in other countries, experiences of the four states with under-21 limits, and what high school and college teachers think would supply good material. A good opponent would recognize that drafting teen-agers who cannot vote is cited as "taxation without representation"—not the straw-man idea "If he's old enough to fight, he's old enough to vote." And a proponent should do better than dismiss the foes' concern about immaturity as "mere prejudice against the young."

THE DECLINE OF EDITORIALS

People spend less time with, and are less influenced by, editorials now than in Horace Greeley's day. More diversions exist both outside and inside the press to steal time from dutiful attention to serious political and sociological discussion. The total press, now including radio and television, devotes less to that journalistic function than did the press of Greeley's day or 50 years beyond. The Columbia Broadcasting System boasted in its 1967 annual report that five CBS-owned television stations broadcast a total of "900 management editorials and replies" during 1967 and that its seven AM-radio stations produced 800. [Compare those 3.5-per-week and 2.2-per-week figures with the number of editorials and letters ("replies") printed in the average daily newspaper.]

More important than the increased competition for attention and the decline in percentage of total press attention has been the development of "responsible" editorial writing. Gone with the welcome loss of vicious diatribes are strong, uncompromising editorials of any kind in most newspapers most of the time. The responsibility that brought sanity to editorial viewpoints has been extended to include caution against riling any important elements within the readership. Exciting writing has been left to men outside the staff, to the exposés of a Drew Pearson or the biting thrusts of a William F. Buckley, Jr. Even the choice of topics has been narrowed for safety's sake. The following example, from a Western newspaper, is all too typical:

LET'S NOT FORGET LAKE HURON

It has been a matter of some small concern to us that the name of Lake Huron does not appear oftener in the news.

We hear much of the other bodies of water in the Great Lakes chain, but seldom of this one. Lake Superior gets into the headlines because of the vast mining industries which depend upon its surface for transportation and because of the storms which sweep across it in bad weather. Lake Michigan comes often to the fore for the same reasons. Lake Erie and Lake Ontario shine by the reflected glory of Niagara Falls and come to attention through the large cities on their shores.

But Lake Huron; unless an airplane falls into it or some other such unexpected event ripples its calm expanse, it doesn't ever get much publicity. It is one of the Great Lakes and as good as any of the other four, and we should like, now and then, to see its name in the paper.

The other two editorials that day were "Kremlin's Plans Go Astray" (a safe villain to attack) and "Women Have Met Challenge Well." The examples might seem extreme, but the daily in question was winning more than its share of editorial-page prizes in regional competition at the time this appeared.

Absolute bottom has been touched by newspapers which present "canned" editorials as their own. Acting as judge in a Middle Western state contest in the 1950s, this author ran across two entries almost word-for-word the same. The topic, town beautification, was harmless. But the implications were frightening. Editors who hoodwink their readers by presenting syndicated writings as their own editorials deserve condemnation. When they submit them as contest entries, editors should have their heads—as well as their consciences—examined. (Comments along those lines led to a new judge the next year.) Agencies supplying these "editorials" mix noncontroversial topics with propaganda in behalf of vested interests. Printing these free offerings with proper credit lines would be legitimate, but neither the propagandist supplying them nor the lazy editor wants to spoil the "grass roots" impact.

United States Senator Lee Metcalf of Montana attacked this practice in a 1965 Senate speech. He charged that one agency in Portland, Oregon, supplied a dozen "editorials" weekly free to 11,000 editors. Private power companies provided the main financing, he said, and every weekly batch contained pieces praising private power or condemning public-power projects. Other interest groups, paying thousands of dollars in fees, also won periodic praise in the mimeographed offerings. Metcalf cited a School of Journalism study in Colorado showing that "one-third of the editors use Industrial News Review editorials, usually as their own, and that some editors used as many as 100 or 200 of the editorials a year." Metcalf named another agency which "for $175 will send your message to 1,199 weeklies and 150 daily newspapers." This practice infects mostly weeklies and a few small dailies. State press associations and journalism schools should move to eradicate the practice.

BRIGHTER EDITORIAL OUTLOOKS

All is far from lost in the world of editorials. Scattered across the nation are daily and weekly newspapers and magazines—and a few radio and television stations (like KDKA in Pittsburgh)—which regularly do their editorial duty. Most major dailies at least occasionally stir their readers with scorching declarations. Indeed, a trend back toward strong editorials has appeared in recent years. More editors are concluding that exciting editorials can help match the new competition, just as specialized reporting has.

An important factor in hard thinking about better editorials has been the National Conference of Editorial Writers, founded in 1947. The NCEW's "Basic Statement of Principles" (see Appendix B) and its quarterly publication, *The Masthead,* have focused attention on ideals and practical improvements, which appear to have picked up momentum in the organization's third decade. Annual NCEW conferences concentrate, as probably no other professional group's do, on critiques of members' efforts. Without imposing narrow "rules," NCEW has struck at cynicism and the ho-hum posture which have threatened the craft. In the very year of NCEW's founding, a Pulitzer Prize-winner airily dismissed questions about the morality of his having written interventionist editorials for a magazine while writing anti-interventionist pieces for a major newspaper during World War II's earliest days. He and others may still believe that editorial writers are mere hirelings, but NCEW efforts have caused editors to think about whether an editorialist should write "against his conscience." The organization has speeded up typographical improvements in editorial pages, spurred papers to get their writers out of the office more often, and encouraged use of bigger staffs. Adoption of such revolutionary breakthroughs as dissenting columns by staff writers are likelier to spread faster and farther with an active NCEW.

Meanwhile, critics have tended to underestimate the powers of the editorial columns. True, Franklin D. Roosevelt won four sweeping presidential victories against newspaper-editorial majorities that once topped three-to-one against him. True, readership studies indicate extremely low percentages even pause over the editorials. But it is also true that positive correlations between editorial stances and public-opinion shifts have been dramatically demonstrated. And the low percentage of readership includes the top percentage of opinion-guiders in most communities.

Press critics like Ben Bagdikian have observed that editorial policies in the 1960s were better tuned to the times than were the traditional isolationism and laissez-faire postures of the 1930s, 1940s, and 1950s. There has been a marked shift away from blind opposition to school levies, improved civil rights, and international cooperation.

An often overlooked power of editorials is their direct influence on government officials. *Life* magazine demonstrated that power with an editorial February 6, 1956, which was credited with leading to the release of the poet Ezra Pound two years later:

AN ARTIST CONFINED

Tokyo Rose got out of jail the other day. This American citizen, who did her considerable best to undermine American morale during World War II, has now finished her sentence as a war criminal. The Nazi storm trooper responsible for the Malmedy massacre of 1944, General Dietrich, is also out of jail, one of a growing line of commutees and parolees.

If their crimes can be atoned or forgotten in 10 years, attention is surely due the case of Ezra Pound, who has been incarcerated for the same length of time. His prison is St. Elizabeth's in Washington, the federal hospital for the insane. He is confined, with the consent of his lawyer, to avoid a treason trial for which he is mentally unfit. He is fit to work on his Chinese translations (he is one of the best translators of poetry who ever lived), to receive friends and disciples, and to reiterate the political and economic nonsense (a weird and ineffective mixture of social credit and anti-Semitism) which he broadcast for Mussolini during the war. Pound's indictment has no statute of limitations. It will never be tried (and Pound will therefore never be eligible for pardon) as long as he stays in St. Elizabeth's. There he sits, busy and batty, free alike of self-pity and remorse.

In France and Italy, where Pound lived for years, the press frequently erupts with appeals to the U. S. government to release and forgive a distinguished old man. They frequently misrepresent the case, which is technically complicated, but they are right that our government has it in its power to quash his indictment. Thereafter his insanity might be redefined (it is not dangerous) so that he could return to Europe if he wants. One Italian deputy made a telling point: "After all, if the U. S. can send us back such characters as Luciano without our asking for them, can't the U. S. also send us Ezra Pound upon our request?"

Seven years ago, before war passions had cooled, Pound was given the Bollingen poetry award. It stirred up a fuss from Congress to Bohemia. Literary men cudgeled such eternal questions as whether poets should be judged by their politics. It would be no service to Pound, or to America, to revive these arguments. If his case is to be reconsidered at all, it should be without hatred or pity, and in the light of justice in comparable cases. These range from turncoats Best and Chandler, who got life, to the repentant P. G. Wodehouse, who was not even indicted.

Our European critics use the Pound case to argue that American civilization is indifferent to its own poets and artists, or has ears only for their praise. Pound turned his back on America in 1907. He led a generation of expatriates and experimenters which, as he once confessed, "was unable to work out a code for action"; in his case fascism filled this gap. As Mark Van Doren put it, Pound "ran out of bounds in his pursuit of a society where artists might live." But meanwhile he has done more to serve the art of English poetry, to keep its practice alive and its standards high, than any living man.

Pound's room at St. Elizabeth's has been called "a closet which contains a national skeleton." There may be good arguments for keeping him there, but there are none for pretending he doesn't exist. The crimes of World War II have aged to the point of requital, parole or forgiveness.

For this reason, if no other, the arguments for quashing the indictment against Ezra Pound should be publicly considered.

—Reprinted by permission from LIFE Magazine, © 1956, Time, Inc.

The same critics who cite undeniable improvement in editorials of late are agreed on the need for much more. Cures for the dulling influence of committee-designed editorials have been suggested by the dozens. Some have called for signed or initialed editorials, to leaven the burden of institutional commitment. Others have suggested empowering individual experts to set editorial policy, basically free of staff interference, in certain designated fields. Still others have proposed use of dissenting columns by editorial writers who disagree with the newspaper's policy. The *Providence Journal* and *Bulletin* created a stir with this in 1967. "One Man's Opinion," by a single writer, was allowed to go beyond editorial policy for sixteen weeks. Although the experiment ended in sharp controversy—the column canceled and the writer moving to another newspaper—it may have pointed a way to elevate editorial-page power. The *Akron Beacon Journal* allowed an editorial writer to back Barry Goldwater for president in 1964 while it supported Lyndon B. Johnson. Sporadic clashes between staff columnists and editorials date back even further.

Provision for restoring local debate to America's editorial columns is as certain to grow in this century's last three decades as the free press is to survive.

FOR FURTHER STUDY

1. Write a letter-to-the-editor. Research both the publication to which you will send it (optimum length, format, and style) and your subject so you can make your point and back it up. Keep a copy so you can compare it with the published version if it gets in.

2. Some of the best editorials appear in general magazines like *Life* and *McCall's* and in politically oriented magazines like *New Republic* and *National Review*. Compare one or more magazine editorials with those in newspapers as to length, literary style, strength of position.

3. Compare one or two newspaper editorials on a given topic with a syndicated column or two on the same topic. (Finding them takes a bit of rummaging.) Compare their relative opinion positions and readability.

4. Sporadic surveys have indicated many readers cannot distinguish between syndicated and local columnists, or even between editorials and columns as such. What could the press do to end such confusion? Check through several newspapers to see whether any do distinguish between local-staff opinions and those they buy from outside.

5. Check the editorials in several days' newspapers to see how many take a position for or against something really controversial (not just for patriotism or against crime).

SUGGESTED READING

CATER, DOUGLASS, *The Fourth Branch of Government*, Boston: Houghton Mifflin Company, 1959. This survey of the Washington press corps includes good attention to the opinion function.

CHILDS, MARQUIS, and RESTON, JAMES B., eds., *Walter Lippmann and His Times*, New York: Harcourt, Brace & World, Inc., 1959. Essays about one of the twentieth century's most influential columnists.

Chicago Tribune, *A Century of Tribune Editorials*, Chicago: The Tribune Co., 1947. Examples of hard-hitting editorials no longer common.

Editor & Publisher, "Directory of Syndicated Newspaper Features," issued each summer as a supplement to a regular weekly issue. This lists 40 classifications of entertainment, news, and opinion features, their authors, and the 300 agencies distributing them.

HEATON, JOHN L., ed., *Cobb of the World*, New York: E. P. Dutton & Co., Inc., 1924. Frank Cobb's editorials in the *New York World*, from 1904 to 1923, are still peerless examples of the craft. Many regard Cobb as the greatest editorial writer ever.

JOHNSON, GERALD W., *The Lines Are Drawn*, Philadelphia: J. B. Lippincott Co., 1958. Reproductions of and commentaries on the Pulitzer Prize cartoons from 1922 to 1958.

KRIEGHBAUM, HILLIER, *Facts in Perspective*, Englewood Cliffs, N. J.: Prentice-Hall, Inc., 1956. A widely used textbook on opinion work in journalism.

The Masthead. Quarterly publication of the National Conference of Editorial Writers, 1725 N St., N.W., Washington, D. C. 20036.

RIVERS, WILLIAM L., *The Opinionmakers*, Boston: Beacon Press, 1965. Deals with both news and opinion dissemination from Washington.

SUNSHINE, JAMES K., " 'The Jim Brown Case,' " *The Masthead*, Fall, 1967 (Vol. 19, No. 3). Describes in detail the *Providence Journal* and *Bulletin's* adventure with a dissenting editorial writer.

VINSON, J. CHAL, *Thomas Nast: Political Cartoonist*, Athens: University of Georgia Press, 1967. Well-illustrated biographical sketch of the man who fathered modern political cartooning.

WALDROP, A. GAYLE, *Editor and Editorial Writer*, Dubuque, Iowa: Wm. C. Brown Company Publishers, 1967. Revision of a long standard textbook on the opinion function of newspapers.

CHAPTER 8

The Role of Advertising

Communist journalists sincerely believe that they work with a free press and that American journalists do not. They argue that capitalists who finance the commercial media (advertisers) control the flow of information and opinion so rigidly that truth is largely suppressed in America. Some American intellectuals agree with half their argument and denounce both their party-controlled system and America's advertiser-financed system with almost equal vigor.

Few serious observers would change the basic American system of financing its major mass media, but arguments about curbing alleged excesses have mounted in the twentieth century's second half. Advertisers are pouring nearly a billion dollars a month into newspapers, television, magazines, and radio. They provide 75 per cent of daily newspapers' revenue in exchange for 60 per cent of their space, more than half of the magazines' revenue for a like amount of their space, and all of commercial radio and television stations' revenue for somewhere between 20 and 25 per cent of air time.

Any challenge to advertising's role must face the hard problem of finding alternatives. Returning to political-party support could hardly handle today's mass circulation. Labor unions and chambers of commerce would provide poor balance even if consumers could be guaranteed one of each medium from both. Government subsidy would surely wreck the Fourth Estate role. Foundations might help, but total expenditures of the thirty-nine largest United States foundations in 1967 were something like 5 per cent of what advertisers spent on the media. Asking consumers to pay double for magazines and three to four times as much for newspapers plus $10 or so per week for radio and TV would surely end mass communications as they now function.

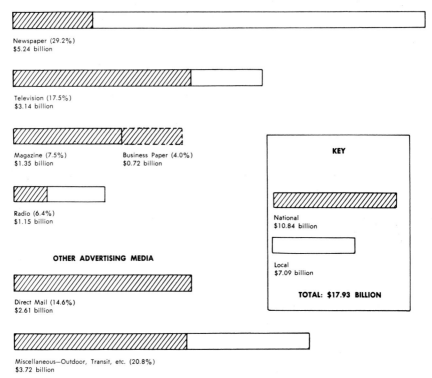

DISTRIBUTION OF ADVERTISING EXPENDITURES
(Estimates for 1968)

MAJOR JOURNALISTIC MEDIA

Newspaper (29.2%)
$5.24 billion

Television (17.5%)
$3.14 billion

Magazine (7.5%)   Business Paper (4.0%)
$1.35 billion $0.72 billion

Radio (6.4%)
$1.15 billion

OTHER ADVERTISING MEDIA

Direct Mail (14.6%)
$2.61 billion

Miscellaneous—Outdoor, Transit, etc. (20.8%)
$3.72 billion

KEY

National
$10.84 billion

Local
$7.09 billion

TOTAL: $17.93 BILLION

—Based on figures compiled under supervision of Robert J. Coen, Director
of Media Research, McCann-Erickson, Inc., and published in February, 1969,
Marketing/Communications. Used by permission.

Figure 8.1. This shows how media shared the total estimated advertising expenditures made in America during 1968. Among the four
journalistic media, radio made the biggest proportionate gain over
1967 totals; television continued to narrow the newspaper lead.

DIRECT ECONOMIC EFFECTS

Advertising-rate ranges offer some perspective on what is involved
in financing press operations. Some typical 1967 national-delivery rates
included $70,000 for a one-minute sales pitch on a televised National
Football League game; $1,000 for a 30-second spot on network radio;
$46,650 for a one-page black-and-white ad in *Reader's Digest*. (By 1970,
Digest rates were to reach $48,475 for one page black and white, and
$58,275 for one page with four colors.)

At the local level, sponsorship of a one-hour show on a single TV station cost up to $10,000; 20-second spots in the top ten markets averaged $1,180 each in prime time (7:30 to 11:00 P.M.). One-minute radio spots averaged $100 during the best time (6:00 to 9:00 A.M.) in the ten biggest markets. A one-page (tabloid-size) advertisement in the *New York Daily News* went for $4,380, and one column inch cost more than $60. The *Los Angeles Times* charged $4,800 for a page (twice tabloid size). Smaller audiences and smaller circulations cost less, of course. A small-city 500-watt radio station might sell a one-minute spot for $4, or half of that in lots of two dozen. A daily under 10,000 might sell one column inch for under a dollar and a full page for under $200.

Competition among the media and between units within each medium for advertising dollars directly affects press performance. Television's concentration on prime-time entertainment, for example, can be attributed to advertisers' attitudes. Most advertisers shy away from sponsoring controversial programs in the first place, and in the second place they want the top ratings that tend to follow quiz games and situation comedies. So long as broadcasters permit sponsors to program choice hours by-the-numbers, viewers will be treated like spoiled children, fed mainly the frothy sweets that first please their undeveloped palates.

The older and wiser print media have kept better control of their formats. Editors generally decide what goes up front and whether the sports department shall use three pages or six in Section A or Section C. Still, advertisers play important roles in the shaping of newspapers and magazines. They make magazines fat before Christmas and thin after, and evening-paper news holes bigger on Thursday than on Saturday. Advertisers help decide which publications can live. An excellent newspaper like the *New York Herald Tribune* died partly because many advertisers preferred to put all their money into New York's other superior morning paper, the *Times*, which had twice as much circulation. (An ivory-tower observer cannot help wondering whether some ads, at one-third less cost, in the thinner *Herald Tribune* might not have reached its smaller circulation with enough greater impact to compensate for that circulation difference.) The numbers-game madness has hit magazines even harder. Television's voracious, new appetite for ad revenues chewed up the old rules during the 1950s, and magazines high on the circulation lists toppled—*Collier's, American, Woman's Home Companion, Today's Woman, Coronet, Liberty*. The new rules dictate that a circulation near 7,000,000—ninth in the nation—means nothing if another magazine like yours is ahead, which is why the *Saturday Evening Post* died in 1969.

Since 1914, the Audit Bureau of Circulations has provided means of checking real circulations against the claims of publishers. In recent decades refined measurements of total-audience profiles—by age groups, sex, income levels, spending patterns—have been developed to give advertisers better pictures of what they are buying. Radio and television have developed rougher estimates through organizations like the A. C. Nielsen Co. Media and media buyers employ polling experts like Lou Harris, George Gallup, and Roper Associates to measure audiences and audience potentials.

An estimated 250,000 persons work full time in advertising—in more than 500 agencies, on the staffs of manufacturers and retailers, and on the media. Advertising men like to say that a million jobs depend on advertising.

In a copyrighted article, February 26, 1968, *Advertising Age* listed 396 advertising agencies which handled $1,000,000 or more in billings for 1967. Led by J. Walter Thompson, at $590,600,000, the list included twenty-one agencies whose world billings exceeded $100,000,000 each. Nine agencies employed more than a thousand persons, Thompson alone listing 2,642. [Figures cited by permission, © 1968, Advertising Publications, Inc.]

Among complex advertising-economic factors affecting the press are third-class mailing rates and regulations. If "junk mail" provides an apparently cheap and handy advertising medium, it can seriously endanger the budget of a struggling newspaper by taking away revenues essential to finance news coverage.

INDIRECT INFLUENCE ON PRESS

Many press critics contend that publications tend to favor moderate-conservative politics in order to please advertisers. The truth is that publishers are businessmen themselves and tend, therefore, to favor conservatism on principle, rather than to curry favor with clients. An equally important truth is that advertisers spend their dollars to reach customers rather than to support editorial policies with which they agree. Two examples illustrate the point. In the early 1940s, Marshall Field's liberal *Chicago Sun* challenged the conservative *Chicago Tribune's* dominance of the morning field in a multimillion-dollar battle of epic proportions. While the political and economic battle raged, Field's giant department store continued to advertise heavily in the *Tribune* for sound business reasons. In 1952, when businessmen clearly favored Republican Dwight D. Eisenhower for president, the *Milwaukee Journal* endorsed Democrat Adlai E. Stevenson. Despite that "anti-business" endorsement and the *Journal's* then-dangerous opposition to Wisconsin's Red-baiting Senator Joseph R. McCarthy, the *Journal* led the nation in newspaper advertising linage. Advertisers could have turned to Hearst's *Milwaukee Sentinel,* which backed Eisenhower and lauded McCarthy, but they did not because the *Journal* was out-circulating the *Sentinel,* 334,000 to 175,000.

Charges of favoring advertisers by suppressing unfavorable stories and playing up favorable ones have more substance, though less than is widely believed. Consumer magazines almost completely blacked out coverage of a "Truth-in-Packaging" bill before Congress in the 1960s, undoubtedly because they feared advertiser displeasure. Most major media maintained discreet silence on automobile-design safety until Ralph Nader's book *Unsafe at Any Speed* created a national sensation that led to congressional hearings. The business-office must ("BOM")—whereby news editors are ordered to give priority to stories promised by advertising salesmen—remains as a disgraceful practice among weaker elements of all four media. Editorial commentary too often steers clear of touchy topics like Sunday-closing laws for fear of offending either Sunday-closed downtown merchants or retailers with suburban outlets. Evidence of "blackmail" advertising policies still crops up occasionally—both in the form of media persecuting nonadvertisers and in the form of advertisers canceling contracts.

Ethical improvement, stronger news media, and enlightened businessmen have combined to reduce advertiser interference with editorial honesty and courage. Competition between the print and electronic media has made suppression less feasible than it was in earlier times. An epidemic threatening a major city on the eve of an expensive "world exposition" could hardly be kept out of all news outlets as such a case allegedly was several decades ago. And the temptation toward such irresponsibility has waned among both journalists and their advertising clients. Sophisticated advertisers recognize increasingly that quality media as vehicles for their messages are more important than stuffing news reports with uninteresting puffs or destroying trust in the media. Influence by advertisers—often only inferred by timid broadcasting and publishing executives—remains a problem, but not an overwhelming one.

ADVERTISING'S OTHER "THREATS"

Although our main concern is with advertising's role in financing the media and the possible implications of that support, other alleged results of journalism's fourth function deserve brief attention. Moves to curb advertising can involve direct threats against press freedom and indirect threats against its economic underpinnings. A partial catalogue of complaints against advertising as it is practiced in America would include:

1. *Offensiveness.* It intrudes by interrupting radio and television programs (every six minutes or less on network TV), cluttering newspaper and magazine pages, and blocking motorists' views of the countryside. Deodorant and mouthwash ads are repulsively numerous. Moron-level sales pitches insult listeners' intelligence. Defenders, including laymen, point to a minority of impressively pleasant ads—offering genuine humor, creative artistry, and educational benefit. They argue that the annoyance in the other cases is a bargain to pay for columns of information and entertainment and 45 to 48 minutes an hour of broadcasting services.

2. *Dishonesty.* People of modest means and intelligence are hoodwinked by "debt-consolidation" loans, "genuine simulated diamonds," and "faster-acting" pills. Everyone is cheated by Sunday-magazine advertisements of half-price carpeting that has been "sold out" when the store opens Monday morning. Actually, real fraud in advertising claims has been nearly eradicated by agencies ranging from Better Business Bureaus to the Federal Trade Commission, and self-policing by advertisers and media operators, who value their long-range powers to sell above any chance to reap quick profits. Hard-headed business attitudes, rather than idealism, have given modern advertising more honesty than is credited to it. Nor are the American masses as gullible about believing extreme advertising claims as critics often assume.

3. *Promoting unwise spending.* High-powered campaigns inspire people without adequate insurance to buy a color-TV set or cause them to choose a new car instead of college for a son. Advertisers reply that such choices are influenced by many factors, of which their appeals are only a part. In a burgeoning economy, people have to keep reaching beyond their old limits to provide sales which in turn create new jobs and eventually enable more people to afford comforts which once were "unwise" luxuries.

4. *Increasing prices.* If General Motors had saved the $200,000,000-plus it spent on advertising in 1967, it could have passed along the savings by cutting prices. This, of course, overlooks the principle of mass production and its lowering of per-unit cost. Competitive advertising also focuses attention on prices, helping inspire sellers to cut their profit margin to remain competitive. Defenders would also argue that consumers get back most of what they pay for advertising through mass-media information and entertainment financed by advertising expenditures.

5. *Aggravation of inferiority feelings.* Sociologists and psychologists have contended that advertising campaigns have added to the anxieties

Steve says advertising raises prices.

But how come that color TV set his fraternity just bought costs $300 less than it used to?

Ten years ago, a typical 21-inch color TV set sold for $700. Today, you can get a comparable set for under $400. With a lot of improvements, to boot. Like automatic fine tuning. And less need for servicing.

What brought the price down so dramatically? Many millions of dollars of advertising, mainly.

Weren't there a lot of technological improvements, too? Yes. But they might have actually *added* to the price—without the vast increase in sales, and volume production, made possible by this advertising.

Maybe you, like Steve, think advertising raises prices, favors big outfits, helps keep useless products on the market. But actual cases prove just the opposite. Advertising lowers prices (like color TV.) Encourages competition. Promotes new ideas. (Contac, for instance.) Helps the imaginative little guy catch up (like Diet Rite Cola, who beat the big cola companies with a good product ...and advertising.)

Interested? Write us. We'll gladly send you more facts about advertising. You'll find they speak for themselves.

In the meantime, keep an open mind.

Figure 8.2. The above is from a series aimed at college students in 1968-69 to rebut some criticisms against advertising. Others in the series, by Compton Advertising of New York, pointed to small-company successes through advertising new-idea products and the effectiveness of public-service campaigns like that of "Smokey the Bear" to reduce forest fires. (Courtesy, Compton Advertising, Inc.)

of people suffering skin problems, obesity, and other minor afflictions, real or imagined. The problem of "keeping up with the Joneses" is magnified by hundreds of advertisements daily. Some critics have even cited television's pictures of affluent living as a root cause in the ghetto riots. The truth is that mass communication in toto, not just advertising, has sparked waves of rising expectations among those who feel inferior. Certainly, it would be difficult to prove that someone driven to self-destruction over skin problems was more the victim of cure-all ads than such factors as cruel peers and family weaknesses.

6. *Helping the rich get richer.* Established concerns can use multi-million-dollar ad campaigns to snow under any newcomers. The answer to this is that a better product, or one with attractive features, can challenge old lines only with advertising. Modest advertising of a better-appealing product can win a place for it against established sellers with enormous ad campaigns. American Motors, under George Romney in the 1950s, sold small Ramblers like hotcakes with an advertising budget only a fraction as large as those of the Big Three, who pushed big cars. Those who attribute unassailable power to advertising should remember the Hershey Chocolate Corporation's dominance without advertising.

Critics have a curious way of dismissing advertising's sales power ("adds to cost") and then ascribing to it powers it does not have ("blocking markets to lesser rivals").

However much Americans might wish to be rescued from advertising's annoyances, they should weigh carefully the dangers of interference against the benefits sought. Banning cigarette advertising from television, for example, might lessen that bad habit's appeal to the young (though England's early experience failed to yield that goal). But in the absence of absolute scientific proof of its threats to health—not just well-informed opinions—might such an action be a precedent for banning ads about other controversial products? Perhaps dairy products' links with too much cholesterol would call for further censorship, just as proponents of banning cigarette ads point to the precedent of no broadcast liquor ads. And if this journalistic function can be "cleaned up to protect gullible citizens," why not have a go at news, commentary, and entertainment?

Gerald W. Johnson, former *Baltimore Sun* editorial writer, gave a good, balanced defense of American advertising in a William Maxwell lecture at Ohio State University in 1957. Declaring that progress toward monopoly in the press appeared inevitable, Johnson said monopoly's "evils are not inevitable." This prominent liberal then used advertising as the model to be followed:

> It seems to me that the American press has a wide-open door behind it through which it can escape from the worst effects of monopoly. That

door is nothing more mysterious than a study of the real nature and effects of its own advertising columns. Coming from me, an admission that anything is to be gained from serious study of advertising means something, for I have spent my life working in the editorial end of journalism, and you know what the editorial end usually thinks of the advertising end.

Nevertheless, I do not share the sorrow of those sociologists who are constantly lamenting the debauchery of the American mind bemused, benumbed, and betrayed by constant exposure to the open and aboveboard propaganda in advertising. I do not quarrel with what they say about advertising. A great deal of it is lying and exceedingly clever lying at that. It has to be clever, for there are laws against the coarser grades. Of the three ordinary kinds, the government flatly forbids lies and damned lies, and looks with a fishy eye on statistics, so the really good copy writer soars into higher levels of mendacity, making his appeal to subtle psychological weaknesses.

But never mind that. Look instead at the visible, tangible results, namely the goods on the shelves of American retail stores. There is little doubt that their general level of excellence is the highest in the world. So are the prices, but so is the income of the purchaser. Put it this way: compare an American who makes a fair living but is not rich, with his opposite number anywhere else. I submit that what the wife of an American automobile mechanic, for instance, takes home in her shopping bag after a visit to the supermarket is, on the whole, better than what the wife of an automobile mechanic takes home in any other country. Perhaps the superiority of one soap over another is a figment of the copy writer's imagination; but travelers agree that *any* American soap is distinctly better than any soap offered elsewhere at an equivalent price.

Yet the learned doctors are offended because, they say, Americans are told more lies about the virtues of competing brands of soap than any other people are told. It may be so, but that is the view of the learned, and the fact remains that the soap is good, which is what impresses me, and impresses the great mass of Americans. In other words, the egghead sees the lies, but the squarehead sees the soap, and whereas one laments the other is content.

One very eminent egghead understood this principle. In the days when our troubles with our southern neighbors were one of our chief worries, Woodrow Wilson said that he got at the truth about Mexico by "balancing lies." I am sure that the American consumer gets at the truth about economic goods through a similar procedure. The lies told about one soap are balanced by counter-lies told about another; and so with cigarettes, automobiles, washing machines and all the other gadgetry magnificently touted in the advertising columns. The upshot is to make the American consumer not the worst swindled but the most discriminating purchaser in the world. Swindled he is, without doubt; but the process is that of making him desire things he does not need, not that of making him buy shoddy goods.

Yet it is precisely in the field of advertising that all ideas are given completely free play. Far from looking at novelty with suspicion, advertising regards it as the pearl beyond price, and the man who can think ahead of the crowd, instead of being burned at the stake, is given a private office with a carpet by Bigelow on the floor.

James Madison believed that this principle applies to political ideas as aptly as it does to the economic market. Read Essay Number 10 in *The Federalist*. Justice Holmes believed it. Read his famous dissent in the Abrams case. Thomas Jefferson believed it. Read his First Inaugural. All the great champions of freedom of the mind, from John Milton to Adlai Stevenson, have believed it.

The promise in our present situation, the bow in the cloud, so to speak, is that the wisest men among American newspaper publishers also believe it, and that the majority of all publishers may come to believe it as firmly as J. S. Mill and Lord Acton did. Just as out of the fury of contending vendors' claims we have emerged with the best market in the world, so out of the fury of contending thinkers' claims we may reasonably hope to emerge with a larger share of truth than we could obtain by any other method.

—Reprinted by permission.

FOR FURTHER STUDY

1. Check through newspapers and/or magazines for examples that *might* reflect advertiser influence—e. g., a long, dull story about the "grand opening" of some store in the news columns and a full-page advertisement farther back. Watch also for the contrary—e. g., the story of a plane crash in a publication carrying advertising from the airline involved. Such simple observations prove little, of course, but they may sharpen your eye for critical reading.

2. What complaints—of your own, or by others—can you add to the list on pages 178 and 180? What defenses?

3. Plan a hypothetical (or real) advertisment to sell some item or service, or to promote an open club party, or to present a political opinion. Check relative costs in more than one medium and try to assess which would best reach the audience you want.

4. Weekend specials at food stores are best handled in newspaper advertising. Make a list of categories most effectively handled in each medium.

5. For class study, Daniel Starch and Staff (Mamaroneck, New York 10544) provides detailed readership studies of advertising in selected issues of certain magazines. If you can arrange to receive one (early September or early January), try to guess which ads will score best when you purchase the magazine; then compare your views with the Starch reports, which usually follow the publication date by six weeks.

SUGGESTED READING

Advertising Age (740 Rush Street, Chicago, Illinois 60611). This weekly provides the most important coverage of the advertising business.

BURTON, PHILIP WARD, and KREER, BOWMAN, *Advertising Copywriting*, New York: McGraw-Hill Book Company, 1952. How to write effective advertising.

DUNN, S. WATSON, *Advertising: Its Role in Marketing*, New York: Holt, Rinehart and Winston, Inc., 1969 (2nd ed.). A good, recent mixture of how it is done and trends in advertising attitudes.

Freedom of Information in the Market Place, Columbia, Mo.: Freedom of Information Center, 1967. An excellent collection of strong attacks on, and defenses of, American advertising-marketing practices. [Paperbound.]

KLEPPNER, OTTO, *Advertising Procedure*, Englewood Cliffs, N. J.: Prentice-Hall, Inc., 1950 (4th ed.). Although somewhat dated, this remains a widely favored basic textbook on overall advertising.

Marketing/Communications (501 Madison Avenue, New York, N.Y. 10022). This replacement of *Printer's Ink* is an important advertising periodical.

MAYER, MARTIN, *Madison Avenue, U.S.A.*, New York: Harper & Row, Publishers, 1958. [Available from Pocket Books.] An unusually balanced look at advertising's role in America.

OGILVY, DAVID, *Confessions of an Advertising Man*, New York: Atheneum, 1963. From inside one of the top-10 agencies, this offers an interesting account of the business.

PACKARD, VANCE, *The Hidden Persuaders*, New York: David McKay Co., Inc., 1957. [Available from Pocket Books.] A long-time best-selling attack on American advertising, especially its use of motivational research.

SANDAGE, CHARLES, and FRYBURGER, VERNON, *Advertising Theory and Practice*, Homewood, Ill.: Richard D. Irwin, 1963. Considered an excellent textbook.

Standard Rate & Data Service (5201 Old Orchard Road, Skokie, Illinois 60076) publishes monthly detailed statistics on ad rates and audience profiles of newspapers, magazines, and radio and TV stations. (A borrowed look at agency copies is students' best approach to this expensive source.)

WEIR, WALTER, *Truth in Advertising and Other Heresies*, New York: McGraw-Hill Book Company, 1963. An expert practitioner calls this "essential to anyone serious about advertising."

CHAPTER 9

The Role
of Public Relations

Modern public relations ranks among the twentieth century's most controversial journalistic developments. Opinions range from highly laudatory to totally damnatory. The former include views of public relations as institutional adoption of the golden rule and getting credit for it. The latter include views like that expressed by Malcolm Muggeridge in a 1961 letter to the *London Times*, recommending that public-relations men be put "under statutory obligation to identify themselves by means of a badge or tie, or, better still, of a clapper or bell such as lepers were forced to use in the Middle Ages."

Muggeridge's facetious suggestion carried a backhanded compliment to the practitioners' effectiveness. As the world has shrunk and public opinion's importance has grown, the need for better communication between all institutions and their publics has skyrocketed. Reasonable critics who understand modern mass communications recognize values in organized public-relations programs. And reasonable defenders admit shortcomings exist in this comparatively new field.

Public relations—good, bad, or indifferent—has existed since man began communicating, of course. Scholars in the field have traced important aspects of modern programs through the centuries. Its formal growth strongly parallels that of government by the people and the spread of literacy. It has been adopted, naturally, by those who would take or keep government away from the people. Truly sophisticated public relations belongs to this century. Ivy Lee, "the father of public relations," and a few others began revolutionizing public relations in the early 1900s. The idea of helping newsmen get to bad news about one's employer, for example, is usually traced to Lee's pioneer efforts with a railroad in 1906. Lee reversed the old cover-up policy and helped reporters reach the scene of a bad accident. It was in that decade that public-relations executives first reached the policy-making level of major corporations—where they could urge adoption of practices in the public interest with a view to winning public favor. It was a significant departure from the attitude reflected in William H. Vanderbilt's legendary reply to a reporter two decades earlier: "The public be damned."

The fabulous success of George Creel's Committee on Public Information in rallying American support for World War I inspired wider adoption of public-relations operations in industry, government, and nonprofit groups. Elmer Davis's Office of War Information in World War II enlarged on and refined the propaganda techniques of a quarter century earlier, helping inspire still further growth in the field.

Meanwhile, expert practitioners were developing improved, many-faceted programs—going far beyond the old press-agentry or mere publicity. Elaborate corporate subdivisions work on both internal and external public relations. Employees, shareholders, community neighbors, customers, and government officials receive special attention. Today, good public-relations programs concern everything from plant or office appearance to basic policy. They involve speech-writing, institutional advertising, production of internal house organs (sometimes separate ones for management and lower-ranking personnel) and external house organs, and legislative lobbying. Our main concern is with press relations, but many of the other activities affect the flow of news and opinion at least indirectly.

Relations between newsmen and public-relations specialists are a curious mixture of animosities and friendly cooperation. The action of Sigma Delta Chi, professional journalistic fraternity, in banning further memberships for men in public relations early in the 1950s reflects the former. The fact that so many ex-newsmen dominate public relations helps account for the latter. (*PR Reporter* found that more than a third of those listed in *Who's Who in Public Relations* in 1965 had started in news work.) An examination of the faults and virtues of modern public relations in terms of its effects on the flow of information and opinion may provide more answers.

THREATS OF PUBLIC RELATIONS

1. *Distortion*. Two basic techniques have been employed to influence news and opinion in the press. One involves supplying the media with conveniently prepared materials—professionally written stories, glossy pictures or mats, tape recordings, and so forth—or making it easy for the media to get the news, especially what the organization wants them to have. The other involves carefully nurturing relations with

reporters and editors so that they will trust the public-relations source and perhaps even want to repay favors.

Modern practitioners, many of them ex-newsmen, know how to mix some negative elements with an emphasis on the positive for stories that appear to satisfy the unbiased-news needs of the media. This has made them potentially more dangerous than the old-line press agents, whose crude techniques were obvious to cub reporters. Cleverly staged events —some of them undeniably newsworthy—can create a falsely favorable image against the day when public judgment might be tested.

Let us examine a relatively harmless example of making "bad news" look better than it is. (Note the italicized portions in this 1964 college press release):

> A tuition increase of $50, *spread over the three-term year,* has been announced by [the college] for the 1964-65 academic year.
>
> The tuition increase will amount to $20 more in the first term *but only* $15 more in each of the other two terms.
>
> In addition, [the college] announced an increase of $30 for room and $30 for board—each at the rate of $10 per term. The increases were approved . . . and were made public *only after* parents had been notified.
>
> This brings to $2210 the total cost for tuition, room and board at [the college]—*still below most schools* with which [the college] is often compared. . . .
>
> Increases were made *necessary* with approval of a budget some $462,500 higher than the 1963-64 budget. . . .
>
> In his letter of notification to parents, [the college president] *pointed out* that "This budget has been developed with great care to provide the best possible educational program and supporting services at the least possible cost."
>
> . . .

One press association wisely put the tuition and room-and-board increases into one paragraph and reported simple facts. The other, however, sloppily left it as it was, which resulted in many papers' cutting after two paragraphs, thus omitting $60 of the $110 increase. One daily used the release verbatim and another eliminated the "but only" in paragraph 2 and presented the remaining unattributed opinions as facts. (The president could not "point out" what is clearly an opinion. The fourth paragraph's assertion should have been checked, or at least attributed to the college.)

The image-building process is so powerful that one football player won All-America honors after a season spent on the bench with injuries; the preseason buildup carried him through. A novel of recent times told, with less than science-fiction exaggeration, of a buffoon elevated to international eminence by clever speech-writers and publicists. The frightening climax was reached when the public-relations hero realized he had created a Frankenstein's monster, who was about to get a critical government appointment. To his horror, he learned that both the public and the buffoon believed in the buffoon's greatness.

It was charged, in hearings before the U. S. Senate's Foreign Relations Committee in 1963, that one agency in New York had gilded the images of Nationalist China, South Africa, and other foreign governments through distribution of subsidized news articles and film documentaries to news media and commercial theaters. Several editors were given free vacation trips to Mexico, one of the clients. The agency insisted that it was promoting only tourism, not political favoritism, and that it had labeled all of its releases so that the news media and theaters could have identified them to their customers.

The editor of a letters column called a nearby race track to check on some allegations made by a complaining reader. He was invited to spend a day at the track. Wined and dined in the inner sanctum, he forgot about the complaining letter. When newspapers are shut down by labor-management disputes many reporters and minor editors are grateful for temporary public-relations jobs, and that gratitude can carry over to critical news developments later on. Norman Isaacs, executive editor of the *Louisville Courier-Journal* and *Times,* has been a leading newspaper critic of newsmen's accepting gifts and expensive favors from public-relations officials.

His criticism puts the burden of that particular "p. r. threat" on news media, rather than on the givers. This suggests that other facets depend upon newspapers, magazines, and broadcast outlets. In truth, neither newsmen nor public-relations officials can afford to practice outright deception on any significant scale. On balance, public relations has been aimed at adjusting focus in the news, and competent newsmen rarely succumb either to raw propagandizing or to "bribes." Much of what is charged to public-relations trickery or blandishments, in the way of favoring certain elements in society, probably belongs to prejudices that precede public-relations work. As in the case of advertising influence, publisher and broadcaster opinions form the critical determinant.

An example of how this works is afforded by hundreds of small-town dailies and weeklies, which present "canned editorials" as their own. Robert U. Brown, publisher of *Editor & Publisher,* has urged state press associations to condemn the practice of printing these free editorials without identifying the sources. The editors are not fooled by this questionable practice, but their readers are.

2. *Cluttering the news.* In the summer of 1968, United Press International Editor Roger Tatarian reported that UPI's foreign desk had received several newspaper requests for coverage of a clothing-designers'

convention in Stockholm, Sweden. Investigation revealed that a public-relations man had prevailed upon a friend to have editors request such coverage. This ridiculous request to burden the wires with copy of limited interest is but one example of a less recognized "p. r. threat." UPI blocked that one, but many less-involved efforts to crowd limited space and time for news succeed.

The public-relations director for a lodge boasted in 1968 that his work had filled 9,000 column inches in San Francisco Bay-area newspapers alone during a single convention. A leading professor in the field of public relations has estimated that more than one-third of the nation's news columns are filled with press releases. A discouraging proportion of that displaces more interesting and more significant material. In view of the tremendous news flow, how does trivia beat out solid news?

Some of it is "sacred cow" matter, e. g., "news" about a college which happens to be the publisher's alma mater or one where he is a trustee. Some gets in because reporters or editors want to do some publicist a favor. Much gets in because it comes in free (whereas other news-gathering costs money), and it is often conveniently packaged. A small-town editor finds it easier and cheaper to cast the mat of a Cypress Gardens bathing beauty than to hire a photographer to get a local picture and then pay for an engraving. The advent of the Teletypesetter has enabled publicists to provide newspapers with stories that can be set into type automatically. (Temptation to edit out puffs is reduced to near zero.) Tape recorders have provided similar avenues for seekers of broadcast-news time.

Some of the dullest space-wasters get in because of the editor's sense of duty. A long, pointless interview with the United Appeals drive chairman—arranged by the public relations director—may eat up 20 per cent of a televised newscast's hard-news time because a worthy cause needs a boost. The business-page editor of an Eastern metropolitan daily once claimed more column inches and stories about industry promotions and business activity for his department than could his counterparts on papers of similar size. "The only trouble," he confessed, "is that nobody reads it."

This cluttering threat is significant because its lack of appeal threatens overall attention to the news and because it crowds out news important to the public.

3. *Helps the powerful.* Like massive advertising, it is charged, modern public relations provides another device for overwhelming new or weaker challengers for public attention and approval. The following skeleton example of an underdog candidate's press release illustrates the contention:

[The candidate's name], [his party] candidate for Congress in the
17th District, which includes, Knox, Licking, Ashland, Richland, Holmes,
Coshocton and Delaware Counties, today called on his [other party]
opponent to repudiate the [other party's] Platform. . . .

The release was a carbon copy on flimsy paper. Incredibly badly written,
it overlooked every news-writing rule and any attention to such editorial
niceties as proper margins, room at the top for a story slug or headline,
dateline, or where the editor could check for facts. His releases were
ignored. By contrast, his incumbent foe won columns of space with professionally polished news releases. The argument is that the incumbent
from the stronger party could avail himself of skillful public-relations
help and the challenger could not.

The charge is applied to big business, big labor, and big government.
Privately owned public utilities, it is argued, can overwhelm critics with
sustained public-relations campaigns, which their foes cannot match.
Enemies of right-to-work laws, seeking repeal of Section 14b of the Taft-
Hartley Act, have contended that nationwide public-relations campaigns
to keep Section 14b have been too well financed to allow for development of counteropinion. The same charge was made for years against
the American Medical Association's massive resistance to "socialized
medicine" and Medicare. Equipped with reputedly the biggest public
relations division of its kind, the AMA hired expert public-relations counsel outside to help fight the Truman, Kennedy, and Johnson administrations' pressure for federal health insurance. Defenders of public relations
point to the fact that Medicare was enacted despite the "p. r. threat";
critics argue that it was needlessly delayed. Defenders also note that
right-to-work laws cover only a minority of Americans, detracting from
the evil-power charge.

Actually, both sides in most contests for public support have access
to expert public-relations help. The federal government was spending
$400,000,000 a year by 1968 on public relations, according to one press
association's estimate. *PR Reporter,* in 1965, estimated American and
Canadian totals, private and public, at one and one-quarter billion dollars. Other estimates, three years later, put the total at two billion dollars.
The 1960 census listed 35,000 persons earning their living at public relations. *PR Reporter* estimated 57,000 in the United States and Canada
by 1965. Estimates in 1968 put the figure as high as 110,000.

Public relations is big business. *PR Reporter* found in 1963 that
nearly a hundred corporations paid their public relations directors more
than $30,000 a year, that 175 public-relations counseling firms had chief
officers in the same range, that 300 corporations budgeted more than
$1,000,000 for public relations annually. More than 1,000 public-relations

counseling firms supply special services to all kinds of endeavors concerned with public opinion.

But public relations, like advertising, is not a magic enterprise. A lone Ralph Nader with one powerful book like *Unsafe at Any Speed* can shake the image of automobile manufacturers who have invested millions in public relations. The late Rachel Carson's *Silent Spring* hit the mass media and public opinion with a force that more than matched years of work by public-relations experts employed by both the federal government and private manufacturers of insecticides.

VIRTUES OF PUBLIC RELATIONS

1. *Open news flow.* Early evening editions of newspapers on November 13, 1965, carried headlines like this: "Cruise Ship Sinks, All Believed Saved." This was over a story about the tragic sinking of the Yarmouth Castle, en route to the Bahama Islands from Miami. Actually, 89 persons had been killed in the fiery disaster, as newscasts and Sunday morning newspapers later revealed. Fire had been reported at 2 A.M., and the ship had gone down at 6:30 A.M. A total of 480 out of a reported

Figure 9.1. Flanked by Executive Vice-Presidents James J. Cassidy (left) and William A. Durbin, Hill and Knowlton President Richard W. Darrow (second from left) and Board Chairman Bert C. Goss (right) review a campaign for a public relations client after weeks of research.

545 passengers and crew members had been picked up by other ships, and an advertising man for the cruise lines had said the firm's information was that no one had been lost.

That kind of public-relations faux pas is almost extinct. Too much time had elapsed to "advertise" such a false hope. One contribution made by ex-newsmen like Ivy Lee, who pioneered twentieth-century public relations, was insistence on elemental honesty. Trying to hold back bad news often makes it worse later, they knew. They recognized that rumors could be worse than the facts, that raising false hopes about victims intensified later bitterness, and that trust—by newsmen and the interested public—is destroyed by falsity that can buy only a bit of valueless time.

Now, public-relations machinery often speeds transmission of bad news. A leading national distributor of dairy products took the initiative in warning the public, through the mass media, of a poisonous batch of cheese while working to get that cheese off grocers' shelves. After a murder occurred on a Midwest campus, the college news-bureau chief worked overtime to supply embarrassing facts and background details to major newspapers and press associations faster than most could other-

Figure 9.2. As in all communications, public relations has turned increasingly toward specialization. Here three Hill and Knowlton financial specialists gather by the teletype to discuss a government economic-policy announcement's possible impact on various clients. (Photograph by Burk Uzzle, © 1968, Magnum Photos)

wise have obtained them. When a reporter from a New York tabloid arrived, panicked administrators wanted to discourage her digging for feature angles. Instead, the news-bureau man provided transportation, arranged interviews, and gave her access to his files. He reasoned, and correctly, that her stories would be less damaging with facts than if she had to rely on rumors.

Such cooperation between reporters and employees of interested parties does influence the final shape of the news in ways sometimes subtle and sometimes worse. But the system sets the stage for better news coverage than existed when all agencies followed the no-news-is-good-news policy whenever things went wrong. Only alert reporters and editors, who can temper their gratitude with reasonable skepticism, can provide protection against fooling the public.

2. *Broader news coverage.* Editors complain justifiably about thousands of publicity releases flowing into their offices. Still, that stream provides an extra supply of tips on news which can be valuable. A speaker at a small-college conference may offer a profound idea; with no reporters covering, the campus news bureau may provide the only chance for wider dissemination of something significant.

Increasingly complex human undertakings have challenged the talents of reporters to understand so that they can relay news to the public. Even science writers need guidance from someone inside the aerospace industry, who has access to researchers and can help translate significant developments into understandable news reports. Organizations involved in both physical and social sciences need inside communicators to relay their stories to the public through the media. The public would remain far less informed if it were not for wide adoption of public relations as an integral part of both private and public organizations.

A special aspect in this broadening has been greater emphasis on the positive. This has been overdone, as we noted in connection with cluttering the news. Yet, any program designed to bring out more of the often hidden bits of good news that are interesting and significant must be counted as a gain. Americans had a need and a right to know when one Peace Corps worker goofed by writing an insulting postcard about the country where she worked. They also had a need and a right to know of some dramatic Peace Corps achievements, and the existence of public relations helped insure that they would hear of those. College towns almost always hear about students who get into trouble, because reporters cover the police stations. They hear about students' tutoring disadvantaged children and entertaining at veterans' hospitals, partly because public relations is operative.

3. *Improved corporate behavior.* A significant minority of corporations involve their public-relations vice-presidents in policy decisions.

However base some might consider such a profit-oriented motivation, the fact remains that an agency seeking to do something good and get credit for it is better than the old public-be-damned operation.

If the public-relations division sells a company on moving against pollution of the air and water, the air and water can be improved along with the company's public image. In an age where big business, big unions, and big foundations rival government agencies in their importance to citizens' welfare, this twentieth-century orientation to public opinion—and therefore public welfare—represents an important contribution by public relations.

Increasingly, public relations has been referred to as a kind of conscience for those who take it seriously. Even monopoly enterprises like telephone companies recognize that public opinion can affect their chances for favorable rates and regulatory laws. If their public-relations executives emphasize this to inspire better service to the public, then the press's power to serve the people has been broadened significantly by this twentieth-century phenomenon.

FUTURE PUBLIC RELATIONS

Continuing growth would appear to be the most certain element in the future of public relations. Listings of public-relations consultants in metropolitan telephone directories have multiplied since World War II. A study of personnel turnover in any major news medium reveals an astounding number of defections to public relations. College courses in public relations have proliferated across the land, reflecting an increase in demand for these journalistic specialists. Hundreds of colleges now offer one or more courses, and thirty-three of the journalism schools and departments listed in the 1968 *Editor & Publisher Year Book* reported special sequences in public relations. The American Council on Education for Journalism had specifically accredited five such sequences in major universities as of 1968.

Equally certain will be further attempts to set professional standards for public-relations work. In 1950, the Public Relations Society of America adopted a "Code of Professional Standards," to which more than 6,000 leading practitioners are pledged. The code inveighs against intentionally disseminating false or misleading information, conflicts of interest in serving different clients, and violating client confidences. In 1963, PRSA adopted a supplementary code for specialists in financial public relations.

Various proposals for licensing public-relations workers have reflected the degree of concern for professional behavior held by some leading practitioners. Such an extreme move seems unlikely, and certainly it would raise questions related to freedom of the press if it were attempted.

Among the more striking actions has been PRSA's establishment of a voluntary accreditation program for its members. The program, launched in 1964, sets eligibility requirements such as a college degree or 10 years' experience and recommendations from fellow practitioners and former clients. It involves both written and oral examinations. PRSA's hope is that use of the "PRSA Accredited" after a practitioner's name will become highly valued by both clients and members, providing PRSA with an instrument for raising standards. About one-fifth of PRSA's 6,000-odd members had been accredited in the program's first five years.

Other organizations, like the 1,000-member American College Public Relations Association, work constantly at improvement of their practices.

However, the major responsibility for making public relations a useful, rather than a damaging, instrument in the flow of information and opinion must rest with newspapers, magazines, and radio and television stations. Understaffed media cannot effectively check against the increased flow of propaganda. Publishers and broadcasters who succumb to "p. r. blandishments" deserve more scorn than the unprincipled hucksters who use them.

FOR FURTHER STUDY

1. Check a newspaper for "p. r. puffs." The business-financial page frequently offers good hunting, if you think about the relative importance of junior-executive promotions in total news available. Stories about colleges, not covered by beat reporters, are another source. Analyze the content to see if it deviates from normal news-story language.

2. Too many newspapers print as news their own "puffs."A typical example would be a story about some subscriber's falling from a stepladder and collecting on his "reader insurance." Does this practice weaken the editor's insistence that others buy advertising space for their hard-sell messages?

3. Interview a reporter or editor about his experiences with public relations. When he accepts free passes to sports events or movies, or when he attends a "press party," does he feel any obligation not to "bite the hand that feeds him"? How much checking does he do on handouts (press releases) before running them?

4. Interview a public-relations practitioner. Ask him about timing problems in giving releases to broadcast and print media and to morning and evening newspapers. Ask him about his evaluation of varying editorial judgments among those to whom he sends stories.

SUGGESTED READING

American Institute for Political Communication, *The New Methodology: A Study of Political Strategy and Tactics*, Washington: AIPC, 1967. [Available in paperback.] Suggests that modern public relations has revolutionized political campaigning. Other interesting case histories include coverage of the U. S. Department of Agriculture's efforts to overcome anti-insecticide opinion stirred by Rachel Carson's *Silent Spring* in the early 1960s.

"The Arts and Uses of Public Relations," *Time*, July 7, 1967 (Vol. 90, No. 1), pp. 40-41. A breezy "Time essay" on the field.

BERNAYS, EDWARD L., *Crystallizing Public Opinion*, New York: Liveright Publishing Corp., 1961 (rev.). This revision of a pioneering work is highly recommended by experts in the field.

CANFIELD, BERTRAND R., *Public Relations: Principles, Cases, and Problems*, Homewood, Ill.: Richard D. Irwin, Inc., 1968 (5th ed.). A widely used textbook in the field.

CUTLIP, SCOTT M. and CENTER, ALLEN H.,° *Effective Public Relations*, Englewood Cliffs, N. J.: Prentice-Hall, Inc., 1964 (3rd ed.). Probably the most widely used textbook in the field.

DARROW, RICHARD W.; FORRESTAL, DAN U.; and COOKMAN, AUBREY O., *Public Relations Handbook*, Chicago: The Dartnell Corporation, 1967. Considered the most comprehensive single volume in the field.

LIPPMANN, WALTER, *Public Opinion*, New York: Harcourt, Brace, & World, Inc. 1922. [Available in Macmillan Free Press paperback.] Public opinion is fundamental to understanding public relations; this is regarded as a classic, especially for news workers.

MacDOUGALL, CURTIS D., *Understanding Public Opinion*, Dubuque, Iowa: Wm. C. Brown Company Publishers, 1966. A more recent, less theoretical approach, aimed directly at newsmen.

Public Relations Journal (845 Third Avenue, New York, N.Y. 10022). This monthly official journal of the Public Relations Society of America reports up-to-date material on the field. Its July number carries the annual Silver Anvil Awards citations for public relations.

STEPHENSON, HOWARD,° ed., *Handbook of Public Relations*, New York: McGraw-Hill Book Company, 1960.

[°The Cutlip-Center and Stephenson books have been keyed into the PRSA Accreditation program's "Study Guide."]

CHAPTER 10

Some Legal Pitfalls

Among the more than half-a-dozen legal categories which directly impinge on journalistic work, the most important—and most complicated —is that of civil libel. Understanding some of the rudiments is important to lay citizens in proper assessment of press performance. Reporters and editors should study the subject, both to protect the press from needless suits and to enlarge their reporting and commenting by recognizing what is safe under the law.

A public speaker who defames an individual may be sued for slander. The publisher or broadcaster who reports the speaker's allegations may be sued for libel—the more serious species of defamation. (Although the "oral" aspect of slander might appear to belong to broadcasting, court decisions have tended to equate broadcasting with publishing because of the mass audiences involved.) Rarely, the same publication or broadcast brings both a criminal-libel indictment and a civil-libel suit. Criminal-libel actions, which have been infrequent, are employed when prosecutors believe that a defamation threatens law and order. This may involve alleged defamation of a government official (as in the *Brooklyn Daily* case mentioned in Chapter 2) or defamation of a dead person (not normally subject to civil-libel action) or any defamation "inciting to violence"—e. g., allegations that might so enrage the victims as to inspire them to attack their foes.

Most libel actions, as we have said, involve civil suits—an individual seeking damages from a publisher or broadcaster for having allegedly harmed his reputation illegitimately. Confusion about civil libel stems from several factors—wildly conflicting court decisions, the fact that many victims ignore libels, the fact that many potential cases are settled outside courtrooms, and ignorance of such factors as "privileged" communication. A brief look at the major defenses against libel damages should provide some understanding. These categories overlap each other, of course, and most libel cases involve elements of several defenses.

MAJOR LIBEL-SUIT DEFENSES

1. *Privilege.* Let us take a hypothetical situation with the fictional Senator J. M. Rail from Chapter 4. If Rail carried out his threat and charged in a Senate speech that D. R. Forp, a State University professor, was a Communist, the fictional professor—no matter how innocent—could not successfully sue Rail for slander. Nor could he successfully sue any publisher or broadcaster who accurately reported what the senator charged. The senator enjoys "absolute privilege" in performing his duties as an elected official—on the Senate floor or in any duly constituted official Senate proceeding. Publishers and broadcasters cover news of such proceedings with "qualified privilege." That "qualified" means that reports must be accurate and fair. (It is theoretically possible that Forp might win damages if he could show that a given publication or station had blatantly ignored significant, related defenses of his loyalty, or had pursued him with distorted coverage indicating malice toward him. If the plaintiff could sustain such charges, the defendant could escape only by proving that Forp was indeed a Communist.)

However, if Rail calls Forp a Communist during a press conference or in some speech outside a duly constituted Senate proceeding, he is open to a slander suit, and any medium which reports his allegation is open to a libel suit. Proving the truth of the charge would offer the only defense for either Rail or those who spread his charge.

Absolute privilege is accorded to official participants during official judicial and legislative proceedings and to "important" government executives in the line of duty. In fact, it means that even individuals wrongly accused of heinous crimes—through gross error—cannot recover damages for such abuse. That special exemption is considered essential to sound government and based on the premise that the common good overrides individual interests in these limited circumstances. Congressional investigations, like that of the Teapot Dome scandals in the 1920s, might be seriously hampered if the investigators were subject to normal slander and libel threats. Judges, lawyers, and witnesses in court sessions must be free of defamation restraints if truth is to be pursued vigorously in the courtroom—where fair-play rules are supposed to be rigidly enforced to protect all participants. And citizens must be able to follow those vigorous pursuits in detail through their press. (Legislators who abuse this special privilege may be censured by their colleagues, for whatever satisfaction that may give their victims. Courtroom witnesses who knowingly lie may be indicted for perjury by the state, but the victims of their lies have no means of recovery.)

So that the public may know what its government does, news reports of such proceedings are also protected, but not absolutely. A newspaper printing complete, verbatim testimony of a trial could acquire almost perfect privilege. Actually, few instances of successful libel suits have occurred when the basic derogatory matter came from absolutely-privileged sources. But legal, as well as ethical, considerations suggest that news media which reported a man's drunken-driving conviction must report his successful appeal of that conviction.

One travesty of civil libel involves the arbitrary gradations of qualified privilege according to government level. It should be as safe to report accurately city-council proceedings as those of a state legislature, but the government-closest-to-the-people myth bends in libel-law records. A New England newspaper was successfully sued for libel after it reported a Council meeting during which a lawyer hired by the village council had been called a "city slicker" for allegedly overcharging the village for legal services. Probably, failure of smaller media to appeal such judgments to higher courts accounts in part for such diluting of qualified privilege at local levels. Some defend the difference as proper protection against the relatively unsophisticated behavior of small-town council members and county commissioners, whose governmental commitments are less than those of their higher-placed counterparts. Privilege in the executive branches ranges from 100 per cent for a presidential press conference to utter confusion down the line.

During the heyday of U. S. Senator Joseph McCarthy's free-swinging attacks on "traitors" in government, many of his defenders said his charges "must be true since he hasn't been sued for libel." Whether they, or McCarthy's Senate colleagues who censured him in 1954, were correct, the not-sued-for-libel argument was erroneous, as an understanding of "privilege" shows.

2. *Fair comment.* The right to criticize duty performance of government officials, the qualifications of political candidates, and the professional competence of authors, actors, and athletes is among the press's most important libel protections. It is essential to cover news of political controversy and to comment with any forcefulness. Except for the Sedition Act of 1798 and a few limited war-time lapses, the United States has adhered to a fair-comment principle quite religiously.

Even so, a great leap forward was made in 1964 when the U. S. Supreme Court unanimously reversed a $500,000 libel judgment against the *New York Times* and four Negro ministers. That landmark decision involved a full-page advertisement (March 29, 1960) which denounced behavior of Montgomery, Alabama, officials in dealing with civil-rights demonstrators. The *New York Times vs. Sullivan* decision in effect knocked out the old "strict rule," which had held that any factual errors, on which strong criticism was based, destroyed the fair-comment protection. Only when errors are made with "malice"—i. e., with knowledge that they are errors, or *with reckless disregard* for accuracy—does the fair-comment defense collapse in an action brought by a public official, the court ruled.

In a sense, the court could be said to have extended to the private citizen a right of political criticism rivaling the "absolute privilege" of government officials. The opinion specifically cited the protection of officials from "the threat of damage suits," and declared: "Analogous considerations support the privilege for the citizen-critic of government. It is as much his duty to criticize as it is the official's duty to administer." (The defense of fair comment here, as in many cases, involved an element of privilege as well.)

In later decisions, the court extended the newly enunciated protection to cover criticism of "public figures" as well as government officials. The extension came when the court in 1967 reversed a $500,000 libel judgment against the Associated Press for having reported that retired Major General Edwin A. Walker of Texas had "led a charge of students against federal marshals" during integration riots at the University of Mississippi in 1962. Lower courts had ruled for the plaintiff because the AP was unable to substantiate its reports of the general's actions during his presence in Oxford, Mississippi.

Unprovable allegations are not, however, always safe press practice in such cases. The Supreme Court in 1967 upheld damages awarded to Wallace Butts, who as University of Georgia athletic director had been accused in a *Saturday Evening Post* article of having passed Georgia football plans to an upcoming opponent. An important difference between the Walker and Butts cases was the factor of time: A press association serving broadcast outlets and dailies has less opportunity to verify details of a running story like the Mississippi campus riots than does a magazine publishing articles of wider choice at a slower pace. If Walker had not made himself a public figure by speaking out on political matters and if he had not been in Oxford, Mississippi, during the rioting, the defendant's appeal might well have lost.

Fair comment does not extend to criticism of the artist's or public figure's personal life or a charge of criminality. Commentators may accuse a governor of "recklessly spending the taxpayers' money" under the fair-comment umbrella, but any charge of embezzling public funds would need to be provably true in court or an accurate report from an absolutely privileged source (a formal indictment or an accusation in the legislature). A reviewer may safely call an author's work "juvenile" even if all better-qualified reviewers hail its "maturity," but an accusation of "plagiarism" is libel per se and would have to be proved in court if the author sued for libel. A critic may safely call a handsome actor "too ugly" for the romantic lead, but dismissing his stage appeal "because he beats his wife" would require another libel defense.

Criticism of public figures, public institutions (like schools), artists, and performers can be caustic—even exceeding the bounds of good taste —but it must be based on substantially accurate facts and it must concern performance offered to the public. The more private the subject's dealings, the less likely fair comment is to cover criticism. Fair comment does not, for instance, extend to criticism of performance by a private doctor or lawyer or retail merchant, as it does to that by a state college's health director or the county's district attorney or an armed services post exchange. One Western college newspaper editor thought fair comment covered editorial charges that a photographer's "prices have steadily risen as his services have steadily declined; his only merit would appear to be his location near campus." The ensuing libel suit was settled out of court for several thousand dollars. Had the case come to trial, the publisher would have had to prove that services had "steadily" declined and that the photographer's "only merit" had been his convenient location.

Had the editor criticized the artistic quality of the plaintiff's photographs voluntarily displayed in the student union building, the defense of fair comment would have been pertinent.

3. *Truth*. Often called the best defense, truth has been left till last because laymen—and some journalists—are often naïve about its application. Actually, a fair and accurate report of a lie made under privileged conditions may be easier to defend than a story the reporter knows to be true. Unless the libel defendant can prove his allegations in a court of law, they cannot be considered "legal truth." The plaintiff may produce more and better witnesses, or the defendant's damning evidence against the plaintiff may not be admissible in court. Just as a prosecutor may legitimately delay seeking an indictment against a known criminal until he has convincing evidence, so a press unit may take time to dig up evidence before exposing scoundrels. The prosecutor knows a poor case may result in "double jeopardy" protection of his quarry, acquitted for lack of evidence. And responsible newsmen know that a successful libel suit against their premature attack may elevate the scoundrel in public esteem, as the vindicated victim of a bullying press.

The worst misunderstanding among laymen has to do with which truth serves as a defense. In those cases where privilege and fair comment are not defenses, truth must cover *both* the allegation and the source of the allegation, if any. For example, in reporting the fictitious

Senator Rail's nonprivileged charge (see second paragraph under "Privilege"), defense against a libel suit by Forp would require proving that Rail made the charge *and that Forp was a Communist.*

A video-taped interview, certified as accurate by the defamer, provides grounds for libel damages against the broadcaster unless he can prove the third party's defamatory remarks are true. A radio station in the Northwest wisely decided not to air its recording of a state legislator's speech because a lawyer defamed in the speech said he would sue the station if it broadcast such defamation. A notarized letter-to-the-editor or a paid-for advertisement still leaves the publisher or broadcaster liable for libel damages. Even if the defendant has taken editorial exception to the defamatory remarks, further indicating that they are not his, his publishing or broadcasting of the defamation is still his responsibility. The fact that the defendant can prove that someone else said it is not a sufficient defense of truth. [The only exception in all this covers broadcast campaign speeches, which cannot be censored by the station. Significantly, news coverage of such speeches does not carry the immunity.]

The key to understanding publisher-broadcaster liability lies in recognizing the relative degree of damage delivered by the original defamer and that delivered by the agency which spreads the defamation. The remarks by the aforementioned legislator were heard by 150 persons in one room; the 5,000-watt station would have carried them to thousands over a three-state area. A defamatory letter may be read by an editor and his secretary; publication can lay it before hundreds of thousands and preserve it in the microfilm or bound-volume files of libraries.

All of which is intended to say that truth is not an easy defense. It is, however, an important defense. The *Chicago Tribune* once called a city alderman a "gangster." When he sued for libel, the *Tribune* proved to the court's satisfaction that the plaintiff was a gangster in the accepted meaning of that word.

Responsible journalists look beyond libel risks in deciding whether to report or comment in given situations, of course. Some sensational derogatory statements, well protected by privilege, may be ignored. Unprovable "truths" are put forward with courage on occasion.

OTHER LIBEL CONSIDERATIONS

Not naming persons defamed in news reports or editorials is a dangerous means of trying to avoid libel suits. A plaintiff may be able to show that many readers or listeners identified him as the unnamed "culprit." This has happened accidentally, both with the person alluded to and with some person not even thought of by the writer. (The "sophomore resident of Stokely Hall who was expelled for cheating" might accidentally point to a sophomore who left school about the same time because of family illness.)

Consent—formal or informal—may protect journalists in reporting derogatory material. (But the willing victim of being lampooned in a lodge paper could successfully sue the station which broadcasts the contents beyond lodge circles.) If B responds to A's attack in kind, the balanced report is safer than either attack by itself. Provocation and the right of reply are important factors.

Headlines present a special problem in libel. Court decisions have ruled both ways—that headlines must be judged by their content alone, and that defamation depends on considering both the headline and story text. Good copy editors look to the former. They sacrifice the specificity of "Burglar Nabbed/In Widow's Home" for "Police Arrest/Burglary Suspect." Both ethics and libel law dictate that he is only a suspect until final court action.

Corrections and retractions present special problems. Where error is clear, both ethical and legal common sense dictate that prompt correction should be made. However, automatic retraction on any demand (as practiced by some media) is editorially debilitating and sometimes legally dangerous. A hasty retraction, as required by some libel-insurance policies, can interfere with other defenses. Thus the prospective defendant may ruin a defense of truth in order to establish mitigation (reduction) of damages. On the other side, refusal to retract may help prove malice on the defendant's part.

Although the general public hears more about dramatic direct-confrontation libel suits like that of Quentin Reynolds against columnist Westbrook Pegler (see Louis Nizer's *My Life in Court*, "Suggested Reading") and *Sullivan vs. New York Times*, the vast majority of actions involve unimportant issues and unknown plaintiffs. They stem from simple errors—sometimes careless, sometimes almost unavoidable. A reporter's copying the wrong line in a police report or composing-room transposition of picture captions can lead to court. An interviewee's ad lib remark during a live broadcast could bring lengthy litigation.

MISCELLANEOUS LEGAL PITFALLS

Invasion of privacy is recognized as a journalistic offense entitling victims to damage claims. Newsworthy persons are entitled to less right of privacy than others, and the right does not protect any participant in the news, willing or otherwise, from reasonable coverage. Trouble arises when journalists begin probing into family affairs and remote connections of persons whose names have been in the news perhaps briefly. Or when "anniversary" features are unearthed to rework details of some tragedy, with unwelcomed reports on what the principals' survivors "are doing now." A particularly loathsome invasion is that involving the unauthorized use of a person's picture to advertise some product or service. Generally, the highest courts have been most lenient with the press when suits involved stories at all connected with legitimate public interest. Thus *New Yorker* magazine successfully defended against a former child prodigy's suit for damages after they interrupted his later obscurity by profiling his life. Exceptions, however, are on record, and confusion may develop even further in this special area than it has in general civil libel. Truth is not an automatic defense, since damage claims are based on invading the plaintiff's wish to be let alone. A story about a plumber's interrupting a housewife in her bath is not of public concern unless she has him arrested in connection with the incident.

Postal regulations concern publishers, though not as much as Federal Communications Commission rulings affect broadcasters. Rules on percentage of space devoted to advertising, rules against promoting lotteries, and wavering restrictions on "obscenity" all impinge on publishers. Magazines, which depend upon second-class mail for about 70 per cent of their distribution, are most concerned. Even with less than 10 per cent dependence, dailies must observe restrictions. As absolute overseer of broadcasting's delivery system, the FCC has vaster regulatory power, which it has so far used with great restraint.

Statutes regulating advertising and copyright ownership are among other legal concerns of journalists. Pirating of newspaper stories by radio stations has been held in violation of "common law" copyright, for example.

CONTEMPT OF COURT

Once ranked under "miscellaneous" in listings like this chapter's, contempt of court threatens to become a bigger issue in this last third of the twentieth century. Simple citations for disturbing courtroom decorum with photographers' shenanigans or reporters racing for telephones have largely faded into history. Battles between the bench and press over picture-taking "near" the courtroom may continue. So will occasional contempt citations for reporting testimony stricken from the record and other defiances of judges' orders. The press's right to criticize judicial performance, though well established by precedent, will continue to be challenged here and there. Two special aspects, however, appear headed for major debate.

One involves a journalist's obligation to reveal sources of information on criminal activity. University of Oregon graduate Annette

Buchanan lost a long fight in 1968 against a $300 fine for contempt in such a situation. She had reported in Oregon's *Daily Emerald* on student use of narcotics. Her refusal to identify students who had given her the information in confidence led to the contempt charge. A minority of states grant reporters and their sources a right of "privileged communication" like that accorded a lawyer and his client, a physician and his patient, or a priest and his communicant. Even journalists are divided on whether they should be free to report scandalous allegations without being held accountable for particulars. Opponents argue that such exemption would enable irresponsible journalists to smear public servants and others. Proponents insist that contempt-citation threats discourage the kind of full disclosure necessary for a watchdog press in a democratic society. Alerting the people to collusion between racketeers and dishonest officials, for example, may be possible only if the press can protect the anonymity of its sources.

By far the biggest contempt-of-court issue facing heated debate is that related to the "Free Press-Fair Trial" controversy. Concern over "trial by the press," which had been growing for decades, reached a climax in the Warren Commission's 1964 report on the assassination of President John F. Kennedy a year earlier. The report cited "irresponsibility and lack of self-discipline" by the press in covering the assassination's aftermath. Typical of stories which bother those concerned with

Figure 10.1 Relman "Pat" Morin is shown dashing for the telephone during court proceedings in Little Rock, Arkansas, at the peak of the school-integration crisis in 1957. News coverage of court matters, as tricky as it is essential, faces growing threats. (Associated Press photograph)

fair trials was this one, which appeared two days after President Kennedy was killed:

> DALLAS (UPI)—Police said Saturday night they have an airtight case against pro-Castro Marxist Lee Harvey Oswald, 24, as the assassin of President Kennedy, including photos of him holding the rifle.
>
> Police were reported showing the photos to the sullen ex-Marine from suburban Irving, Tex., who has steadfastly maintained his innocence and has also denied slaying a Dallas policeman.
>
> The photos, police said, show him with both the rifle used to kill President Kennedy and the pistol used to kill pursuing Patrolman J. D. Tippitt shortly after the assassination.
>
> "This case is cinched," said Homicide Chief Capt. Will Fritz.
>
> When he was brought down from a cell in city jail to a room where he was shown the photos, Oswald was the picture of confidence, smiling and loudly complaining about prison treatment. When he was taken back up to his cell he looked frightened. . . .

Such prejudiced reporting, it is argued, makes a fair trial difficult for a defendant. The fact that Oswald was "found guilty" by the Warren Commission's investigation after Oswald was slain by Jack Ruby (the same day that story appeared) did not detract from the fact that prejudice against the suspect had been built up unfairly among prospective jurors, critics maintained. Perils include both difficulty in convicting the guilty and the danger of convicting the innocent.

The American Bar Association soon thereafter appointed a committee, headed by Massachusetts Supreme Judicial Court Justice Paul C. Reardon, to recommend pretrial safeguards against prejudicial publicity. In 1968, the ABA adopted, by a more-than-two-thirds majority, four recommendations of the Reardon Report. Briefly, these would forbid lawyers, court officials, and police from releasing other than a suspect's vital statistics and the arrest circumstances. No reports of confession or previous criminal record, etc., would be allowed, and no statements like that of the Dallas homicide chief in paragraph 4 of the foregoing example. No interviews or picture-taking of the person in custody would be permitted without his written request. Most controversial from the press's point of view are recommendations for excluding the public and press from various preliminary hearings and encouragement of using contempt powers to protect the defendant from unfavorable publicity. Judges would be encouraged to cite the press for any report a judge considered aimed at influencing the trial's outcome or for reporting any information from closed proceedings—no matter how obtained.

As each of the fifty states decides—in its bar association, legislature, and court system—whether to follow the ABA recommendations, the contempt-of-court pitfall will be profoundly affected for all of the media.

Meanwhile, as in every legal-problem area, press performance can help reduce or widen that pitfall.

FOR FURTHER STUDY

1. Find stories which might embarrass principals identified in them. Estimate which defense would be most important if libel suits were filed. (For example: arrest of a reputable citizen—privilege; criticism of artist's performance—fair comment; letter-writer's charge that a neighbor dumps garbage in the street—truth.)

2. A person clearly libeled by a small daily may choose not to sue because of the qualified-privilege defense. Why? (Hint: What happens to the defamatory remarks when the suit is filed?)

3. Read the First and Sixth Amendments to the U. S. Constitution. How does press coverage help guarantee part of the Sixth Amendment?

4. Note the prejudiced phrases in the story from Dallas about President Kennedy's accused killer. Since a prosecutor is likely to present more "prejudiced" material against a defendant in court, why do some lawyers object to disseminating such prior to the trial?

5. A wire story from California reports an Eastern governor has been arrested for drunken driving. Should news media in his state take more precautions than an editor in Nebraska before running the story? Why?

6. John A. Stormer's *None Dare Call It Treason* (published in 1964 by Liberty Bell Press, Box 32, Florissant, Missouri) created a sensation summarizing "charges" against citizens. Note the number of footnotes— "References," pp. 238-248—from congressional hearings and the like. What libel defenses would these suggest?

SUGGESTED READING

ASHLEY, PAUL P., *Say It Safely: Legal Limits in Publishing, Radio, and Television*, Seattle: University of Washington Press, 1966 (3rd ed.). A superb, brief treatment of press law.

The Associated Press, *The Dangers of Libel* (AP Traffic Department, 50 Rockefeller Plaza, New York, N.Y. 10020). A 26-page pamphlet available at low cost, giving excellent tips on avoiding libel.

EMERY, WALTER B., *National and International Systems of Broadcasting: Their History, Operation and Control*, East Lansing: Michigan State University Press, 1969. The most comprehensive coverage of broadcast law.

FRANKLIN, MARC A., *The Dynamics of American Law*, Mineola, N.Y.: The Foundation Press, Inc., 1968. The first 191 pages cover a libel case in revealing detail. [That chapter is available in paperback.]

GILLMOR, DONALD M., and BARRON, JEROME A., *Mass Communication Law: Cases and Comment*, St. Paul, Minn.: West Publishing Co., 1969. This and the Nelson-Teeter book, listed below, are the two best comprehensive volumes on press law.

HACHTEN, WILLIAM A., *The Supreme Court on Freedom of the Press*, Ames: Iowa State University Press, 1968. In dealing with the broad topic of its title, this volume provides a superior view of the best judicial thinking on press law.

MEYER, SYLVAN, "We call It Privilege, They Call It Freedom to Smear," *Nieman Reports*, December, 1965 (Vol. 19, No. 4), pp. 9-14. This appeal for more reporting of libel cases underlines the dangers of laymen's why-don't-they-sue assumptions.

NELSON, HAROLD L., and TEETER, DWIGHT L., JR., *Law of Mass Communications: Freedom and Control of Print and Broadcast Media*, Mineola, N.Y.: The Foundation Press, Inc., 1969. An updated revision and extension of the late Professor Thayer's book listed below.

NIZER, LOUIS, *My Life in Court*, Garden City, N.Y.: Doubleday & Company, Inc., 1961. [Available in Pyramid Books paperback.] Chapter 1 on the Quentin Reynolds-Westbrook Pegler libel case is as exciting as it is informative on the subject of libel. Chapter 4 covers a little known, but classic, libel case—also rewarding.

————, *The Jury Returns*, Garden City, N.Y.: Doubleday & Company, Inc., 1966. [Available from Pocket Books.] Chapter 4's account of John Henry Faulk's suit against those who blacklisted him in broadcasting offers good background on libel law and a bonus on another threat to freedom, all in most readable form.

PEMBER, DON R., "Privacy and the Press: The Defense of Newsworthiness," *Journalism Quarterly*, Spring, 1968 (Vol. 45, No. 1), pp. 14-24. An especially valuable discussion of the invasion-of-privacy problem for the press.

SHAPIRO, FRED C., "Annals of Jurisprudence: The Whitmore Confessions," *New Yorker*, Feb. 8, 15, and 22, 1969 (Vol. 44, Nos. 51, 52; Vol. 45, No. 1). Reviews questionable police work and press coverage.

THAYER, FRANK, *Legal Control of the Press*, Mineola, N.Y.: The Foundation Press, Inc., 1962 (4th ed.). Among comprehensive treatments, this was perhaps best known and most widely used as a textbook in journalism schools until recently. (See Nelson and Teeter listing above.)

Criticisms of the Press

With the possible exceptions of politics and public schools, no American institution draws more criticism than does the press. Among privately operated ventures, certainly, it has no peer in either the number or intensity of attacks made on it. Since its own functions include criticizing other institutions and reporting others' criticisms, the press should expect both backlash and the perils of getting caught in cross fires. And the press, in toto, does expect and accept this way of life.

Among unfair—or meaningless—charges leveled at the press, particularly newspapers, is one to the effect that it reacts badly to criticism. It is unfair in that it implies that other enterprises accept criticism in better fashion. Nothing in the records supports the implication. Organized medicine could claim no sufferance laurels in its response to proposals like Medicare. The legal profession's reaction to the 1966-67 best seller *How to Avoid Probate* was hardly generous. Nor was that of public-school officials when books like *Quackery in the Public Schools* and *Why Johnny Can't Read* were going the rounds. The professional journals and professional meetings of no other group match those of the press in percentage devoted to criticism from both practitioners and laymen. No one even expects other enterprises to promote lay criticism with such a device as letters-to-the-editor.

Of course, the press should welcome—in fact, encourage—criticism. And this side of the millenium, negative press over-reaction to critics can be counted as a serious fault. That was proved when a major newspaper group dropped the editor of its best daily after he criticized smug one-paper-town operations in 1960. It has been underlined upon every revival of the program, "CBS Views the Press." But, as is true with several press faults, better perspective is needed for measuring the real thinness of the press's skin. In fact, a case can be made against too much positive press reaction to some complaints. Important news has been suppressed by editors who have been overly generous to shortsighted do-gooders, who wanted less "bad news." The blandness of most editorial columns and widespread noneditorializing by broadcasters are partially caused by kind response to critics.

A list of press faults, real and alleged, could occupy an entire book larger than this one. For our purposes, a few categories will be briefly treated.

BIAS IN THE PRESS

Newspapers, as the major purveyors of news and opinion, draw most fire for bias. But all media, in proportion to their volume of hard news and commentary, are subjected to it. *Time* magazine has in effect pleaded guilty to the charge; both of the other major news magazines have been accused of the fault. *Reader's Digest* has been worked over on this count in several books, including John Bainbridge's *Little Wonder* (see "Suggested Reading"). Despite equal-time rules and practices, broadcasters have suffered under this lash.

Edward L. Bernays, public relations counsel, found a heavy concentration on this as the major alleged newspaper fault in a comprehensive survey made in 1952. His report to the National Newspaper Promotion Association was based on questionnaires returned by 213 daily-newspaper publishers and 171 "opinion leaders" from industry, religion, science, education, and other fields. Asked to rank deviations from newspaper ideals in order of their prevalence, publishers gave first place to "political bias" with 22 per cent, and the laymen ranked "slanting the news" first with 33 per cent. Publishers gave third place to "slanting the news" (20 per cent), and laymen gave second to "political bias" (18 per cent). Thus the bias-slanting categories totaled 42 per cent for publishers and 51 per cent for laymen—far ahead of the six other categories (failure to perform public service, response to economic pressures, bias and self-interest of the publisher, pressure groups, sensationalism, miscellaneous). Adding the "bias . . . of the publisher," which seems logical, would run the totals to 49 per cent for publishers and 57 per cent for laymen. If "response to economic pressures" meant a resultant bias, as seems probable, the grand totals reach 67 per cent for publishers and 66 per cent for laymen. Thus "bias" (for several different reasons) headed the list of newspaper faults in the view of two-thirds of the publishers and outside "opinion leaders" alike.

It is important to underline the fact that neither group was charging typical newspapers with this fault. They were saying only that among deviations which they saw, bias was the most frequent. Actually, only

44 per cent of the laymen answered no to a question: ". . . does the American newspaper press [in 1952], taken by and large, meet the ideals [of impartiality and independence]?" Only 25 per cent of the publishers said no.

So long as mere humans write and edit the news, bias is inevitable. The question, of course, is whether those who process news and views try to be fair and how talented they are in their attempts. Like beauty, bias is often in the eye (or ear) of the beholder. Yet there is no denying that bias, far beyond the unavoidable limits, does show up too frequently.

In his survey of the 1952 presidential-campaign coverage, Professor Nathan B. Blumberg found six out of thirty-five major newspapers guilty of slanting the news to favor a candidate (see "Suggested Reading," Chapter 2). A gross example of unfairness turned up during the 1968 Democratic presidential primaries. The *Indianapolis Star,* strongly opposed to Senator Robert F. Kennedy's candidacy, reprinted a *New York Times* editorial, which criticized the primaries system for giving an advantage to candidates with access to the most money. With no indication of having edited it, the *Star* omitted a 30-word clause decrying favorite-son Governor Roger D. Branigin's access to political funds. This made it appear that the *New York Times* had aimed only at Senator Kennedy's family fortune, when it had done otherwise. That journalistic sin was compounded when Kennedy aides' protests brought only a countercharge of "bellyaching" from the publisher.

This kind of shocking bias is isolated, and it appears to have been in decline for some years. Even in the Indianapolis case, important balance was maintained by the total press effort. The ethics of the *Star's* surgery on the *New York Times* editorial was widely challenged by media available to Indianans. Inside the *Star* itself (and its sister *Indianapolis News*), syndicated columnists and letter-writers countered the unbalanced news treatment of the candidates. Interestingly, one of the six papers which scored worst in Blumberg's *One Party Press?* study in 1952 has since, under a new publisher, been winning national acclaim for its journalistic integrity and general excellence.

Probably a majority of "bias" charges against the press are unreasonable, but enough survive the reasonableness test to rank that fault as a major threat to effective journalism. Unseen bias—favored treatment of traditional "sacred cows" and failure to explore relatively uncharted problem areas of society—may present a larger danger than the crude, old-fashioned bias, which is difficult to put over in today's mass media.

Reaction to television coverage of the disgraceful violence at the 1968 Democratic Convention in Chicago underlined a desperate need for effective rebuttal against unfair bias charges. Tens of thousands of letters—from citizens with no firsthand information—denounced network

Figure 11.1. NBC Newsman John Evans, shown interviewing another man injured during the August, 1968, Democratic Convention demonstrations, was one of 36 reporters and photographers clubbed by Chicago policemen. More frightening than that unusual attack on newsmen by uniformed officers was the strong public endorsement of those attacks, even after investigations showed that the attacks were made against orders by superior officers. (Used by permission, Wide World Photos, Inc.)

coverage of police brutality. As sincere as they were blindly prejudiced against the demonstrators, those citizens refused to believe what they saw on live TV. Exhaustive after-the-fact confirmation of hoodlum behavior by some Chicago policemen only brought more denunciations of the press. Many either applauded all police behavior or refused to believe documentation that policemen purposely attacked news photographers as part of a scheme to cover their disobedience of superior officers. The press can always expect disfavor when it transmits bad news, but the long-lived depth of reaction against this instance of "telling it as it was" signals real danger to press freedom. The beating of thirty-six newsmen, praised or dismissed by citizens, belongs in a police state—not the United States of America. The press itself must take some of the blame. More direct efforts toward building public confidence are needed. The *Minneapolis Star* and *Tribune's* practice of checking back with citizens after stories about those citizens have been printed has helped build such confidence. (It is a good check on the newspapers' performance, too.)

"MONOPOLY" IN THE PRESS

Concentration of press ownership in fewer hands threatens the likelihood of differing approaches to the news and differing editorial viewpoints. The number of competing daily newspapers has been declining steadily since the first decade of this century. While the population more than doubled, the total number of dailies dropped from about 2,200 in 1910 to 1,752 by 1968. Meanwhile, mergers among surviving dailies have reached such a point that 95 per cent of America's cities depend on single-ownership newspapers. One corporation owns both dailies in Milwaukee, the nation's eleventh largest city. The Scripps-Howard group operates both dailies in Memphis, the twenty-second largest city.

Mergers beyond single cities—called "groups" or "chains"—have grown even faster than the number of newspapers has declined. A leading expert on newspaper groups, Professor Raymond B. Nixon of Minnesota, summarized group-ownership trends in the June 1, 1968, *Editor & Publisher*. His figures reveal a relative explosion of growth during the 1960s. Between 1910 and 1961, such operations grew from 13 groups with 62 newspapers to 109 groups with 552 newspapers. During that half-century then, growth for each decade averaged about 19 groups and 96 newspapers. Between 1961 and (early) 1968—only two-thirds of a decade—50 groups and 276 newspapers were added. By early 1968, a total of 159 groups controlled 828 dailies, covering 58 per cent of America's total daily-newspaper circulation. Half of the groups extended to more than one state: Thomson Newspapers owned 36, scattered across 20 states; Scripps-Howard had 17 in 10 states and the District of Columbia; Newhouse had 23 in 10 states, stretching from Massachusetts to Oregon. Ranking them by "seven-day circulation" (cumulative weekday plus Sunday totals), Nixon listed 35 groups which circulated more than 1,000,000 copies a week. Table 7 lists the top 10 groups (which accounted for 29 per cent of all weekday circulation), identifying each with its largest holding and noting the number of states involved. [Material in this paragraph derived by permission, © 1968, Editor & Publisher Co.]

Radio and television stations, of course, have replaced some elements of the competition lost with the shrinkage and linkage of newspapers. Professor Guido H. Stempel, III, reported in *Columbia Journalism Review* (Spring, 1967) that twice as many communities had local journalistic competition in the mid-1960s as had any fifty years earlier. He also found that 88 per cent of the communities with single-ownership dailies were served by competing broadcast units. Thus, the 95 per cent of "monopoly" cities was potentially reduced to about 52 per cent when both print and broadcast media were counted. However, he noted: "If [broadcast] competition in a given community is not significant so far as local news and opinion is concerned, it is perhaps time the public demanded that it become significant. The opportunity for significant competition exists."

TABLE 7

LEADING DAILY NEWSPAPER GROUPS
(As of early 1968)

GROUP (STATES INVOLVED) [LARGEST PAPER]	No. of. DAILIES	TOT. CIRC. WEEKDAY	No. of SUNDAYS
1. Tribune Co. (3) [*New York Daily News*]	7	3,620,520	5
2. Newhouse (10) [*Cleveland Plain Dealer*]	23	3,190,180	14
3. Scripps-Howard (11)[a] [*Cleveland Press*]	17	2,504,466	7
4. Hearst (6) [*Los Angeles Herald-Examiner*]	8	2,080,647	7
5. Knight (4) [*Detroit Free Press*]	7	1,390,117	6
6. Gannett (5) [*Rochester* (N.Y.) *Times-Union*]	29	1,290,710	8
7. Cowles (6)[b] [*Minneapolis Star*]	11	1,108,637[c]	7
8. Ridder (7) [*Seattle Times*]	16	1,143,847	10
9. Times Mirror Co. (1) [*Los Angeles Times*]	3	964,702	2
10. Ochs Estate (2) [*New York Times*]	3	914,576	2

[a]Counting the District of Columbia
[b]Plus Puerto Rico
[c]Sunday circulation puts Cowles ahead of Ridder.

—Table based on study by Raymond P. Nixon, used by permission. © 1968, Editor & Publisher Co.

The potential diversity of nearly 7,000 radio and television stations has been curbed by the same corporate-merger tendencies that beset newspapering. The Federal Communications Commission has blocked giant combines by limiting groups to a maximum of seven radio stations (they may be joint AM and FM operations) and seven television stations (only five may be VHF) each. The *1968 Broadcasting Yearbook* listed 318 groups, each of which controlled at least two TV stations or at least three AM-radio stations.

Joint newspaper-broadcast operations exist in most major cities, and —as of late 1968—publishers of magazines and newspapers owned more than one-fourth of America's commercial TV stations. In fact, newspaper groups control broadcast groups, carrying the no-competition danger toward its ultimate. Seven of the ten names in Table 7 showed up in *Broadcasting Yearbook*'s list. For example, the Tribune Co. owned TV stations in New York, Chicago, Denver, and Duluth, Minnesota, and four radio stations.

Joint ownerships within a medium and among media worry students of the democratic press for several reasons. Reduction of competition enables surviving publisher-broadcasters to offer their customers less, since those customers have little or no choice. News-processing budgets can be cut because readers and listeners have no way of learning what they are missing. Advertising rates can be fixed at high levels on a take-it-or-leave-it basis. Most important, mass-media monopolists can slant the news and suppress opinions they dislike.

An illustration was offered in June, 1968, when *Reader's Digest* stopped publication of a controversial book by Funk & Wagnalls, a publishing house it had acquired a couple of years earlier. The book, Samm Baker's *The Permissible Lie*, called for an internal cleansing of the advertising business. A *Reader's Digest* executive explained that the author's critical view of advertising clashed with the *Digest*'s view, and that the *Digest* could not allow a subsidiary to circulate such heretical ideas. The incident ended happily when Baker found another publisher and the *Digest* turned over Funk & Wagnalls plates and 5,000 printed copies free to Baker. The danger is that one day not enough independent publishing houses will remain to circulate clashing views. If a few giants, dedicated to the status quo, control great networks of magazines, newspapers, broadcast outlets, and book-publishing houses, how can democracy's essential dissenters air their views on an effective scale?

The danger was also illustrated during the peak of controversy swirling around Wisconsin Senator Joseph R. McCarthy's charges that Communists had infiltrated the United States government. Some editors of the sixteen Hearst newspapers then scattered across ten states, from Boston to Los Angeles, supported McCarthy vigorously. Hearst's *Milwaukee Sentinel*, for example, traded heavily on that position in its competitive battle with the anti-McCarthy *Milwaukee Journal*. But one day, in the early 1950s, Hearst headquarters ordered a lockstep editorial blast at McCarthy, thus imposing one view on millions of newspaper readers from coast to coast. All two-and-one-half-million subscribers to seventeen Scripps-Howard newspapers in ten states and the District of Columbia were urged to vote for the same presidential candidate in 1968. Editors in the East, South, Middle West, and West had to abide by a majority vote among themselves—no matter what their regional political atmosphere or their staff or individual-editor views might have suggested.

Trends toward monopoly are not all bad, of course. Efficient pooling of resources can result in one good operation's replacing two bad ones. In a limited market, concentration of advertising revenues can enable the surviving publisher or broadcaster to hire a bigger and better staff. He is less beholden to individual advertisers than when he was competing on a marginal budget. He is potentially better able to give a sometimes fickle public more of the things it should have instead of wasting space or time on silly contests or sensational, audience-attracting "news" and low-level entertainment. Solid performance by "monopoly" newspapers like the *Louisville Courier-Journal, Milwaukee Journal,* and *Kansas City Star* prove that single ownerships need not spell doom for good journalism. Broadcast stations owned by the ABC, CBS, and NBC networks are operated more like journalistic show pieces than scruffy money-grubbers.

Still, the flat analogy that press units should be merged willy-nilly as other segments of enterprise have been in recent years is an outrage. Peddling dairy products and peddling news and views, as the First Amendment implies, are of different import in this democratic society.

EMPHASIZING TRIVIA AND "SENSATIONALISM"

Significantly, the aforementioned Bernays study found that nearly one out of eight laymen considered "sensationalism" the chief fault of newspapers, but no publisher so ranked it. This reflects the impossibility of even defining that loosest of all charges made against the press. To some, any bad news is "sensationalism." To others, it means over-emphasis on bad news, but these more thoughtful critics disagree widely on when the line is crossed.

Crime coverage probably presents the focal point of this alleged fault. Among major U. S. dailies, the *Christian Science Monitor* and *New York Daily News* offer perhaps the widest range in editorial attention to crime. However badly critics might rate the *Daily News* on this count, it is a fact that crime does not lead news-space categories. A surprisingly small percentage of New York City's 50-odd murders per month get major attention in that tabloid's columns. America's typical newspapers and newscasts devote even less attention to this prime ingredient of sensationalism. Some charges of sensationalism are actually carry-overs from earlier periods, like the 1930s, when crime got a bigger press. Some fans of the *Christian Science Monitor* agree that its ignoring of crime would be dangerous for all news media to emulate.

Trivia, as represented by broadcasting's stress on entertainment, probably chokes the press more threateningly than does any stress on sensationalism. Handouts from publicity agents, the "booster" attitude inspired by Chamber of Commerce colleagues, and a desire to avoid offending important groups have inspired a dangerous blandness in both news coverage and commentary by most mass media at the local level.

Bernays put it another way. By analyzing his survey answers in terms of all criticisms, not just those listed first, Bernays found that "failure to perform public service" was most frequently cited by publishers in his 1952 study. He noted a correlation between newspapers rated best by his respondents (see Chapter 12) and the newspapers' reputations for leadership in public service. The *St. Louis Post-Dispatch*, for example, pioneered in obtaining smoke abatement long before air-pollution became a fashionable topic. It holds the record for most Pulitzer Prizes for "meritorious public service."

In the years since Bernays made his survey, newspaper attention to public service has grown. Perhaps competition from television—and some dramatic network television efforts of that kind—has inspired greater overall newspaper attention to public service. Dwight E. Sargent, curator of Harvard University's Nieman Foundation, told the 1968 American Newspaper Publishers Association convention that "there is more crusading today than ever before in newspaper history." He cited the record number of entries in the Pulitzer Prize categories for public service and investigative reporting, which averaged 166 annually between 1966 and 1968.

The idea that the press should do more than record events as they happen has taken wide hold. The fact that all of the nearly 3,000 communities with at least one mass medium harbor uninvestigated problems should serve as a challenge, rather than an indictment for America's press.

MISCELLANEOUS CHARGES

Because the press operates a private business dependent upon profits, alleged business failings loom large in the catalogue of criticisms. No industry appears to suffer from labor-management disputes on the scale that daily newspapers do. Strikes and shutdowns lasting for months have shaken newspapers' operations in big cities from coast to coast since World War II. The Detroit newspapers set a new record of more than nine months in 1967-68, "proving" that people can get along without them. Regardless of whose fault it is—selfish publishers or shortsighted union men—labor-management difficulties in newspapering rank as a disgraceful drag on an effective press. Antiquated production methods ultimately deny to modern Americans what they need from a modern press. Editorial pay scales began moving toward competitive levels only in the late 1960s.

Secrecy within the press is a peculiarly ironic fault in an institution dedicated to "the people's right to know." A law requiring public disclosure of who owns all press units, and those owners' possible conflicts of interest, would violate the First Amendment's spirit. But voluntary disclosure, as an ethical obligation, would represent a noble gesture by the caretakers of the people's press. Reports on internal staff dissension, like those which occasionally leak to the public, should be commonplace. When an editorial writer left the *Louisville Courier-Journal* in disagreement with its views on the Vietnam-war policy, the newspaper reported this to its readers. Such revelations should be regularly made in newspapers, magazines, and broadcast news, but silence or outright dishonesty is the traditional treatment.

Tolerance of criticism by the press is better than critics generally charge, but meaningful response has been too near zero. Only one publisher (Louisville's *Courier-Journal* and *Times*) moved with alacrity to adopt A. H. Raskin's exciting suggestion in 1967 that newspapers should appoint an ombudsman to represent the public on their editorial staffs. Louisville Publisher Barry Bingham's proposal that the media experiment with "local press councils" languished for years until the Mellett Fund underwrote a handful of modest college-operated efforts with small newspapers in late 1967.

Broadcasting's general neglect of news-dissemination and its reluctance to provide editorial commentary remains a major press fault. Kenneth A. Cox and Nicholas Johnson, members of the FCC, dissented to renewal of seventeen (out of 101) Oklahoma radio and TV station licenses in 1968 on grounds of too little news and public-affairs programming. In their shocking 215-page document, they made clear that Oklahoma was picked at random for their study, that it was probably typical of other states in terms of its broadcast attention to significant journalism. Their effort might provide a starting point for Professor Stempel's aforementioned suggestion that the public should demand local-news competition by broadcasters. Meanwhile, News Director Gordon Kilgore of KDTH in Dubuque, Iowa, summed up the situation in a speech before the Northwest Broadcast News Association in 1968: "I am convinced that for every good radio news operation there are four lousy ones." [As quoted in the *RTNDA Bulletin*, published by the 1,000-member Radio Television News Directors Association.]

FOR FURTHER STUDY

1. Analyze carefully coverage of and comment on some controversial situation about which you have felt (or have heard) that a press unit has been unfair. Measure space or time totals and placement and other factors in the total press attention to both sides. (Suggestion: Finding bias favorable to your side may provide a fairer test.)

2. Check this chapter's Table 7 totals against the current *Editor & Publisher Year Book*'s "group newspapers" listings. Have any of the groups added holdings and moved into more states? Check the current

Broadcasting Yearbook for "Group Ownership of Broadcast Stations" and your state's listings under "Newspaper/Magazine Ownership of Stations."

3. Who controls the media on which you depend? Ask newspaper publishers or editors and station general managers; then check the latest *Editor & Publisher Year Book* and *Broadcasting Yearbook* for any intra-media and intermedia links.

4. Evaluate the news stories offered in one issue of a newspaper or one local newscast by comparing what was presented with what could have been available. (Check against an Associated Press or United Press International file for that day, or against the *New York Times* or some other superior newspaper, to find major stories omitted.) How much of the total represents "trivia"—insignificant events of interest to few people?

5. Many a charge of "sensationalism" boils down to a complaint that media emphasize news unfavorable to a particular group—public officeholders or teen-agers, for example. Examine the files of an alleged offender over a period of time, measuring "good" and "bad" reports. (In a number of cases, records show a surprising balance of favorable news, indicating that news-consumers themselves tend to concentrate on the unfavorable.)

SUGGESTED READING

PERIODICALS

Columbia Journalism Review (602 Journalism, Columbia University, New York, N.Y., 10027). This quarterly contains the most interesting current commentary on all four major journalistic media.

Nieman Reports (77 Dunster St., Cambridge, Mass. 02138). This quarterly, published by the Society of Nieman Fellows, prints slower-paced commentaries, concentrating on newspapers.

[See also: Hausman, Linda Weiner, "Criticism of the Press in U. S. Periodicals, 1900-1939: An Annotated Bibliography," *Journalism Monographs*, August, 1967 (No. 4). Obtainable from School of Communication, University of Texas, Austin, Tex. 78712, this offers a wide selection of critiques of historical interest. Among other things, the listings suggest that the press has improved significantly.]

❀   ❀   ❀

BAGDIKIAN, BEN H., "Journalism's Wholesalers," *Columbia Journalism Review*, Fall, 1965 (Vol. 4, No. 3). An examination of how exclusive syndication of features handicaps would-be competitors in newspapering.

BAINBRIDGE, JOHN, *Little Wonder: Or, The Reader's Digest and How It Grew*, New York: Reynal and Hitchcock, 1946. Based largely on a series in *New Yorker*, this volume dissects America's most widely circulated magazine.

BRUCKER, HERBERT, *Freedom of Information*, New York: The Macmillan Company, 1949. Probably the best defense of American newspapers between book covers.

CHRISTENSON, REO M., and McWILLIAMS, ROBERT O., *Voice of the People: Readings in Public Opinion and Propaganda*, New York: McGraw-Hill Book Company, 1962. [Available in paperback.] An excellent collection of 107 articles. Chapters III, IV, VII, and XII offer especially pertinent articles.

FRIENDLY, FRED W., *Due to Circumstances Beyond Our Control . . .* , New York: Random House, Inc., 1967. [Available in Vintage paperback.] A biting criticism of television's dedication to the trivial.

KENDRICK, ALEXANDER, *Prime Time: The Life of Edward R. Murrow*, Boston: Little, Brown & Co., 1969. Both a tribute to the great broadcast journalist and a challenge to radio and television management.

LIEBLING, A. J., *The Press*, New York: Ballantine Books, Inc., 1964 (Rev.). This paperback collection and extension of Liebling's "Wayward Press" articles in *New Yorker* is a delightful, albeit devastating, attack on newspaper shortcomings.

LINDSTROM, CARL, *The Fading American Newspaper*, Garden City, N.Y.: Doubleday & Company, Inc., 1960. A long-time newspaper editor criticizes failures to change, but offers hope for the future.

MATTHEWS, THOMAS S., *Name and Address: An Autobiography*, New York: Simon & Schuster, Inc., 1960. A magazine editor's reminiscences include exposure of *Time*'s inner workings.

RIVERS, WILLIAM L., and SCHRAMM, WILBUR, *Responsibility in Mass Communications*, New York: Harper & Row, Publishers, 1969 (Revised). Criticism of both electronic and print media in depth.

RUCKER, BRYCE W., *The First Freedom*, Carbondale: Southern Illinois University Press, 1968. Includes a strong attack on concentration of newspaper ownership.

TEBBEL, JOHN, *Open Letter to Newspaper Readers*, New York: James H. Heineman, Inc., 1968. A good job of separating unsophisticated criticisms from legitimate concerns and exploring little-recognized problems of newspapers.

"What's Wrong with the Press?" *Newsweek*, Nov. 29, 1965 (Vol. 66, No. 22), pp. 55-60. Typical of periodic attacks on newspapers, this offers a good cross section of the usual complaints.

WHITE, LLEWELLYN, *The American Radio: A Report on the Broadcasting Industry in the United States from the Commission on Freedom of the Press*, Chicago: University of Chicago Press, 1946. This pretelevision critique contains still valuable material.

[For additional readings, see: PRICE, WARREN C., *The Literature of Journalism*, Minneapolis: University of Minnesota Press, 1960 (2nd Printing). Pages 281-292 list the classics by George Seldes and others.]

CHAPTER 12

Press Status and Outlook

In this last third of the twentieth century, American journalism faces an exciting mixture of what Gerald Johnson aptly called "peril and promise."

Viewed historically, press performance in delivering information matches American advances in most other services. The volume and breadth of news coverage, and the speed with which it is delivered to most of America's nearly 60,000,000 households, are clearly modern-day marvels. Stimulating commentary has not kept pace—on a mass scale—but that phase of journalism is far from moribund. Local editorializing on the air has been growing, and newspapers are attacking the blandness that has marked local editorials during the first two-thirds of this century. Press freedom from government controls ranks exceptionally high, but several ominous threats have grown with the complexities of modern society.

Among all nations in the world, America has no superiors and few peers in news-dissemination. American press commentary ranks among the top dozen (where freedom and journalistic sophistication are sufficiently developed to produce it). Relative excellence—as compared with that of the British and Scandinavian presses, for example—could be judged only in subjective ways. The United States is the only major power indulging itself in a "high" degree of press freedom (see Table 8, pp 222-223), but its printed media have been outranked in total freedom by both the Swiss and Scandinavian presses since World War II.

Evaluation of the American press often suffers from unfair comparisons, both historical and geographic. Evaluators are prone to romanticize about the giants of American journalistic history, instead of comparing the general run of the press then with the general run of the press today.

And they are wont to compare the United Kingdom's *London Times* and *Guardian* with America's lesser journalistic lights—overlooking London's multimillion-circulation *Daily Mirror, Daily Express,* and *Daily Mail* on the one side and papers like the *Louisville Courier-Journal, Milwaukee Journal,* and *Los Angeles Times* on the other side.

More than a half dozen nations outrank the United States in per-capita newspaper circulation, but the comparison breaks down on several counts. American dailies are much larger than those of other nations, adding weight to its 1.05 copies-per-household score. (In one recent year, Americans used more than 3.5 times as much newsprint per person as did the Japanese, who led in circulation per capita.) America's own drop from more than 1.30 newspapers per household since the century's second decade has been counterbalanced by the rise of radio, news magazines, and television. The fact that daily newspapers continue to sell twenty-one copies for every twenty households, as television nears saturation and radio moves well past it (see Table 9, page 232), speaks more significantly for journalism's role in American life.

STATUS OF FREEDOM

Freedom is the first essential for effective journalism in a democratic society. Thus, America's position in the highest of three freedom categories—as determined in the most comprehensive study of the world's press—offers the best promise for now and the future. But the total Table 8 listing (pp. 222-223) suggests peril, too, both because of a free press's need for more company and because of apparent slippage over recent decades. Table 8 is based on research carried out by the Freedom of Information Center at the University of Missouri's School of Journalism. The very existence of the Center and its support by 140 sustaining members represents promise. Nearly 100 of those are newspapers, broadcasting units, and organizations like the American Society of Newspaper Editors and the American Book Publishers Council. The fact that more benefactors of freedom have not supported the Center's work suggests some peril, also.

The Center made its first survey of 115 nations in 1966-67 and ranked 94 of them in seven categories for 1966. A year later, it rechecked the 94 and was able to confirm or alter the status of 84. The Center plans annual "updata" surveys and full-scale studies every fifth year. More than 1,000 questionnaires were mailed to native journalists, foreign correspondents, and journalism professors familiar with the countries for the first survey. A total of 537 "usable" replies provided an average of 5.7 ratings per country, roughly balanced between native and foreign judges. For the 1967 follow-up, 560 questionnaires were mailed, and 260

TABLE 8

Relative Press Freedom as of 1967

PICA (Press Independence and Critical Ability) Ranking
by Freedom of Information Center

Rank	Western Hemisphere	Europe	Middle East	Africa	Asia
1. Free— High Degree 4.00 to 2.51	Canada Costa Rica Guatemala Peru United States	Belgium Denmark Finland Netherlands Norway Sweden Switzerland			Australia Philippines
2. Free— Moderate Controls 2.50 to 1.51	Bolivia Colombia Ecuador El Salvador Honduras Jamaica Panama Uruguay (1)*	Austria France Ireland Italy United Kingdom West Germany	Cyprus Turkey		Japan Malaysia New Zealand
3. Free— Many Controls 1.50 to 0.51	Argentina Brazil Chile Dominican Republic Mexico Venezuela (1)		Israel (2)	Kenya Rhodesia Uganda Zambia	Ceylon India Singapore (2)

222

	Asia	Africa	Middle East	Europe	Western Hemisphere
4. Transitional 0.50 to −0.50	China [Taipei] (3) Indonesia South Korea South Vietnam Thailand (3)	Ghana Malawai (3) Tanzania (3)	Lebanon (3) Morocco (3)	Yugoslavia	
5. Controlled— Low Degree −0.51 to −1.50	Burma (4) Laos (4) Nepal Pakistan (4)		Iran	Spain	
6. Controlled— Medium Degree −1.51 to −2.50			Iraq (5) Jordan (5) Syria U.A.R. [Egypt]	Czecho- slovakia (7) Greece (3) Portugal (5)	Haiti
7. Controlled— High Degree −2.51 to −4.00	Cambodia (5) China [Peking] North Korea	Ethiopia		Albania Bulgaria East Germany Hungary (6) Poland Romania U.S.S.R.	Cuba

UNRANKED (insufficient information): *Western Hemisphere*—Nicaragua, Paraguay; *Middle East*— Afghanistan (5), Algeria (7), Libya, Saudi Arabia, Sudan, Tunisia (5), Yemen; *Africa*—Burundi, Cameroon (6), Central African Republic, Chad (7), Congo [Kinshasa] (4), Dahomey, Guinea, Ivory Coast, Liberia, Malagasy Republic, Mali, Niger, Nigeria (4), Rwanda, Senegal (6), Sierra Leone, Somalia, South Africa (3), Togo, Upper Volta (7); *Asia*—Mongolia, North Vietnam

*(NOTE: 1966 ranks are shown in parentheses in the 20 cases where they were changed—one improvement, 19 drops—and in the 10 cases where new data were unavailable.)

—Table based on FoI CENTER REPORT NO. 201, courtesy, Freedom of Information Center, School of Journalism, University of Missouri.

"usable" replies obtained—an average of three judgments per country. It was possible in a majority of cases (but not all) to have 1966 judges indicate stability or change for the follow-up study of 1967, the Center reported. Phrased negatively, here are the criteria on which judges scored the press of each country:

1. Legal controls—official censorship, forced retractions, etc. (excluding libel and obscenity laws).
2. Extra-legal controls—threats, violence, confiscation, etc.
3. Government licensing, certification, or appointment of news and editorial personnel.
4. Government licensing of print media.
5. Government processing of foreign news agencies' reports.
6. Government controls over domestic news agencies.
7. Government favoritism in releasing news.
8. Government control of distribution (excluding postal service).
9. Lack of press criticism of local and regional governments and officials.
10. Lack of press criticism of national government and officials.
11. Government, or government-party, ownership of media.
12. Bans against opposing political-party publications.
13. Libel and privacy laws.
14. Requirements that newsmen name sources when called before courts of law.
15. Organized self-regulation—press councils, courts of honor.
16. Government control of newsprint.
17. Government control of foreign exchange—as it affects media—and government controls on buying printing or broadcasting equipment from abroad.
18. Government subsidies—or bribes—to press.
19. Government loans to media.
20. Press dependency on government advertising.
21. Government control or influence in broadcast programming.
22. Advertising's influence over broadcast news and documentary programming—including content and volume of such programs.
23. Labor-union power to influence editorial policy or suspend publication.
24. Chain ownership of press units.
25. Number of economically insecure press units.

Judges scored each criterion on a numerical basis, and each judge's 25 scores were averaged. In turn, all averages for each country were averaged to two decimal places for placement on a nine-point continuum, from 4.0 for freedom to −4.0 for control. For the 1967 updating, judges were asked only to indicate any degree of change over the preceding year. (In addition, Communist countries were judged on adjusted criteria. Criteria 12-25 were removed in favor of nine different criteria: lack of published information not conforming to government-party policy, lack of published critical letters and controversial petitions, lack of published commentaries criticizing governmental decisions and administrative measures, lack of press self-management, degree to which central media police lower-level media, extent of jamming of foreign broadcasts, allocation of newsprint on bases other than demonstrated reader preference, published retractions in cases where readers have made unfounded criticisms of the press, and lack of public access to publications from countries with ideologies contrary to the government party's.)

The Center has pointed out that its measurement of "press independence and critical ability" (PICA) was made from a western point of view. It has also admitted that its follow-up studies may tend to emphasize the negative. The 1967 study responses indicated some slippage for 70 per cent of the countries, enough in nineteen cases to drop nations from one to three rankings. (However, events in 1967—a military takeover in Greece, and war in the Middle East—probably justified most of the shifts downward.)

The PICA rankings were grouped so that three were considered in the "free" range, one was called "transitional," and three were considered "controlled." Findings for the first two studies showed:

RATING 1966	NATIONS	POPULATION (PER CENT)
"Free" (1-3)	55	1.50 billion (45.2%)
"Transitional" (4)	10	.43 billion (13.0%)
"Controlled" (5-7)	29	1.30 billion (39.2%)
Sub-Totals	94	3.23 billion (97.4%)
Unranked	21	.09 billion (2.6%)
TOTALS	115	3.32 billion (100%)

RATING 1967		
"Free" (1-3)	47	1.43 billion (43.3%)
"Transitional" (4)	11	.31 billion (9.0%)
"Controlled" (5-7)	26	1.40 billion (41.1%)
Sub-totals	84	3.19 billion (93.4%)
Unranked	31	.22 billion (6.6%)
TOTALS	115	3.41 billion (100%)

Study of Table 8 should underline both promise and peril again. The American press is setting a noble pace for others. Its leadership of the Inter-American Press Association deserves some credit for eleven Latin American countries' scoring within the three free-press rankings. Top rankings for seven European countries and the Philippines and Australia in the Pacific provide good foundations for building press freedom worldwide. However, the second-class freedom of the United Kingdom's press and the same for France, Italy, and West Germany reflect disturbing weakness in the free world's commitment to the most basic freedom of all. The "transitional" rankings of major allies like Nationalist China, South Korea, and South Vietnam are at least embarrassments to the free world's leader. A high degree of press freedom served less than 10 per cent of the world's population in 1967. Such a minority position is inevitably more difficult to hold than would be a position shared by many.

Obviously, the American press should step up its campaigns on behalf of freedom. It must perform in a manner which will inspire public confidence, as against public inclination to endorse performance controls. It must move against both government and private threats to its essential independence—from increased restrictions on court coverage to advertiser control of prime broadcasting time. Group operation of press units must be checked from within to maintain real freedom and to forestall legal limits which might bring something more than mere curbing of the chains. The best defense calls for an offensive against press-freedom curbs—e. g., all-out attacks on inadequate or unobserved public-records laws, refusal to stand by when the presidential press conference is neglected (as it was during the Lyndon Johnson Administration), imaginative experiments with taped broadcasts of trial proceedings (to expand, rather than contract, press coverage of the people's courts).

Two great breakthroughs of the 1960s inspire confidence in the future. The 1964 *New York Times vs. Sullivan* victory in the Supreme Court substantially reduced dangers in press discussion of public officials' performance. Subsequent court rulings have extended the new protection to include reporting and commenting on "public figures." Enactment of the Federal Public Records Law established a new beachhead for advancing the people's right to know. Despite its flaws and the press's curious slowness to employ the new law, it has helped turn back some of the secrecy tide loosed during the Cold War era. Sam Archibald of the Missouri School of Journalism's Freedom of Information Center office in Washington reported two examples in July, 1968. Archibald cited the law to force State Department declassification of a twenty-four-year-old "secret" document, "The President's Power to Use Armed Forces Abroad Without a Declaration of War," and make it available to the public. He also pried loose the *Handbook for Congressional*

Foreign Travel, which had been published by the State Department, Agency for International Development, and the U. S. Information Agency, and stamped "Limited Official Use."

IMPROVING PERFORMANCE

The breadth and volume of American news-disseminating efforts are almost too enormous to comprehend. The Associated Press and United Press International each were reportedly spending nearly $1,000,000 a week to serve their clients in 1968. Each listed more than 1,200 American dailies and more than 3,000 radio and television clients. The Associated Press also served 4,200 foreign newspaper and broadcast units, and UPI served 2,200. Employed by AP were 3,500 persons full time and "many thousands of part-time reporters and photographers"; in addition, AP had access to all news gathered by staffs of its newspaper and broadcast members on a cooperative basis. Its daily files totaled 5,000,000 words, including duplications on its world circuits. United Press International employed 10,000 full- and part-time in 238 bureaus to process 4,500,000 words daily on all its circuits. In addition, of course, thousands of reporters and correspondents work directly for newspaper groups, broadcasting networks, and individual newspapers, magazines, and radio and TV stations.

Overall performance in any enterprise is judged in part by the best it has to offer. All four media have recognized leaders, but assessment of "best" newspapers has been attempted most often. Out of lists

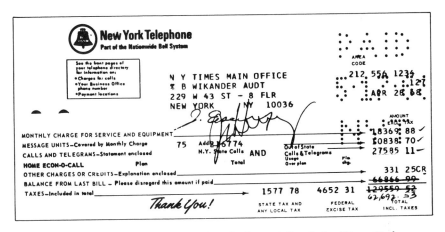

Figure 12.1. This April, 1968, telephone bill of the **New York Times,** showing two months' totals of $129,559.52 (more than $2,000 a day) provides a clue to that newspaper's greatness. (Courtesy, **New York Times**)

compiled from surveys of publishers, teachers, and others, six major
dailies have shown up most often—the *New York Times, Christian Science
Monitor, St. Louis Post-Dispatch, Milwaukee Journal, Washington Post,*
and *Louisville Courier-Journal.* Others frequently mentioned during the
last few years include the *Wall Street Journal, Baltimore Sun, Chicago
Daily News, Kansas City Star, Atlanta Constitution,* and *Los Angeles
Times.* Close observers note that others, less widely known, serve better
than some which make the lists regularly. Several with less than 50,000
circulation have won high praise from experts—the *York* (*Pa.*)
Gazette & *Daily,* the *Madison* (*Wis.*) *Capital Times,* the *Lewiston*
(*Idaho*) *Tribune,* and the *Santa Barbara* (*Calif.*) *News-Press* (which,
under former Publisher Thomas M. Storke, won a Pulitzer Prize for
exposing the John Birch Society in 1962). In summarizing one survey
of "best" newspapers, Public Relations Counsel Edward L. Bernays
quoted a typical response: "I know of many a good weekly or daily in
the 'under 15,000 circulation' category. . . . They have more real influence in the area which they claim to influence and more down-to-
earth news coverage of their community in precise ways and touchy
situations than any metropolitan daily."[1]

Programs encouraging press excellence range from fellowships for
extra study by news workers to prizes for outstanding performance. More
than 300 journalists, mostly men, spent a paid school year on leave to
study at Harvard under Nieman Fellowships between 1938 and 1965.
The fellowships average more than twelve a year. Nieman Foundation
Curator Dwight E. Sargent said in 1968 that there were "at least 12"
such programs for sending newspapermen back to college. Between
1946 and 1968, more than 5,000 newspaper workers had taken two-week
seminars at Columbia University's American Press Institute, which seeks
to promote excellence in every phase of newspapering. In 1958 special
fellowships were established by CBS for broadcast-news workers at
Columbia University.

Led by the Pulitzer Prizes in publishing and the Peabody Awards
in broadcasting, more than 100 annual contests are aimed at promoting
superior journalism. Increasing entries in the most meaningful contests
reflect conscious effort toward improved performance. The Lasker
Awards in Medical Journalism, for example, grew from a handful of
entries in 1950 to 200 from newspapers and 50 from magazines in 1968.
Pulitzer Prize officials have reported record numbers of entries in the
public-service categories of late. The 130 sets of awards listed in *Editor
& Publisher Year Book* include categories for promoting world peace,
racial and religious brotherhood, conservation of natural resources, and

---

[1]Quotation reprinted by permission, © 1960, Edward L. Bernays.

Figure 12.2. AP correspondent Peter Arnett (sans helmet) and the man who took this picture during a Viet Cong ambush of U. S. Marines in South Vietnam represent the ultimate in man's effort to keep his fellowman informed. (Associated Press photograph)

dozens of other worthy causes. Lawyers, educators, political scientists, and others offer prizes for helping the public understand their specialties. (A minority of the contests are publicity-seeking gimmicks, such as one designed to promote cigar smoking.)

Beyond contests in importance, conscientious individual efforts to set new standards are impressive. The Louisville newspapers in 1967 appointed the first newspaper ombudsman to investigate reader complaints from a position inside the staff. John Herchenroeder, as assistant to Executive Editor Norman Isaacs, investigates complaints in minute detail, sees that corrections are made when necessary, and corresponds at length with complainants. The process develops two-way education, in that it makes reporters and editors better aware of reader concerns—sometimes resulting in review of news policy—and it educates readers about newspaper responsibilities which they could not have understood without detailed explanations. The program has produced a much higher level of dialogue between the newspapers and their readers by directly encouraging inquiries and complaints and by having those complaints processed by one specialist with power to act on them.

A number of media have moved to adjust their coverage of police news out of concern for the "fair trial" problems. Notable among the earliest efforts was the 1966 policy declaration of the *Toledo Blade* and *Times*, which won a commendatory resolution from the Association for Education in Journalism in 1967. The Toledo newspapers' policy established voluntary restrictions on coverage of criminal proceedings, but provided for important exceptions. Five primary categories were included: (1) Accused persons are identified by name, age, and address, but no prior criminal record is included. (2) The time, place, and circumstances of arrest are reported; the fact that the accused has made a statement may be reported, but no "confession" is reported. (3) The charges and identity of complainants are reportable, but no statements by officials or lawyers on either side "construed as detrimental or beneficial to the accused." (4) Grand jury indictments and trial dates are reported, but not names of jurors selected for the trial. (5) Newsworthy trials are covered in detail, but inadmissible evidence and courtroom arguments made in the jury's absence are not reported.

Exceptions are made at the editors' discretion. The policy provides these in case the community becomes alarmed by "a wave of violent crimes," or the newspaper detects "efforts to shield" a public official facing charges or any evidence of a breakdown in law enforcement or "lapse of conduct expected of a public official." The policy also allows for exceptions in cases where other media ("particularly from out of town") arouse the public "through sensational reports."

Some newsmen sincerely question the wisdom of policies like those of the Toledo newspapers. They argue, for example, that the full why of a suspect's arrest should be reported to protect citizens against unwarranted arrests and to help the public evaluate police performance. Some critics, on the other hand, scoff at the policy because of its loopholes. Readers of the Toledo newspapers, which had already won praise for restraint in covering the journalistically infamous 1954 arrest and trial of Dr. Sam Sheppard, have observed real changes in handling crime news. Whatever one's view of the self-censorship, none can deny the nobility of intent exhibited by broadcasters and publishers adopting such policies.

In addition to the wholesome volume of critical analysis produced inside journalistic associations, recent years have seen a growth in sophisticated evaluation of press performance from outside. Notable among these has been the American Institute for Political Communication—"a non-partisan, non-profit organization dedicated to improving the flow of government and political affairs information to the American people through independent study, analysis, and reporting of the dissemination process." Its monthly *Political Communication Bulletin* reports closely on performance of public-opinion polls, performance of syndicated and network commentators, general press treatment of government and political news, and the federal government's behavior regarding press access to news. (Table 6 in Chapter 6 presents an example of AIPC work.)

The Mellett Fund for a Free and Responsible Press began underwriting experimental "local press councils" in 1967. Pilot projects were set up in Bend, Oregon, and Redwood City, California, under Professor William L. Rivers of Stanford University, and in Cairo and Sparta, Illinois, under Professor Howard R. Long of Southern Illinois University. Publishers and citizens representing cross sections of the communities meet to discuss mass-communications problems in their own cities. This effort at improving communication between newspapers and their readers poses some dangers. When he was *Washington Post* executive editor, James Russell Wiggins, for example, commented: "It might not be a good thing, in many cases, to mobilize more completely the collective contemporary opinion of a community through advisory committees, likely to be on the side of a present majority." As has been demonstrated by press performance since the latter colonial days, editors have an obligation beyond reflecting mere majority views. The press-council experiments must find safeguards against any tendency toward tyranny by the majority.

Concerns about television's "vast wasteland" performance inspired a three-pronged attack by outside groups in 1967. The Carnegie Commission on Educational Television, after a year's study, offered a 12-point program for strong public broadcasting. A National Citizens Committee for Public Television was formed five months later to push a

program for government financing of public network television. The
Ford Foundation undertook a multimillion-dollar "Public Broadcast
Laboratory" program, linking 119 educational-TV stations to present
programs of substance. By November, President Lyndon B. Johnson had
signed the Public Broadcasting Act of 1967, which laid some groundwork
for federal aid to build a stronger public-broadcasting program for both
radio and television. The Columbia Broadcasting System and the Carnegie Corporation pledged $1,000,000 each to the Corporation for Public
Broadcasting established by the act. Again, details of the public-broadcasting plans have met with opposition. A primary one, advanced by
Broadcasting magazine and others, is that political pressures will keep
programming away from controversial issues—the very ones that need
airing. Others fear that the program will serve as an excuse for commercial television to ignore significant issues, thus reducing its much
larger audience's already limited attention to democracy's most important problems.

These recent signs of ferment in journalism offer real hope for improvement of America's mass media. Meanwhile, the people continue to
rely heavily on all four. Table 9 shows how audiences have continued

TABLE 9

20-YEAR GROWTH OF MASS MEDIA

MEDIUM	1947-48	1952-53	1957-58	1962-63	1967-68
Newspapers					
morning	328	327	309	318	327
afternoon	1,441	1,459	1,453	1,451	1,438
Circulation	51.7 mil.	54.0 mil.	57.8 mil.	59.8 mil.	61.6 mil.
Magazines					
general,[a]	239	258	270	274	276[b]
farm					
Circulation	141.0 mil.	163.0 mil.	183.3 mil.	203.2 mil.	225.7 mil.[b]
Radio					
AM stations	1,621	2,391	3,195	3,810	4,156
FM stations	458	580	537	1,081	1,753
Radio Homes	40.0 mil.	45.0 mil.	48.9 mil.	52.3 mil.	58.8 mil.
Television					
all stations	17	129	544	579	644
TV Homes	1.6 mil.	23.4 mil.	43.0 mil.	51.3 mil.	56.0 mil.

[a]Single titles and groups not separated.
[b]Figures for 1966, latest available at time table was constructed.
Figures are from *Editor & Publisher Year Books,* Magazine Publishers Association reports, and *Broadcasting Yearbook.*

to grow for newspapers, magazines, radio, and television. Outlets have continued to expand in broadcasting, and stability is clearly established in the print media since World War II.

IMPROVING PERSONNEL

College degrees, once frowned upon in newsrooms, have become almost mandatory. In fact, this facet of personnel qualification has changed so much that media-encouraged education beyond the bachelor's probably rivals in volume the percentage of college-educated news workers of 50 to 75 years ago.

Manpower shortages, aggravated by the mushrooming growth of electronic journalism and public relations, have forced major improvements in newspaper pay scales since the 1950s. The American Newspaper Guild in 1946 set goals of $50 per week for beginners and $100 per week for journeymen (those with five or six years' experience). By 1968, the Guild had moved its goals to $167.50 for beginners and $335 for journeymen. Already in hand was a *New York Times* contract setting a $250-a-week minimum for journeymen, as of the spring of 1969. More than three dozen dailies had contracted for journeyman minimums of $200 or more per week. The *Detroit Free Press* contract, signed in 1968, called for $132.15 for beginners by 1971, and reporters and copy editors with five years' experience will get at least $226.10. Sub-editors will get $244.51. The *Wall Street Journal* had led a major breakthrough in 1956 when it jumped beginners' pay to $100 a week. The attractions of news work for years gave media owners the advantage of an "employers' market." But continuing losses of experienced reporters and editors (23 per cent of Nieman Fellows, for example, between 1938 and 1964) to other fields and necessary staff expansions have forced salaries up. (Reporter minimums rose twice as fast as the cost of living from 1954-1966, one study indicated.)

Recruitment measures have multiplied since the late 1950s. The outstanding effort of recent years has been made by the Newspaper Fund, endowed by Dow Jones and Company (publishers of the *Wall Street Journal* and the *National Observer*). Begun in late 1958, the Fund financed workshops, summer sessions, and graduate study for more than 4,800 high school teachers in its first nine years. Between 1960 and 1967, it awarded scholarships to 687 students at colleges offering no journalism programs in return for those students' spending a summer on newspaper editorial staffs. It encouraged summer internships for both journalism and nonjournalism students by offering prizes of $100 to $500 for outstanding summer interns from 1965-1968. The Fund began a special internship program in copy editing in the summer of 1968.

As frequently (and often unfairly) denounced as the field it has tried to serve, college education for journalism has played a significant role in "professionalizing" mass communications. And, as in the industries it serves, its programs have ranged from inept to magnificent. Outlandish criticism by editors and educators in other disciplines has receded since journalism education's beginnings in this century's first decade, but controversy is as certain to remain with it as it is with journalism itself. In fact, journalism professors disagree among themselves and compete as fiercely for advancement of their special interests and differing views as the most philosophically-opposed editors. A brief look at journalism-education organizations demonstrates this.

Most college journalism teachers come together in the Association for Education in Journalism (AEJ), which was formed in 1951 from an overall organization, begun in 1912, and two groups of journalism-school administrators, which operate independently but maintain affiliate status within AEJ. The AEJ's twelve special interest divisions reflect the range of specialties and, to some degree, cleavages among the hundreds of teachers. Divisions include newspaper, magazine, radio-television, photojournalism, graphic arts, advertising, public relations, history, international communications, mass communications and society, communication theory and methodology, and secondary-school journalism. Educational commitments range from concentration on how-to-do-it training to emphasis on esoteric research in communication theory. Other clashes involve the educators' role in press criticism—some opposing the critical approach, some demanding much more of it, and some ignoring that issue.

Accrediting and its goals form potentially the most divisive issues. Again, extremists offer uncompromising positions not accepted by the majority but nonetheless producing disputes. One extreme holds that accreditation of journalism schools violates the First Amendment's spirit by moving toward something akin to "licensing" practitioners. The other holds that efforts should be made to close down all schools without accredited sequences. (One proposal called for a maximum of one college per state allowed to grant journalism degrees.) A middle course has been steered between the two. Working with industry associations, AEJ and its two administrator affiliates have operated the American Council on Education for Journalism to set accreditation policy and direct a separate ACEJ Accrediting Committee, which arranges educator-practitioner evaluations of programs for which accreditation is sought. The Council in 1969 included nine educators and nine practitioners (one each from groups like the American Society of Newspaper Editors, Magazine Publishers Association, and National Association of Broadcasters). By then the Council had approved from one to six sequences each at fifty-six colleges.

Those fifty-six colleges formed the American Association of Schools and Departments of Journalism. And sixteen of them also belonged to the sixty-six-member American Society of Journalism School Administrators. Those sixteen joint memberships and the fact that both groups support the Council financially and elect members on the Council reflect the basic mood of cooperation and compromise in journalism education. Most Society members who have not sought accreditation—either out of choice or because they feared their operations were too small to qualify—believe the Council's basic standards have improved journalism education even for schools not directly involved. Just as the American Newspaper Guild's wage minimums have competitively benefitted editorial workers on non-Guild papers, the Council's standards on budget minimums and teaching loads have been reflected in many nonaccredited operations. The Council's long-time "maximum" of 25 per cent on journalism courses has affected curriculum-planning in all schools.

Moderate dissenters from accrediting's status quo on both sides continue to agitate for change. Some among those with accredited sequences seek to promote the value of accreditation by refusing to accept transfer credits from the others or by requiring make-up work for graduate students enrolled from the other schools. They have succeeded in limiting certain benefits to those with accredited sequences—e. g., some industry-financed scholarships for journalism study and the Hearst Foundation writing awards for undergraduates. Dissenters on both sides have quarreled with the looseness of sequential accreditation's being translated into "accredited schools." In 1968, for example, six of the fifty-five were accredited only in sequences like advertising, technical journalism, "community journalism," or television. A total of twenty-one others were accredited in news-editorial alone. Yet, only fourteen of the fifty-five advertised just their accredited sequences in *Editor & Publisher Year Book* listings, thus diluting the significance of accrediting overall. One sampling of seventeen "accredited schools" found them listing seventy-four sequences, of which only thirty-five were actually accredited. The Council has tried to police exaggerated claims, but with little success. One state university's catalogue, for example, devoted two pages to what accreditation involved, clearly implying that its news-editorial and radio-TV programs were included when, in fact, only its advertising program was so blessed.

Whatever the quarrels, a majority of journalism educators have approved the principle of accrediting. By setting high standards and involving practitioners in both the policy-making and policing, the Council has helped establish the relatively new discipline in America. The fact that units without accreditation have prospered indicates that freedom of choice has remained also.

The total growth of journalism education is borne out in *Journalism Quarterly* reports on enrollments. In 1948, during the postwar "GI Bulge," 73 colleges reported a total of 16,619 majors. Twenty years later, 118 colleges reported a total of 24,445. Media managers have learned to compete with other recruiters for the growing crop of specially educated graduates. And journalism education's contribution to maintaining America's free press was an undeniable fact.

Those who accept special education for journalism as worthwhile may differ on its greatest value—attracting more college students into journalism, or producing employees already trained in basic techniques, or broadly contributing some professional status to the craft. This author, who entered newspaper work without benefit of an undergraduate major and who has worked frequently with newsmen in the years since, would cite two special benefits:

1. Sharp reduction (though not elimination) of cynicism among editorial workers. Journalism—as much as the ministry, medicine, or any profession—needs idealism, and good education for journalism can supply that elusive ingredient. More important, by placing journalism's faults in perspective, journalism education can shield tomorrow's beginners from early discouragement as they move toward positions where they can influence policy in better directions. Those who begin with only "stars in their eyes" are more inclined either to go along with the system or chuck it than are those who have both commitment and some real understanding of publishing and broadcasting pitfalls.

2. Better opportunities to instigate needed changes. With some appreciation of journalistic history, some grasp of press law, some mastery of techniques (protection against the can't-do-it-that-way syndrome), and some research experience, the journalism-educated novice is more inclined and better able to help bring changes than is his innocent counterpart. His timing and choice of targets are likely to be more effective than those of the beginner who is yet to be annoyed by the inverted-pyramid straitjacket and awed by libel-law mysteries. He should have a better inspiration from the examples of innovators like Benjamin Day, Horace Greeley, Joseph Pulitzer, Adolph Ochs, Henry Luce, and Edward R. Murrow. All other things being equal, the journalism graduate—knowing the rudiments and more of his craft from the start—can get a better hearing than can the new reporter who has to be told the difference between proofreading and copy editing and why defamatory remarks from one rostrum are more libel-prone than those from another.

Journalism graduates or not, young people offer an especially bright hope for an effective fourth estate in America. The change from yesterday's "Apathetic Generation" to today's "Activist Generation" happens to coincide with a sharp upturn in journalism enrollments in the 1960s. Reports from newspaper recruiters indicate that this has been more than mere coincidence. An opportunity to do something significant is increasingly cited as the primary concern of prospective employees, recruiters have reported.

The generation that has manned the Peace Corps and VISTA offers the best guarantee of continued strength and needed improvement for journalism in a democracy.

PROMISING SIGNS OF SUCCESS

Lacking historical perspective, one can only estimate the significance of recent specific changes in America's press. Several indicators of revolutionary change appear to have emerged during the 1960s.

An important dimension—a kind of "fifth estate"—has been added to the total press picture. Now watching the watchdog, so to speak, are publications like *Columbia Journalism Review* (started in 1962), the *Political Communication Bulletin* (1966), and the *Chicago Journalism Review* (1968). Their small circulations reach an elite among the opinion-shapers. Probably most important among those are the press managers and practitioners. Just as government officials sometimes respond directly to thoughtful editorials, so also do journalists react to published professional criticisms and suggestions.

The tendency of public-relations agencies to refrain from unethical practices is strengthened by a *Columbia Journalism Review*'s exposé of a leading agency's attempt to suppress a book unfavorable to a client. The tendency of a network newscaster to balance opinion-polling results is strengthened by a *Political Communication Bulletin*'s box-score comparison of his handling with those of his competitors. Errant publishers and broadcasters react with less arrogance to sophisticated analyses of their performance than they do to lay criticisms, which are often based on ignorance.

Produced by working newsmen, *Chicago Journalism Review* is perhaps the most astonishing of the "fifth estate" thrusts. The monthly collection of inside stories on Chicago newspaper and broadcast policies and practices was started after the 1968 Democratic National Convention in Chicago. Some Chicago journalists charged that their bosses were knuckling under to Mayor Richard Daley's administration by whitewashing police brutality. One charge had it that organized press photographers, for example, had to commend police performance publicly or lose police cooperation, essential to their working in the city. Backed by a $2,500 grant from the Center for the Study of Democratic Institutions and some smaller donations, the *Review*'s offerings have ranged widely.

In one 1969 article, for example, it hit both the *Chicago Tribune* and the competing *Chicago Daily News*—the latter for skipping a Drew Pearson column which had attacked the *Tribune's* bid to buy FM-radio station WFMT.

If working newsmen continue to risk their employers' wrath and the publishers continue to tolerate such "disloyalty," a new age may have dawned in American journalism. Other cities' newsmen may join forces to enlarge this search for greater journalistic truth.

Another phenomenon of the 1960s was the rise of the "underground press." Except on the most authoritarian high-school and college campuses, the term is a misnomer in that its producers do not operate secretly. With goals ranging all the way from wider use of four-letter words to better treatment of the poor, these rebels-in-print have shaken The Establishment. At the very least, they were part of the upheaval that forced the traditional press to take more notice of the military-industrial complex and pay better attention to problems of the ghettos. (One observer has even suggested that the *Louisville Courier-Journal* might not have printed a four-letter word in its complete text of a 1969 federal report had it not been for the pioneering of papers like the *Berkeley Barb.* Executive Editor Norman Isaacs later apologized for having followed the text exactly, as British papers like the *London Times* and *Guardian* have done in printing court testimony for years.)

Life magazine's muckraking efforts in the 1960s typify a mass-medium effort some scholars believed had disappeared half a century earlier. One 1969 exposé led for the first time in history to the resignation under pressure of a U. S. Supreme Court justice. Another was credited with toppling a two-term U. S. senator in the 1968 elections.

The "new honesty" has touched even the trade press, where idealists would not ask for it. Professor Theodore Peterson reported the 1964 effort of *Fleet Owner* (strictly for truck-fleet operators) to expose the menace of truck drivers' staying extra hours on the highways by using amphetamines to keep them "awake." (Peterson's account of this biting-the-hand-that-feeds-it undertaking was carried in the summer, 1965, issue of *Columbia Journalism Review.*)

For many reasons, maintaining a herd of journalistic sacred cows was more difficult in the 1960s than it had been in any previous decade.

Improving personnel has been the biggest single factor, of course. Contributing to that factor have been closer ties between colleges and the outside world. According to a report by Professor John Hulteng of Oregon, thirty-five colleges across the nation presented sixty-four seminars for working journalists during 1968 alone on topics ranging from better crime coverage to improving presentation of foreign affairs. After years of rather timidly viewing the 1947 Hutchins Commission

Report on a Free and Responsible Press, journalism educators took a harder look in the 1960s. The University of Washington's School of Communications visited commission members in the twentieth-anniversary year and presented an updated report of their views.

Increasing attention has been paid to the monopoly threat in the last third of the century. The FCC has challenged joint newspaper and TV-station ownerships from Cheyenne, Wyoming, to Boston, Massachusetts. One joint publishing venture—in Chattanooga, Tennessee—was voluntarily dissolved in the 1960s. Although mergers and group expansions continued, serious efforts to adjust that trend were growing as the 1970s dawned.

Meanwhile, the mass-communications business continued to prosper, outpacing the general business boom of the 1960s in several respects. Between 1946 and 1968, for example, newspaper advertising revenue grew nearly eleven per cent faster than the Gross National Product. Employment on newspapers grew more than eleven per cent faster than total employment. Television's gains in both departments were spectacularly greater, and radio—which had suffered most from TV's earlier impact—was recovering rapidly. Magazines continued circulation and ad-sales gains, but at a significantly slower pace.

Even technological research, long neglected by newspaperdom, showed signs of breaking through. After years of 66-word-per-minute transmission, for example, the Associated Press was perfecting systems aimed at 2,400 words per minute—more than thirty-six times as fast. With more complete copy almost instantly at hand, the AP's Ted Boyle wrote in the fall, 1968, *Journalism Educator*: ". . . within the next few years we are going to have vastly improved newspapers—newspapers on which there will be less physical work and a lot more time for thinking." The improved use of satellite transmission and continued refining of all its equipment by the television industry defies description.

If Americans hold to basic press freedom, American journalism will be equipped to serve its critical functions in the crises which confront the world.

FOR FURTHER STUDY

1. Compare self-criticism in journalism with that in other fields by browsing through copies of *Broadcasting* and *Editor & Publisher* and then doing the same with periodicals like the *Journal of the American Medical Association* and the *American Bar Association Journal*.

2. Check the *Reader's Guide to Periodical Literature* for evaluations of performance in all media—look under "press" (newspapers), "magazines," "radio," and "television."

3. Transpose Table 8's rankings to a world-outline map; pencil color No. 1 countries solid blue, No. 2 blue lines, No. 3 blue dots, No. 4 blue and red dots, No. 5 red dots, No. 6 red lines, No. 7 solid red. If you do not have access to Freedom of Information Center releases (see "Suggested Reading"), send 25 cents and an addressed, stamped envelope (7 x 10) to obtain the latest PICA rankings—usually issued in May each year. Compare your map and make changes accordingly.

4. Study the PICA criteria (page 224). On which would the United States rank lowest? Should any criteria be added? Any removed (No. 15, for example)? How many relate to "press independence" and how many to "critical ability"? How would your campus media rate on that list?

5. Consider Criteria 21 and 22 with relation to the Corporation for Public Broadcasting provided in the 1967 law and advertising's control of broadcast programming. Review Table 7 in Chapter 11 and consider its implications with relation to Criterion 24.

SUGGESTED READING

PERIODICALS

The Center Magazine (available only on a membership basis, Center for the Study of Democratic Institutions, Box 4068, Santa Barbara, California 93103). With one-third of the Center's fellows ex-journalists, this bimonthly is heavy on press critiques.

Chicago Journalism Review (11 East Hubbard Street, Chicago, Illinois 60611). This pioneering monthly by Chicago newsmen adds to public discussion of press performance.

Columbia Journalism Review—see Chapter 11 list.

Freedom of Information Center Reports (Box 858, Columbia, Missouri 65201). The monthly report and bimonthly *FoI Digest* give the best coverage of press freedom's overall status.

The Journalism Educator (Department of Journalism, University of Nevada, Reno, Nevada 89507). This quarterly offers an amazing variety of generally short pieces, only a fraction of which are pedagogical.

Journalism Quarterly (School of Journalism, University of Minnesota, Minneapolis, Minnesota 55455). The main repository for scholarly research in mass communications.

Nieman Reports—see Chapter 11 list.

Political Communication Bulletin (American Institute for Political Communication, 422 Washington Building, Washington, D. C. 20005). These monthly reports on press performance are up-to-date and unique.

*   *   *

BOROFF, DAVID, "What Ails the Journalism Schools," *Harper's*, October, 1965 (Vol. 231, No. 1385), pp 77-88. A typical attack on journalism education, but based on more observation than most.

BOYLE, TED, "Today, 66 Words per Minute from AP—Tomorrow, 2,400," *The Journalism Educator*, Fall, 1968 (Vol. 23, No. 4).

HOHENBERG, JOHN, *The News Media: A Journalist Looks at His Profession,* New York: Holt, Rinehart and Winston, Inc., 1968. An excellent cataloging of press problems aimed at uplifting the fourth estate.

———, ed., *The Pulitzer Prize Story,* New York: Columbia University Press, 1959. Newspaperdom's achievements reflected from 1917. (Lists of winners since this publication can be found in current edition of *The World Almanac.*)

LYONS, LOUIS M., ed., *Reporting the News,* Cambridge, Massachusetts: Harvard University Press, 1965. [Available in Atheneum paperback.] Choice articles from 17 years of *Nieman Reports,* including an account of Thomas M. Storke's exposé of the John Birch Society and Edward R. Murrow's castigation of television and radio for failures to do more with news and views. The editor's introduction provides good background on the Nieman program and related matters.

MERRILL, JOHN C., *The Elite Press: Great Newspapers of the World,* New York: Pitman Publishing Corp., 1968. Professor Merrill takes a fresh look at "quality" (good and free) and "prestige" (good, but restricted) newspapers in assessing newspaper journalism worldwide.

RESTON, JAMES, *The Artillery of the Press: Its Influence on American Foreign Policy,* New York: Harper & Row, Publishers, Inc., 1967. [Paperback.] Includes a stimulating plea for more attention to the press's most serious customers.

SVIRSKY, LEON, ed., *Your Newspaper: Blueprint for a Better Press,* New York: The Macmillan Company, 1947. A dated, but still meaningful, examination of news needs for the future.

Appendixes

Magazine Circulation

ONE HUNDRED GENERAL AND FARM MAGAZINES LEADING IN A.B.C. CIRCULATION, FIRST HALF OF 1967

(NOTE: These standings, rather than later ones, were chosen to represent the first such Audit Bureau of Circulations period inside the last third of the twentieth century.)

1.	Reader's Digest	17,104,119
2.	TV Guide	12,342,732
3.	McCall's Magazine	8,567,495
4.	Look	8,212,303
5.	Life	7,417,712
6.	Better Homes & Gardens	7,128,371
7.	Family Circle	7,005,769
8.	Ladies' Home Journal	6,929,734
9.	Saturday Evening Post	6,747,424
10.	Woman's Day	6,355,874
11.	National Geographic	5,588,865
12.	Good Housekeeping	5,557,015
13.	Redbook	4,423,002
14.	Playboy	4,253,305
15.	Time	3,710,574
16.	American Home	3,594,010
17.	Farm Journal	3,043,302
18.	American Legion	2,514,836
19.	True	2,495,182
20.	Boys' Life	2,450,720
21.	True Story	2,234,428
22.	Newsweek	2,090,563

23. Parents' Magazine 2,031,419
24. Senior Scholastic Unit 2,022,167
25. Junior Scholastic 1,735,414
26. Popular Mechanics 1,630,212
27. U. S. News & World Report 1,580,536
28. Popular Science 1,522,555
29. Outdoor Life 1,500,296
30. Workbasket 1,475,958
31. Mechanix Illustrated 1,436,326
32. Seventeen 1,418,978
33. Elks 1,412,465
34. Field & Stream 1,408,710
35. Argosy 1,381,626
36. Sports Afield 1,361,443
37. Scouting 1,354,894
38. Successful Farming 1,330,203
39. Sports Illustrated 1,310,950
40. Glamour 1,300,881
41. Progressive Farmer 1,265,488
42. V. F.W. Magazine 1,214,694
43. NewsTime 1,193,067
44. House & Garden 1,184,614
45. Grit 1,172,659
46. Photoplay 1,115,322
47. Esquire 1,062,290
48. Presbyterian Life 1,055,575
49. Columbia 1,044,519
50. Holiday 1,039,274
51. American Girl 1,017,993
52. Ebony 996,247
53. Co-Ed 994,729
54. House Beautiful 981,168
55. National Enquirer 933,456
56. Cosmopolitan 889,175
57. Sport 874,544
58. Sunset 860,209
59. TV-Radio Mirror 843,345
60. Nation's Business 815,072
61. Modern Screen 806,936
62. Ingenue 806,208
63. Our Sunday Visitor 803,028
64. 'Teen 764,643
65. Modern Romances 759,532

66.	Hot Rod Magazine	731,980
67.	Simplicity Fashion Magazine	702,534
68.	Mademoiselle	676,340
69.	Young Catholic Messenger	617,460
70.	Flower & Garden Magazine	610,160
71.	Catholic Digest	602,151
72.	Lion	595,767
73.	Together	593,500
74.	True Confessions	576,006
75.	McCall's Pattern & Home Decorating	556,267
76.	Lutheran	545,663
77.	National Observer	539,508
78.	Business Week	535,529
79.	Motor Trend	510,121
80.	Saturday Review	490,784
81.	Family Handyman	477,451
82.	New Yorker Magazine	473,275
83.	Pageant	473,168
84.	Forbes	470,982
85.	Hairdo	462,330
86.	Motion Picture	462,255
87.	Capper's Weekly	460,782
88.	Fortune	457,294
89.	Vogue	444,497
90.	Popular Photography	429,897
91.	Harper's Bazaar	427,064
92.	Farmer-Stockman	426,443
93.	Rotarian	422,350
94.	Scientific American	419,367
95.	Westways	417,044
96.	Christian Herald	401,394
97.	Coronet	400,439
98.	Home Garden	400,100
99.	Car & Driver	393,304
100.	Popular Electronics	386,803

(Reprinted by permission of the Magazine Advertising Bureau of the Magazine Publishers Association, Inc.)

Journalistic Codes of Ethics

AMERICAN SOCIETY OF NEWSPAPER EDITORS

CANONS OF JOURNALISM
(Adopted in 1924)

I. *Responsibility.* The right of a newspaper to attract and hold readers is restricted by nothing but considerations of public welfare. The use a newspaper makes of the share of public attention it gains serves to determine its sense of responsibility, which it shares with every member of its staff. A journalist who uses his power for any selfish or otherwise unworthy purpose is faithless to a high trust.

II. *Freedom of the Press.* Freedom of the press is to be guarded as a vital right of mankind. It is the unquestionable right to discuss whatever is not explicitly forbidden by law, including the wisdom of any restrictive statute.

III. *Independence.* Freedom from all obligations except that of fidelity to the public interest is vital.

1. Promotion of any private interest contrary to the general welfare, for whatever reason, is not compatible with honest journalism. So-called news communications from private sources should not be published without public notice of their source or else substantiation of their claims to value as news, both in form and substance.

2. Partisanship in editorial comment which knowingly departs from the truth does violence to the best spirit of American journalism; in the news columns it is subversive of a fundamental principle of the profession.

IV. *Sincerity, Truthfulness, Accuracy.* Good faith with the reader is the foundation of all journalism worthy of the name.

1. By every consideration of good faith a newspaper is constrained to be truthful. It is not to be excused for lack of thoroughness or accuracy within its control or failure to obtain command of these essential qualities.

2. Headlines should be fully warranted by the contents of the articles which they surmount.

V. *Impartiality.* Sound practice makes clear distinction between news reports and expressions of opinion. News reports should be free from opinion or bias of any kind.

This rule does not apply to so-called special articles unmistakably devoted to advocacy or characterized by a signature authorizing the writer's own conclusions and interpretations.

VI. *Fair Play.* A newspaper should not publish unofficial charges affecting reputation or moral character without opportunity given to the accused to be heard; right practice demands the giving of such opportunity in all cases of serious accusation outside judicial proceedings.

1. A newspaper should not invade private rights or feelings without sure warrant of public right as distinguished from public curiosity.

2. It is the privilege, as it is the duty, of a newspaper to make prompt and complete correction of its own serious mistakes of fact or opinion, whatever their origin.

VII. *Decency.* A newspaper cannot escape conviction of insincerity if while professing high moral purpose it supplies incentives to base conduct, such as are to be found in details of crime and vice, publication of which is not demonstrably for the general good. Lacking authority to enforce its canons, the journalism here represented can but express the hope that deliberate pandering to vicious instincts will encounter effective public disapproval or yield to the influence of a preponderant professional condemnation.

RADIO TELEVISION NEWS DIRECTORS ASSOCIATION

CODE OF BROADCAST NEWS ETHICS
(Adopted in 1966)

The members of the Radio Television News Directors Association agree that their prime responsibility as newsmen—and that of the broadcasting industry as the collective sponsor of news broadcasting—is to provide to the public they serve a news service as accurate, full and prompt as human integrity and devotion can devise. To that end, they declare their acceptance of the standards of practice here set forth, and their solemn intent to honor them to the limits of their ability.

I. The primary purpose of broadcast newsmen—to inform the public of events of importance and appropriate interest in a manner that is accurate and comprehensive—shall override all other purposes.

II. Broadcast news presentations shall be designed not only to offer timely and accurate information, but also to present it in the light of relevant circumstances that give it meaning and perspective.

> This standard means that news reports, when clarity demands it, will be laid against pertinent factual background; that factors such as race, creed, nationality or prior status will be reported only when they are relevant; that comment or subjective content will be properly identified; and that errors in fact will be promptly acknowledged and corrected.

III. Broadcast newsmen shall seek to select material for newscast solely on their evaluation of its merits as news.

> This standard means that news will be selected on the criteria of significance, community and regional relevance, appropriate human interest, service to defined audiences. It excludes sensationalism or misleading emphasis in any form; subservience to external or "interested" efforts to influence news selection and presentation, whether from within the broadcasting industry or from without. It requires that such terms as "bulletin" and "flash" be used only when the character of the news justifies them; that bombastic or misleading descriptions of newsroom facilities and personnel be rejected, along with undue use of sound and visual effects; and that promotional or publicity material be sharply scrutinized before use and identified by source or otherwise when broadcast.

IV. Broadcast newsmen shall at all times display humane respect for the dignity, privacy and the well-being of persons with whom the news deals.

V. Broadcast newsmen shall govern their personal lives and such nonprofessional associations as may impinge on their professional activities in a manner that will protect them from conflict of interest, real or apparent.

VI. Broadcast newsmen shall seek actively to present all news the knowledge of which will serve the public interest, no matter what selfish, uninformed or corrupt efforts attempt to color it, withhold it or prevent its presentation. They shall make constant effort to open doors closed to the reporting of public proceedings with tools appropriate to broadcasting (including cameras and recorders), consistent with the public interest. They acknowledge the newsman's ethic of protection of confidential information and sources, and urge unswerving observation of it except in instances in which it would clearly and unmistakably defy the public interest.

VII.   Broadcast newsmen recognize the responsibility borne by broadcasting for informed analysis, comment and editorial opinion on public events and issues. They accept the obligation of broadcasters, for the presentation of such matters by individuals whose competence, experience and judgment qualify them for it.

VIII.   In court, broadcast newsmen shall conduct themselves with dignity, whether the court is in or out of session. They shall keep broadcast equipment as unobtrusive and silent as possible. Where court facilities are inadequate, pool broadcasts should be arranged.

IX.   In reporting matters that are or may be litigated, the newsmen shall avoid practices which would tend to interfere with the right of an individual to a fair trial.

X.   Broadcast newsmen shall actively censure and seek to prevent violations of these standards, and shall actively encourage their observance by all newsmen, whether of the Radio Television News Directors Association or not.

NATIONAL CONFERENCE OF EDITORIAL WRITERS

BASIC STATEMENT OF PRINCIPLES
(Adopted in 1949)

Journalism in general, editorial writing in particular, is more than another way of making money. It is a profession devoted to the public welfare and to public service. The chief duty of its practitioners is to provide the information and guidance toward sound judgments which are essential to the healthy functioning of a democracy. Therefore the editorial writer owes it to his integrity and that of his profession to observe the following injunctions:

1. The editorial writer should present facts honestly and fully. It is dishonest and unworthy of him to base an editorial on half-truth. He should never consciously mislead a reader, distort a situation, or place any person in a false light.

2. The editorial writer should draw objective conclusions from the stated facts, basing them upon the weight of evidence and upon his considered concept of the greatest good.

3. The editorial writer should never be motivated by personal interest, nor use his influence to seek special favors for himself or for others. He should hold himself above any possible taint of corruption, whatever its source.

4. The editorial writer should realize that he is not infallible. Therefore, so far as it is in his power, he should give a voice to those who disagree with him—in a public letters column and by other suitable devices.

5. The editorial writer should regularly review his own conclusions in the light of all obtainable information. He should never hesitate to correct them should he find them to be based on previous misconceptions.

6. The editorial writer should have the courage of well-founded conviction and a democratic philosophy of life. He should never write or publish anything that goes against his conscience. Many editorial pages are the products of more than one mind, however, and sound collective judgment can be achieved only through sound individual judgments. Therefore, thoughtful individual opinions should be respected.

7. The editorial writer should support his colleagues in their adherence to the highest standards of professional integrity. His reputation is their reputation, and theirs is his.

Sample Stylebook

(This is an abbreviated version of a stylebook used by a typical college student newspaper.)

ABBREVIATION

1.1 ADDRESSES—When street number is given, abbreviate: 21 N. Washington St., 31 W. Green Blvd., 6 Mason Ave. But: He lives on North Washington Street. (Exception: Abbreviate all in headlines.)

1.2 ATHLETIC TIMES AND DISTANCES—Abbreviate minutes and seconds and feet and inches in athletic results. Ex: Pole Vault: 1. Sloan (OWU) 12 ft. 11 1/2 in.; Time: 1 min. 29 sec.

1.3 CHRISTMAS—Do not abbreviate Christmas.

1.4 CLASSES—Class of '18 may be used for Class of 1918.

1.5 DATES—Abbreviate the months of the year except March, April, May, June, and July when used with the days of the month, as Jan. 1, Feb. 2, Aug. 3, Sept. 4, Oct. 4, Nov. 5, Dec. 6. Never abbreviate days of the week. Ex: Monday, Sept. 23; May 10.

1.6 DEGREES—Abbreviate college degrees when they follow a name. Ex: Alice Jones, M.A.

1.7 MILITARY—Military titles are abbreviated only when they directly precede proper names. Ex: Adjt. John Jones, Brig. Gen. Charter Smith, Capt. Doe, Col. Grubb, Maj. Fenbirk, 2nd Lt. Williams, Pvt. Small, Sgt. Friday.

1.8 NAMES—Do not abbreviate Christian names. Write a name as the person signs it. Ex: William J. Jones or W. John Jones.

1.9 NUMBER—Abbreviate "number" when followed by numerals. Ex: No. 96.

1.10 ORGANIZATIONS—Spell out the name of an organization or company except in specific cases when the body uses an abbreviation as in

Wm. C. Brown Co. Organizations—except those known by abbreviations, like YWCA, AWS—should be spelled out the first time they appear in a story. When in doubt about an organization's familiarity, spell out. Never abbreviate "Co." in the plural.

1.11   PER CENT—Spell out "per cent"; use figures before it and no period after. Ex: Approximately 10 per cent was collected. (% may be used in tabular matter and in headlines.)

1.12   PERSONAL, PROFESSIONAL—These professional and personal titles are abbreviated when used before the name: Asst., Atty. Gen., Dr., Lt. Governor, Messrs., Mlle., Mr., Mrs., Prof., Supt., the Rev., the Rev. Mr.

1.13   POLITICAL AFFILIATION AND STATE OF CONGRESSMAN—Abbreviated like this: Sen. Eugene McCarthy (D.-Minn.); (D.-Ohio); (R.-N.D.).

1.14   STATES, TERRITORIES, POSSESSIONS—States of the United States when used after the names of cities are abbreviated. Do not abbreviate when used alone. Ex: In Kentucky; but, at Lexington, Ky. Always spell out names of United States territories and possessions.

Ala., Alaska, Ariz., Ark., Calif., Colo., Conn., D.C. (District of Columbia), Del., Fla., Ga., Hawaii, Idaho, Ind., Iowa, Kan., Ky., La., Me., Mass., Md., Mich., Minn., Miss., Mo., Mont., N.C., N.D., Neb., N.H., Nev., N.J., N.M., N.Y., Ohio, Okla., Ore., Pa., R.I., S.C., S.D., Tenn., Tex., Utah, Va., Vt., Wash., Wis., W.Va., Wyo. Spell out provinces of Canada.

1.15   TIME—Do not capitalize abbreviations, "a.m." and "p.m." Write 3 p.m. (not three o'clock in the afternoon); write midnight and noon (not 12 midnight or 12 noon); write 8 p.m. today (not 8 p.m. tonight).

1.16   TITLES—(See Rule 1.12.)

CAPITALIZATION

2.1   ACADEMIC COURSES—Capitalize specific courses such as History 71 or American Colonial History. Do not capitalize general subjects: a chemistry course; the mathematics classes. Language designations—English, German, etc.—must be capitalized, of course.

2.2   BOOKS, PLAYS, POEMS, PERIODICALS—Capitalize the first and succeeding key words in titles of books, plays, poems and periodicals, etc. Ex: "Of Mice and Men," "A Streetcar Named Desire," "Trees," New York Times, the Delaware Gazette, The Transcript.

2.3   CLASSES—Do not capitalize the class levels, freshman, sophomore, junior, senior, except when referring to one as an organization, as the Freshman Class.

2.4   DATES, SEASONS, TIME—Capitalize days of the week and months of the years. Do not capitalize seasons of the year. Ex: Monday, January, spring, summer, winter, fall.

2.5   COMMITTEE—(See 2.12).

2.6   DEGREES—Capitalize college degrees when in abbreviated form but not when written out. Ex: B.A.; bachelor of arts.

2.7   DIRECTION—Do not capitalize points of the compass as north, south, east, west unless they designate a definite region. Ex: He lives in the Midwest. He lives north of here. He is a Southern Democrat.

2.8   FEDERAL, STATE AND MUNICIPAL DEPARTMENTS—Capitalize names of federal, state and municipal departments and bureaus, as Department of Agriculture, State Insurance Department, Bureau of Vital Statistics, Delaware Fire Department.

2.9   GEOGRAPHICAL LOCATIONS, BUILDINGS, STREETS—Capitalize in full. Ex: Olentangy River, Delaware County, Edgar Hall, Sandusky Street, William Street Church, Gray Chapel, Orchard Heights, Selby Field.

2.10 HOLIDAYS, SPECIAL OCCASIONS, ERAS, ETC.—Capitalize: New Year's Day, Mother's Weekend, Homecoming Weekend, April Fools' Day, 20th Century, Dark Ages, the Depression.

2.11 LEGISLATIVE BODIES—Capitalize names of national and state legislative bodies. Ex: Congress, House of Representatives, House, Senate, Parliament, Chamber, General Assembly, the Legislature.

2.12 ORGANIZATIONS, COMPANIES, COMMITTEES, SCHOOL DEPARTMENTS, ETC.—Entire names should be capitalized. Ex: Sailing Club, Department of Physics, Physics Department, Student Council, Board of Trustees, Federal Bureau of Investigation, Johnson Seed Co., Student Y, Publicity Committee.

2.13 POLITICAL PARTIES AND PHILOSOPHIES—Names of political parties should be capitalized. Political philosophies should not be. Ex: Communist Party, Republican Party, Democrats, Progressives; democracy, communism, fascism, socialism.

2.14 TITLES—Capitalize titles when they are part of the name but not when they are in apposition. Exception: President when it refers to the President of the United States is always capitalized. Ex: University President Elden T. Smith; Elden T. Smith, president; Coach Frank Shannon, Chairman Tad Smith, C. E. Evans, professor of history; Mike Ward, Student Government president.

2.15 UNIVERSITY, COLLEGE AND HIGH SCHOOL—Capitalize when used as part of a title. Ex: University of Kentucky, Salem High School, Ohio Wesleyan University, Millersburg Military Academy.

Do not capitalize when used in the plural, as the state universities of Kansas, Montana and Texas.

FIGURES

3.1 AGES—Use figures for all ages, as 9 years old; 3-year-old girls.

3.2 ATHLETIC RECORDS AND BETTING ODDS—Use figures for athletic records, scores and betting odds. Ex: jump of 20 ft. 2 in. (no comma after feet); Missouri 3, Kansas 0. Olson is a 7-5 favorite in his fight with Gavilan.

3.3 BILLION—The U.S. debt limit was $200-billion.

3.4 CIPHERS OMITTED AFTER DECIMAL POINT OR COLON—Except for the purpose of lining up tabular matter, omit ciphers. Ex: 5 a.m., $1, 5 per cent (not 5.0). Use ciphers only where needed for clarity —Ex: His grade point rose from 1.98 to 2.00. Ciphers can precede decimal point when needed—Ex: It dropped from 1 per cent to 0.5 per cent.

3.5 COMMA—Years, street and license numbers, etc., are not pointed off with commas. Ex: 1915; 1055 Delmar Ave.; City Ordinance 45555; but, 1,456 men.

3.6 DATES—Do not use ordinals in dates. Ex: Write Jan. 14 (not Jan. 14th.)

3.7 DECADES—Spell out (the Nineties) or use figures (the 1890s).

3.8 DIMENSIONS—Figures consisting of two or more factors use the word "by." Ex. A lot 70 by 100 feet (not 70 x 100 feet).

3.9 FOLD, ODD, A—Spell out round sums, indefinite numbers and periods of time preceded by "a" and sums terminating in the compounds "fold" and "odd." Ex: Forty-odd bushels; a dozen or so; a hundred and one reasons; one-hundredfold; a year and a day.

3.10 MILLION—Population of the U.S. is 200-million.

3.11 MONEY—When the sum is in cents, use figures with "cents" spelled out, as 10 cents, 5 cents. When writing sums totaling millions, use as follows: $4.6-million (not $4,600,000); $12-million (not $12,000,000), unless clarity requires it, as in the budget climbed from $968,000 to $1,212,000.

3.12 NUMBERING—When numbering points in an article, use numerals.

3.13 ORDINAL NUMBERS—Except as modified elsewhere, write out ordinal numbers under 10. Use figures for numbers 10 and above. Ex: first, third, ninth; 10th 22nd, 123rd, Second Division, 88th Congress. Do not use ordinals in dates.

3.14 PER CENT—Use figures for per cents, as 5 per cent.

3.15 STATISTICAL MATTER—In matter of a plainly statistical character the various items will go in figures. Ex: The report gave 364 cases, as follows: Scarlet fever, 1; croup, 11; diphtheria, 27; measles, 7. Won, 7; lost, 5; total, 12.

3.16   STREETS—Use figures for street numbers, 10 W. Fontaine Ave.; 1049 N. Ninth St. Spell out numbered streets through Ninth; use figures for 10th and above. Ex: Ninth Street, 81st Street, 107th Avenue.

3.17   SUMS BELOW AND ABOVE 10—Except as modified elsewhere, sums below 10 are spelled out; 10 and larger, use figures. Fractional sums are written out except when used with scores, as 6 1/2-3 1/4. Where both a number before 10 and a number above 10 appear in the same sentence, both shall be put into figures. Ex: Deaths for the week number 9, as against 14 the preceding week.

3.18   THOUSANDS—Comma denotes thousands (1,182) except as in Rule 3.5

3.19   VOTING—Use figures for votes, as Williams 34, Jones 17, Brown 5.

PUNCTUATION

APOSTROPHE

4.1   BUSINESS NAMES—Business names usually take the possessive. Ex: Wilson's, People's, Bun's. But Wilson Brothers basement does not take the possessive form.

4.2   HOLIDAYS—Holidays showing possession call for apostrophes as indicated in Webster's Dictionary. Ex: Dad's Weekend, Mother's Day, April Fools' Day, Washington's Birthday, New Year's Day, St. Valentine's Day.

4.3   PLURALS—Plurals of letters take the apostrophe; plurals of figures do not. Ex: A's, B's; 5s, 10s, 700s, 1920s.

4.4   POSSESSIVES—Use 's after singular possessive (Bill's; Ed Jones's). (Note: Edwards Gym is not a possessive form.)

4.5   SHORTENED WORDS AND YEARS—Words in shortened forms that have become well established do not take the apostrophe. Shortened years do except when hyphenated. Ex: Alpha Sig, Alpha Gam, Panhel, cello, phone, etc.; rock 'n' roll; the Class of '28; but, Class of 1900; 1928-29.

COLON

4.6   INTRODUCING A LIST—Omit colon after forms of verb "to be" which introduce a list. Ex: The new members are Gus Bell, Ted Kluszewski and Jim Greengrass, but, The new members are as follows: Gus Bell, Ted Kluszewski and Jim Greengrass.

4.7   SCRIPTURE REFERENCES—Use colon between chapter and verse in references to Scripture. Ex: Hezekiah 10:6-18.

4.8   TIME—Use colon in writing time of day when not on the hour. Ex: 9:59 a.m.; but, 10 a.m.

A colon may also be used in shortened statements of time involving hours, minutes, and seconds; Ex. 1:42:28; 2:01 1/2.

COMMA

4.9   PERSONAL NAMES, SCORES, VOTES, ETC.—If inserted parenthetically, set off by commas. Other names and titles may or may not be, according to circumstances. Omit the comma between the names of teams and their scores when written together. Ex: James Gordon and his son, Charles, were present. Cincinnati won, 2-0, in the 11th inning. Iowa 21, Notre Dame 0. The measure was defeated, 28-17, on a strict party vote.

4.10   POSITION RE QUOTES—Comma always precedes closing quotes. Ex: "Church for Everyone," "Healing" and "What Price Passion?" were his sermons for February.

4.11   SERIES—Unless required by preceding punctuation, omit comma before "and" in a series of connected phrases. In a series separated by semicolons, last punctuation before the and is a comma: Dan Jones, president; Bob Smith, secretary, and Barbara Doe, treasurer. He ate apples, bananas and grapes.

4.12   WHO, WHICH, BUT, ETC.—Omit the comma before who, which, but, etc., when the connection is close and immediate. Ex: The men who were in the swamp surrendered. We tried but they were too tall.

DASH

4.13   MECHANICS—When typing a dash, use two typed hyphens for each dash.

4.14   AVOID OVERUSE AND MISUSE—Dashes may occasionally replace parentheses or the semicolon to connect closely related thoughts, but sparingly.

HYPHEN

4.15   Hyphenating will be used for clarity, with compound modifiers for example. Terms should not be hyphenated if there is no distortion of meaning and no ambiguity. Ex: 18-year-old freshman, author-teacher Marshall, soldier-statesman Eisenhower.

4.16   DATES—Use hyphen to signify preposition "to" between dates. Ex: Aug. 15-29, 1970-71.

4.17   FRACTIONS—In spelled-out fractional numbers hyphenate the numerator and the denominator. Ex: One-half the money was gone; three-fifths; thirty one-hundredths (0.30); thirty-one one-hundredths (0.31); six and seven-eighths.

4.18   NUMBERS—one-hundred; 2-million; 3.4-billion, two-thousand.

4.19   ONE AND TWO QUALIFYING NUMBERS—A single number preceding and qualifying a noun will be hyphenated with the noun to form an adjective; do not compound if there are two or more numbers. Ex: One-minute intervals; 10-pound gun; 10 days' leave (or 10-day leave), 80 to 90 acre farm; one to three inch boards, 3-week-old baby, 10-month-old child; he was given two weeks' vacation, he had a two-week vacation, 100-yard dash; 120-yard low hurdles.

4.20   RELATIONSHIPS—Hyphenate the relationships "step," "half" and "in-law" and the term "great" indicating degree in direct line of descent. Also, hyphenate "grand" in the collateral branches. Ex: Great-grandfather, great-grandmother, step-father, half-sister, son-in-law, brother-in-law; grand-nephew; grand-uncle.

4.21   SCORES—Hyphenate scores of athletic events. Ex: 28-7, 6 1/4-4.

PARENTHESES

4.22   Use parentheses when inserting directions or explanations to reader. Ex: Jane Jones (above), daughter of James Jones. (Portrait by De Longe). Sen. Robert La Follette (R.-Wis.) took the stand.

4.23   POSITION—When an entire sentence is in parentheses, the period should precede the final parenthesis.

PERIOD

4.24   ABBREVIATIONS—Ordinarily omit the period after an all-capitalized abbreviation. Some exceptions are a person's initials, the name of a country or state, the United Nations, the District of Columbia, and college degrees. Ex: NATO, CIO, AMA, IFC, ROTC, MUB, OSU, ATO, DG. ODK, CBS, WSLN, NSA, GOP, GI, GIS, TNT, SOS: but, U.S., R.I., U.S.S.R., U.N., Washington, D.C., B.A., M.S., Ph.D.

4.25   POSITION RE QUOTES—When used with quotation marks, the period always appears inside the closing mark. Ex: Howard Pease is the author of "Road Kid."

QUOTATION MARKS

4.26 ATHLETIC AWARDS—Omit quotation marks with athletic awards or letters. Ex: The varsity W.

4.27 BOOKS, PUBLICATIONS, ARTICLES, SPEECHES—Do not quote the title of a sacred book, or titles of regularly published newspapers or periodicals. Quote titles (but not the characters) of other books. Titles of articles appearing in a newspaper or periodical should be quoted. "Rosemary's Baby" was reviewed in The Transcript.

4.28 DEBATES, RESOLUTIONS, SIGNS, ETC.—Quotation marks enclose questions for debate, resolutions, signs, mottoes.

4.29 DIALOGUE—All direct dialogue should be in quotation marks except when in Q. and A. form. Use the quotation at the beginning of each paragraph of a continuous quotation, but at the end of the last paragraph only.

4.30 MUSIC, PLAYS, POEMS, PICTURES—Use quotation marks around titles of musical compositions, operas and the several musical parts which they include, and the titles of plays, poems and pictures. (See 4.32 for exception.)

4.31 NICKNAMES—Omit quotations with nicknames, except when used with the full name. Ex: Thomas "Tommy" Manville; F. Lawrence "Larry" Howe; but, Larry Howe.

4.32 PROGRAMS—Omit quotation marks in material set in regular program style.

SEMICOLON

4.33 IN SERIES—Separate compounded appositives. Ex: Tom Jones, sophomore; Bill Brown, junior, and Phil Smith, freshman, were given recognition. (Note that semicolon drops to comma before the and in a series.)

4.34 POSITION RE QUOTES—Logic dictates position—Ex: He read "The Press"; it made him furious.

SPELLING

5.1 Follow Webster's preferred spelling in all cases. Check directories on all names.

TITLES

6.1 APPOSITIVES—Do not use unwieldy titles preceding a name as Vice-President for Academic Affairs Robert P. Lisensky. Make it Robert

P. Lisensky, vice-president for academic affairs; Mike Ward, Student Government president.

6.2 BOOKS, PLAYS, ADDRESSES, ETC.—Capitalize the important words in titles of books, magazines and newspaper articles, addresses, plays, poems, pictures, and signs, but not in slogans or mottoes. Ex: "World Peace and Former German Emperor"; "The Strange Adventures of Madam X"; "Portrait of a Dying Swan"; the headline said "Korean to Speak"; he saw a sign, "Horses for Sale"; slogan, "All for one, one for all"; his motto is, "Do others or they'll do you."

6.3 BUSINESS TITLES—Do not use the man's business or trade as a title, (as Grocer Smith, Butcher Jones, Carpenter Wilson), but write Coach Les Michael, Chairman Tom Jones.

6.4 CIVIL, PROFESSIONAL, RELIGIOUS, MILITARY TITLES—These titles are capitalized only when used with the name and not in apposition. "Acting" and "former" are not capitalized. Ex: Col. Grubb, President Hoover, former President Lyndon Johnson, the Rev. John J. Smith, Brig. Gen. Robert F. Williams, Vice-President Dawes; Ohio's acting Governor Smith, who has filed for the office of state senator, was formerly mayor of Northhampton, Mass.; the President and Mrs. Nixon received the prince of Wales and the duke of York.

6.5 DOCTOR—Use "Dr." only for practitioners of healing arts. Never use "Dr." when referring to professors on this faculty or visiting professors, except as part of a direct quotation. Ex: Dr. Henderson has resigned as University physician; He said, "Dr. Spencer is my favorite professor."

6.6 MISS, MRS.—Do not use "Miss" or "Mrs." the first time the name is used in an article except in case of husband and wife written together. Exception: When married woman uses husband's first name, write as Mrs. Sam Jones the first time the name is used. When repeating a woman's name (including student) in an article, use the proper titles. Ex: Helen Taggart, Mrs. E. G. Taggart, Mrs. Taggart. Ex: Margaret Forsythe, dean of women; Miss Forsythe; Alsa King, women's representative, Miss King; Patricia Nixon; Mrs. Richard M. Nixon; Mr. and Mrs. F. E. Ayer.

6.7 MR.—The title "Mr." is used in only three situations: (1) when a man and his wife are mentioned together, Ex: Mr. and Mrs. James Smith; (2) obituaries; (3) when only the last name of a minister is being used, the Rev. Mr. Allen.

6.8 NAMES—Always give first name or initials when first referring to a person. When repeating the name in the article, use only the last name. Repeated women's names carry "Miss" or "Mrs." Ex: Mary K. Murphy, Miss Murphy.

6.9   PROFESSORS—Use a faculty member's full title in apposition the first time the name is used. Ex: C. E. Jones, instructor in Spanish, translated the letter.

Write John Doe, assistant professor of English; Thomas Smith, instructor in history; Marion E. Burton, lecturer in journalism.

6.10   REVERSED TITLES—Reversed titles, commonly used and accepted as such, will be capitalized. Reversed titles carrying abbreviation "No." and which are only in occasional use are not capitalized. The terms "page," "column" and "paragraph" always lowercase. Ex: Grade A, Highway 51, Style 2228, Room 441, passenger train No. 4, Truck Company 2, Grade 1-A, page 3.

6.11   REVEREND, FATHER—Reverend as a title should always be preceded by "the." Ex: The Rev. William Brown, the Rev. Mr. Brown. Use "Father" as the title of a Roman Catholic priest. Do not abbreviate "Father" or "Rabbi."

6.12   TITLES OF NOBILITY—English titles of nobility will be capitalized only when they precede the Christian name. Other foreign titles will be capitalized when they are followed by such prefixes as de, di, le, von, etc. Ex: Duke Edward of York; the duke of York; Prince Von Bismark; Duc De La Rouchefoucould.

6.13   TITLES OF RESPECT—Titles of respect are not capitalized. Ex: His honor the mayor; your honor; his excellency Cardinal Spellman; your majesty.

A Sample
Headline Schedule

This is part of a typical newspaper headline schedule, reprinted by permission from the *Toledo Blade's* Stylebook. Below are the type styles and sizes used for "display" heads on major first-page or section-page stories. (For example, a 4-column 36 Tempo Heavy line would count about 26 units; an 8-column 72 Tempo Heavy, about 26 units; an 8-column 72 Tempo Heavy Condensed Caps, about 30 units. Note: 72-point type is one inch high, and 36-point type is one-half inch high.) Following the display listings are actual examples of some of the most frequently used 1-column and 2-column heads. (The *Blade* dropped its old 42-point No. 1 head some years ago and began using No. 2 for top-of-the-page 1-column headlines.)

Type face	Count per column
24 Metro Medium (regular, italic)	11
30 Metro Medium (regular, italic)	10
36 Tempo Heavy (regular, italic)	6½
36 Tempo Bold (regular, italic)	7½
42 Tempo Heavy (regular, italic)	6
42 Tempo Bold (regular, italic)	6¼
48 Tempo Heavy (regular, italic)	5¼
60 Tempo Heavy (regular, italic)	4¼
72 Tempo Heavy (regular, italic)	3¼
60 Tempo Heavy Cond. Caps	4½
72 Tempo Heavy Cond. Caps	3¾

	Count for 8 cols.
84 Tempo Heavy Cond. Caps	28
96 Tempo Heavy Cond. Caps	26

—No. 0—

Doctors Name Aid

14 pt. Metro

—No. 2—

Verdict In Land Sale Overruled In District Court

New Trial Ordered In Wood County Acquisition Case

TOP—34 pt. Erbar
DECK—14 pt. Metro regular
—3 lines

—No. 3—

Malaysia Gains Filipino Accord

Nations To Discuss Consular Exchange

TOP—34 pt. Erbar
DECK—14 pt. Metro regular
—2 lines

—No. 4—

Fund Bill Signed For Mental Health

$4.8 Million Slated For Centers, Staffs

TOP—28 pt. Erbar
DECK—14 pt. Metro regular
—2 lines

—3 Line No. 4—

U.S., Britain Face Loss Of Military Bases In Libya

Nation To Refuse To Renew, Extend Existing Treaties

TOP—28 pt. Erbar
DECK—14 pt. Metro regular

—No. 5—

Cleveland Blast Shatters Windows

18 pt. Metro regular

—3 Line No. 5—

Election Board Employees Work Despite Holiday

18 pt. Metro regular

—No. 6—

Cleveland Man Dies In Traffic Accident

14 pt. Metro

—No. 6 Italic—

Put Stub In Voter? That Can't Be Right

CLEVELAND (AP)—Ray C. Miller, clerk of the Cuyahoga board of elections ordered a quick correction after reading a newly printed booklet of in-

14 pt. Metro Italic
TYPE—1 col. 9 pt. light indent

—No. 7—

2 Air Force Craft Crash Within Day

Newfoundland Area Twin Mishaps May Have Taken 33 Lives

TOP—30 pt. Metro
DECK—14 pt. Metro regular

—No. 8—

Paying Legal Costs Urged For Innocent

Goldberg Notes Expenses Can Ruin Acquitted Person

TOP—24 pt. Metro regular
DECK—14 pt. Metro regular

—No. 8-A—

Bright Idea Pays $5,000 To Employee

Chevrolet Worker's Other Suggestions Had Earned $500

TOP—24 pt. Metro Italic
DECK—14 pt. Metro Italic

—No. 9—

Victims Of Fire To Thank Helper

18 pt. Metro Italic

(3 lines with twin 1 col. drops)

Rival Bill Offered As Johnson Vows Medicare Drive

6 GOP Senators Propose Public, Private Plan

President Gives Pep Talk To Senior Citizens

TOP—2 col. 36 pt. Tempo Medium
(Note correct type designation is Tempo Bold, but to
avoid confusion with Tempo Heavy, use above designation)
DECKS—1 col. 18 pt. Metro

Panamanian-U.S. Talk Deadlocked

Demand For Review Of Treaty Rejected; New OAS Meeting Set

TOP—2 col. 36 pt. Tempo Medium
DECK—2 col. 18 pt. Metro
TYPE—Set 5 lines 2/9 light, break 1/9

—No. 11—

Seizure On Vessel Protested By U.S.

40 Americans Are Removed From Ship In Beirut; On Way To Israel

TOP—2 col. 36 pt. Tempo Medium Italic
DECK—2 col. 18 pt. Metro Italic
TYPE—Set 5 lines 2/9 light, break 1/9

—No. 12—
(3 lines)

825-Acre North Adams Area Added To City In '64's First Annexation

Council Acts On Reynolds Corners Tract With 3,020 Residents, Property Valued At $8 Million For Taxation

TOP—2 col. 30 pt. Metro
DECK—2 col. 14 pt. Metro
TYPE—Set 5 lines 2/9 light, break 1/9

—No. 12—

Taft Candidacy Is Issue For Court, Brown Says

Secretary Of State Says Petition Flaws May Disqualify Rival In GOP Senate Race

TOP—2 col. 30 pt. Metro
DECK—2 col. 14 pt. Metro
TYPE—Set 5 lines 2/9 light, break 1/9

—No. 12—
(3 lines with two 1 col. drops)

New York Enters City With 4.3-Inch Snowfall; Deep South Hard Hit

| Death Of Shoveler, Rash Of Accidents Blamed On Weather | Dixie Areas Left Stunned As Storm Moves Northward |

TOP—2 col. 30 pt. Metro
DECKS—1 col. 14 pt. Metro
TYPE—All 1/9

—No. 13—

Landless Farming Seen In Food Role Of Future

*Plants Grown In Nutrient Solution
Able To Supply Less Fertile Regions*

TOP—2 col. 30 pt. Metro Italic
DECK—2 col. 14 pt. Metro Italic
TYPE—All 1/9

—No. 14—

Chief Government Witness Subpenaed By Hoffa Lawyers

Defense Cross-Examination Aimed
At Discrediting Partin's Testimony

TOP—2 col. 24 pt. Metro regular
DECK—2 col. 14 pt. Metro regular
TYPE—All 1/9

—No. 15—

President Gives Ballroom Diplomacy Two-Hour Whirl

Dancing Texan Still Going Strong As Last Of Guests Leaves White House

TOP—2 col. 24 pt. Metro Italic
DECK—2 col. 14 pt. Metro Italic
TYPE—All 1/9

—No. 16—

Steeds' Illness Unhorses Police

SAN FRANCISCO (Æ)—For the first time in the 75-year history of Golden Gate Park not a single mounted policeman patrolled there today.

HEAD—18 pt. Metro Italic
TYPE—1/9 light indent
RULE—Round corner

—1-10-10 Folo Head—

(Preceded by a 3-em dash only if it introduces a new dateline, or in the case of a local story following a wire story.)

Other Nations Agree To Join Cyprus Force

10 pt. Bodoni Italic

Forecast Good For Mills Race

Prospect of good weather is in store for sailors competing today in the 45th annual Merrill B. Mills Trophy race over a 67-mile triangular course in Lake Erie.

Starting at Toledo Harbor Light, Cruising Class C gets off at 12:30 p.m. and will be followed by Cruising Class B at 1 p.m., and Cruising Class A at 1:30 p.m.

HEAD—18 pt. Metro Italic
TYPE—1/9 boldface indent
RULE—No. 12, Top & Bottom
(NOTE: The above style is for Sports Department.)

Omitted from this reprinting are No. 7-A (same as No. 7, but in italics), 3-Line No. 9, and Top No. 10 (same as two-line No. 10, but with a 1-column drop) plus more than 50 examples of un-numbered headlines for obituaries, women's pages, stories continued inside, and other special situations.

Index